THE ERIE CANAL

TRAVELER'S GUIDE

RESTAURANTS, PUBS, AND ATTRACTIONS WITHIN A STONE'S THROW OF THE CANAL PATH

LARRY WEILL

BOOKS

T0370203

North Country Books
An imprint of The Globe Pequot Publishing Group, Inc.
64 South Main Street
Essex, CT 06426
www.globepequot.com

Distributed by NATIONAL BOOK NETWORK

British Library Cataloguing in Publication Information Available

Library of Congress Cataloging-in-Publication Data Available

ISBN 9781493089079 (paperback) | ISBN 9781493089086 (epub)

To the countless men, of all ethnicities, origins, and backgrounds who struggled to fell the trees, gouge the dirt, and blast the rock to create the Erie Canal, toiling with primitive hand tools, through oppressive heat, malaria-ridden swamps, and risk-filled rockfalls. Thousands perished in this massive challenge that would open the frontier for our fledgling country's economy. You are not forgotten.

CONTENTS

INTRODUCTION

A NOTE ABOUT NAMES

In this book, you will see many names and terms relating to the Erie Canal and the trail(s) that run along its banks. The primary trails discussed are the Empire State Trail and the Erie Canalway Trail. While these two trails often coexist on the same stretch of pavement or gravel, they are not "one and the same." A marker for both trails is shown on page viii. The Empire State Trail is a 750-mile expanded trail system or network that crosses the entire state of New York from New York City all the way to the border with Canada. It also runs across the state horizontally (mostly east-west) from Albany to the point where the Erie Canal enters the Niagara River, and then south into the city of Buffalo. It was completed in 2020 and is the longest multiuse trail in the United States.

The Erie Canalway Trail is the name given to the portion of the Empire State Trail that follows (roughly) the Erie Canal from Albany to Buffalo, even though the canal ends in Tonawanda.

While hiking or biking along the Erie Canalway Trail, you are always on the Empire State Trail as well. Within the chapters of this book we sometimes simply refer to it as "the Canal Trail" or even just "the trail." These are roughly akin to nicknames for the same pathway and should not be confused with another route.

RESTAURANTS, PUBS, AND ATTRACTIONS ON THE ERIE CANAL

The Erie Canal was completed in October 1825. While the canal's use as a primary means of moving commercial goods across the state has been replaced by trucks and trains, its recreational usage has increased exponentially over the years.

The Erie Canalway Trail that parallels the waterway has become a mecca for hikers, bikers, and runners of all ages. On any given day one can meet fun-seeking travelers and exercise fanatics as they follow the time-tested path along the canal. Some choose to limit their excursions to a short one to two miles, while others (especially bikers) cycle their way from the Pacific Ocean en route to the East Coast. It's all good and everyone is welcome.

What's also impressive is the selection of places to eat, drink, and play along the way. In almost every city, town, and hamlet it is possible to find a host of appetizing locations to satisfy your hunger and quench your thirst. These vary from the sophisticated and (sometimes) posh culinary establishments and bistros to the more rudimentary pubs, where local beers are served by the pint. Whatever you want, it is usually possible to find it "within a stone's throw" of the Erie Canal.

Also situated across the stretch of paved and unpaved pathways are countless activities, parks, museums, and more. A great many of these offer free entry to anyone venturing along the trail, although not all of them are readily visible from the canal.

Thus, the question arises: when writing a guidebook such as this, how close to the canal does a restaurant, bar, or attraction have to be in order to be included in the discussion? If the dis-

Both trail signs on the same marker pole, located in Ellicott Park in North Tonawanda, New York.
PHOTO BY LARRY WEILL

tance specified was one mile, the list would include thousands (or possibly tens of thousands) of locations. Even a half mile seemed a bit too far. So, with a little bit of thought and imagination, the "stone's throw" used as a measuring stick was determined to be 445 feet and 10 inches.

Why?

THE STORY BEHIND THE DISTANCE

Why 445′10″? Glen Edward Gorbous was an aspiring Canadian baseball player who was signed to a minor-league contract as a nineteen-year-old athlete in 1950. After several years in the minors, he finally made it to the major leagues in 1955, where he played for Cincinnati and then for Philadelphia. His statistics were unremarkable, and his mediocre batting average (.238) and power hitting (total of four home runs) led to his demotion in May 1957. At that time, he was traded to St. Louis and assigned to play for the Double A Omaha Cardinals.

Although unable to perform to major-league standards, Gorbous did have one very unique talent: he could throw a baseball an astonishing distance. Some thought he could throw a ball farther than anyone who had ever played the game. So, on August 1, 1957, at the age of twenty-six, the team arranged an exhibition at their stadium in Omaha to see if Gorbous could do just that.

The previous record for a throw was 445'1". Gorbous, on his fourth attempt, launched a rocket throw of 445'10", thus breaking the record by nine inches. According to *Guinness World Records*, that is a mark that still stands today.

CAVEATS TO THIS BOOK

As mentioned, this book is intended for use as a guide to those individuals who are hiking, biking, or boating the Erie Canal. For that reason, the restaurants, pubs, and attractions listed on these pages have been selected because they would be of interest to anyone traveling on the canal or its associated pathway.

In organizing this book, I started on the western end of the Erie Canal and worked my way east. The official "starting point" I selected was the location where the Erie Canal meets the Niagara River. From a geographical viewpoint this makes sense, as the Erie Canal is the main focus of this book rather than any of the connected waterways. The reason I am explaining this is because the Empire Trail (which parallels the canal for hundreds of miles) does continue for quite some distance beyond the terminus of the canal. It eventually winds its way into the city of Buffalo, extending as far south as the bottom of Erie Basin. At that point, it turns northeast before reaching its end at Cathedral Park. These lengths of trail are not connected to the Erie Canal and are not discussed in this book.

The sole exception to the parameters listed above is the Erie Canal boat *Seneca Chief*, which is berthed at Commercial Slip in downtown Buffalo. This newly constructed re-creation of the boat used by Governor DeWitt Clinton to inaugurate the canal in 1825 was too significant to leave out of this book.

For practical purposes, the number of eating and drinking establishments that line the Erie Canal are too numerous to mention. An exhaustive listing would require a book several times the size of this volume and would be impractical for most readers. Because of this, a certain selectivity was employed to narrow the focus and restrict the compilation to a manageable number. However, it is important to stress that the inclusion of any businesses and attractions in this book does not imply that they are recommended above any others, or that a restaurant not listed on these pages is unworthy of inclusion. An attempt was made to mention the better-known restaurants, pubs, and attractions whenever possible, although this is certainly not a guarantee.

Chain coffee shops, fast-food restaurants, and most chain restaurants are not included in this book, regardless of their proximity to the canal.

It is important for people planning on dining at a restaurant or pub to know that not all establishments accept either credit cards or even cash. Some restaurants along the canal have a strict policy of accepting cash only. Others will accept credit cards, but have a two-tiered price structure: they will charge 2 to 3 percent more for payment by credit card. Most restaurants and pubs state their policy on their menu. A few locations accept only credit cards and not cash, so it's best to call ahead and ask.

The locations referenced in this book are only those found on the actual Erie Canal or the Canalway Trail. Businesses found on the Oswego Canal, the Champlain Canal, and the Cayuga-Seneca Canal have not been included for the sake of managing the number of entries.

Likewise, restaurants and other establishments located in places where the original canal existed (prior to reroutes) have also been omitted from this book. Even without considering the two main expansions of the Erie Canal to widen and deepen the waterway, sections of the canal have been moved and rerouted several times to circumnavigate cities and bodies of water.

Also left out of this volume are the sixty-eight different locks, aqueducts, drydocks, bridges, and culverts found along the route of the canal. (Note: this is just the Erie Canal. There are a great many more locks and features found on the other feeder/side canals.) While they are all interesting and of historical significance, it is doubtful that most travelers would plan a stop based around any one such component of the waterway. There is information available online for those interested in any one of these sites.

There are numerous locations provided throughout this text regarding "attractions" rather than restaurants and pubs. Attractions are businesses, historic sites, or activities that canal travelers might find of interest to add to their itinerary. These include such things as tour boat cruises or boat/bicycle rental companies, interesting side trails focusing on nature, bizarre or unusual sites, or items of extraordinary historical significance. (There are so many boat/canoe/kayak rental firms along the canal that this book refers readers to the Canal Corporation's website, where a comprehensive listing is provided.)

Another category of attractions not listed in this book is "parks." In almost every section of the Erie Canal it is possible to find a municipal or state park, and many locks along the waterway also have their own green space. These are too numerous to list, and most hikers/bikers will pass through them whether they intended to do so or not. A few parks that contain extraordinary structures or relics from the canal's past have been included in this book. Also, parks of a more unusual nature (i.e., "bark parks" for exercising Fido) may appear here as well.

The majority of parks located along the canal and Canalway Trail are "general use" parks, open to the public the entire day. The hours of use for most of these tracts is "dawn to dusk," although different hours may be posted on a sign or inside a park kiosk. Please be respectful of any park rules that appear on the park's signs, and always carry out your own trash.

It is also important to note that the author cannot vouch for the accuracy of the proximity of 445′10″ from any of the subjects in this book to the actual edge of the Erie Canal. Some of the restaurants had balconies situated directly over the canal banks, while other businesses were located through dense brush and vegetation, often situated on private property. A best attempt was made to apply the same standard to all businesses and attractions, although some were much tougher to estimate than others. (The author does not own a 445′ tape measure.)

Another important point to mention for hikers and bikers coming off the canal path to find some of these restaurants and other establishments is that some of them will be harder to reach than others. While they are all located within "a stone's throw" of the canal, some of them are situated on the other side of the canal from the pathway. In at least one case, the "attraction" (the Mohawk Valley Welcome Center) is on the other side of the New York State Thruway from the canal path, which would create a very hazardous (and also illegal) crossing. In most cases, there are multiple bridges crossing the canal in the towns and cities along the Erie Canal. Users of this book can walk or bike across these bridges to safely access the other side. However, safety should always be considered at all times. Please obey all laws and traffic rules when traveling along the routes lining the canal.

Speaking of rules, the locations of authorized camping spots have changed somewhat over the past one to two years. Make sure that your intended campsites are still approved by the state and canal authority, as some previously authorized locations have become off-limits for overnight camping.

Individuals who already hike or bike the canal know that many of the bridges that span the canal are under construction to repair years of damage and corrosion. Many of these bridges are not canal-run lift bridges but municipal structures built on city/town streets for the simple purpose of getting from one side of the waterway to the other. Please note that the majority of these crossings are still open to pedestrians or cyclists, even if they are closed to automobile traffic. Common sense applies when crossing these spans on foot, as they may be covered in construction equipment and debris.

Other sections of the Canalway Trail are closed for short distances to effect repairs to overpasses, drainage culverts, embankments, and more. Those areas may reroute hikers and bikers onto city/town roads, so take care to avoid vehicular traffic.

Users of this book will also discover that there are many more businesses (restaurants, pubs, etc.) associated with some counties and stretches of the canal than others. Unfortunately, this is unavoidable, as there are just some townships, cities, and counties that are more developed than others. At times one can drive alongside the Erie Canal for ten to twenty miles without encountering a single business. In other locales, there are attractive-looking restaurants and bistros lined up one after another, making it difficult to decide which to include and which to leave out. (Impartiality? Forget it! That goes out the window very early in the process.) Most of the larger cities (i.e., Rochester, Syracuse, Schenectady, etc.) have a huge array of restaurants, cafés, breweries, and other such businesses lining the sides of the canal as it passes through their towns. But other localities of lesser size are also blessed with a plethora of places to dine, drink, and sightsee. Examples of this are Lockport, Fairport, and Sylvan Beach. These towns thrive off the Erie Canal and the annual flow of hikers, bikers, and boaters who visit the communities. Reporting on all of the restaurants, pubs, and attractions in each of communities would be impossible.

Another category of events and "attractions" along the canal includes the many festivals and fairs that are conducted in different locations, especially during the warmer months. Some of these events occur for extended periods of time and are not limited to one specific location. An example of this is the Erie Canalway Challenge, which takes place each year in February. This event is conducted over the entire length of the Erie Canal and is designed to get individuals and families out of the house and into the great outdoors. The primary objective is physical activity and exercise, and people can hike, bike, run, roller skate, or paddle. (Paddling on the Erie Canal in February might be difficult.) You keep track of your own miles and try to attain goals of different mileages.

This is only one example of the many events along the canal that take place in almost every town and in almost every month of the year. If you are hiking, biking, or boating the canal, it might take some planning for you to arrive at a specific location for a specific event. However, there is a table in the back of this book that lists as many events as we could find. It is organized chronologically throughout the year, along with the event locations. Note: Festivals and other events vary from year to year, so please confirm the events and dates before planning your schedule.

There are a few exceptional areas across the state where the canal path is located at an extended distance from the canal itself. For example, the route of the Canalway Trail south of Oneida Lake is usually eight to twelve miles south of the canal, which passes through the middle of Oneida Lake. This is important because the canal and the trail are used by two distinctly different groups of travelers. Most hikers and bikers will be found on the canal trail rather than in the water—likewise, very few boaters will be found piloting their vessels down the asphalt pathway! In order to accommodate both sets of canal voyagers, I have tried to list restaurants, pubs, and attractions within proximity to either the canal or the path, for convenience to the reader. Additionally, when the canal transits across sections of much larger bodies of water (i.e., Oneida Lake), I have included the businesses and points of interest to boaters along the entire shoreline of the lake, even though this information will be irrelevant to the hikers and bikers on the canal path. (A separate note on the safety implications of transiting Oneida Lake is found at the end of this introduction.)

One other reference included in this book is a listing of boating services, including marinas, boat docks, electricity, water, fuel, repair services, and more. There are many locations that offer these services, and they are all listed on the New York State Canal Corporation's website. See "Public Harbors and Marinas" at the back of this book for more details.

Explanation of photographs: Due to constraints on the number of pages in this volume, it has been important to limit the photographs to a maximum of one per business. This is unfortunate, as many of these old, historic pubs and restaurants have magnificent architecture and woodwork on display in their interiors. However, an attempt has been made to show the exterior (front) of the building or storefront wherever possible. This has been done to provide the user (hikers/bikers/boaters) with a visual guide to locating that particular business.

Finally, please note that certain information pertinent to individual restaurants and pubs does change on an annual basis. For example, days and hours of operation may vary from month to month or season to season. Likewise, restaurants that offer outdoor dining, whether on a scenic rooftop or on a deck or patio overlooking the canal generally cease offering those options once the summer ends. For these reasons, it is always best to call ahead whenever possible to confirm the current accuracy of this information. (Some restaurants may even close permanently between seasons.) Phone numbers and street addresses have been included for every restaurant and pub for your convenience.

IMPORTANT INFORMATION TO BIKERS—WHAT IS BFNY?

BFNY stands for Bike Friendly New York, and it is a designation that can be earned by a restaurant, pub, accommodation, retail business, or other establishment to notify bicyclists of its policy of supporting and encouraging cycling activities.

Bicycling is the second-most-popular outdoor activity in the United States. Literally tens of millions of people enjoy cycling for exercise and as a mode of transportation. Many of these same individuals use their bicycles as a way to tour across their community or across the nation.

Seeing the BFNY sticker on the outside of a business identifies that entity as a location where you can be sure to find certain amenities to support their activity. Most restaurants and pubs that have earned the BFNY designation have space reserved in front of their business for parking bikes, along with a bike rack for locking them in place.

Many BFNY restaurants also offer the following:

- Menus posted in front of the restaurant (many have vegetarian/vegan options available)
- Restrooms (for customers)
- Energy bars and "quick bites" to go
- Free water bottle fill-ups
- Charging ports for electronic devices
- Some offer discounts to cyclists/trail users

Although not listed here, many businesses also offer bicycle repair kits, which can be used to make minor repairs. These kits normally contain a flat tire kit, rubber gloves, a hex wrench set, a multitool device, screwdrivers (Phillips and flathead), cleaning supplies, chain lube and grease, and a pedal wrench.

Businesses are not required to offer all services to cyclists, so inquire about availability upon arrival.

IMPORTANT NOTICE TO BOATERS TRANSITING ONEIDA LAKE

This guide provides many descriptions of restaurants, pubs, and attractions located around the perimeter of Oneida Lake. The reason for these individual write-ups is that the Erie Canal passes directly through the middle (lengthwise) of Oneida Lake, which is a large body of water, measuring roughly twenty-one miles in length and five miles across. The intent of this guide is to provide information to boaters on the canal about possible locations to pull up to a dock for a meal at one of these locations around the lake.

However, there is a danger involved in leaving the plotted track of the canal as it transits across the lake from Brewerton to Sylvan Beach, or vice versa (from east to west). The average depth of Oneida Lake is twenty-two feet, and it reaches a maximum depth of fifty-five feet in some places. But this water depth varies greatly from point to point in the lake and decreases rapidly as one approaches many of the shorelines. While conducting interviews at many of the restaurants and pubs around Oneida Lake, several of the business owners warned that there were only a few feet of navigable water approaching their own docks. Extreme care must be taken by the boat owners to avoid grounding on the lake bottom or running into other submerged obstacles in the water.

Boaters who are using small boats, canoes, paddleboats, and other platforms with very limited draft should be safe in most of these locations. Anyone using a deeper draft boat of any kind should carry some form of sounding device to measure the water depth and avoid going aground or striking underwater obstacles.

Maps detailing potential shoal waters and other submerged hazards are available online from organizations such as the Oneida Lakes Association, at www.oneidalakesassociation.org.

SPECIAL ATTRACTION: THE ERIE CANAL BOAT *SENECA CHIEF*

The *Seneca Chief* (page xvi) is berthed at the Commercial Slip at Canalside in downtown Buffalo. The Commercial Slip is located at 44 Prime Street, Buffalo, New York. *Seneca Chief* is the "Flagship of the Erie Canal Bicentennial," and thus is featured in this book. The boat is a special project that will sail across the entire Erie Canal and will serve to commemorate Governor Clinton's initial sailing on the first iteration of this vessel.

The *Seneca Chief*, docked at the Commercial Slip in Buffalo the day after its christening (May 25, 2024). Phone/Address: (716) 881-0111/Commercial Slip at 44 Prime Street, Buffalo, New York 14202.
PHOTO BY LARRY WEILL

HISTORICAL BACKGROUND

The *Seneca Chief* is a major nautical and historical project that attempted to replicate the canalboat used by Governor DeWitt Clinton in his inaugural sailing of the Erie Canal in 1825. Clinton was the sixth governor of New York State and was the major driving force behind the planning and construction of the Erie Canal. It was under his reign as governor that he convinced the state legislature to provide $7 million for the construction.

On the voyage aboard *Seneca Chief*, he sailed from the west end of the newly completed Erie Canal to the location where the canal merged with the Hudson River. He then continued on his ten-day passage, heading south on the Hudson until arriving in New York Harbor on November 4, 1825. Off the coast of Sandy Hook, Clinton then poured a bucket of water that had been brought from Lake Erie into the Atlantic Ocean, thus "wedding the waters."

The effort to re-create this boat was a monumental task because it required vast amounts of research before any construction was started. One problem in building a duplicate craft involved the lack of photographic references. Even the predecessor of photography, daguerreotype, was not in use until the 1840s. This meant that the details of building such a craft were derived from whatever records, plans, and archived sketches that could be found in museums and libraries.

The following two paragraphs are taken from the Buffalo Maritime Center's exhibit:

At present, it is unknown why the boat was named *Seneca Chief*. The naming of the boat probably fell in line with the attitude of the time and can be perceived as a stinging honor towards the people pushed aside.

Today's Erie Canal Boat Project replicates a historic vessel from a time and culture different from our own. Comparing the influences and perspectives of the people of 1825 in relation to our own helps us understand the past more fully and guides our future actions. Today, the boat's name, *Seneca Chief*, is an opportunity to share the story of the Haudenosaunee and the Erie Canal.

BUILDING THE NEW *SENECA CHIEF*

Coordinating this massive effort is the Buffalo Maritime Center (BMC), a community-based nonprofit organization focused on "life lessons through community boatbuilding, preserving maritime culture, and exploring the waterways of Western New York." (Taken from the mission statement of the BMC website.) They successfully mobilized and utilized hundreds of volunteers who were engaged in every aspect of the work, from research to hands-on boatbuilding. To increase interest and awareness of this mission, the boat was constructed in public view inside the Canalside Longshed. It is interesting to note only two professional shipwrights were involved in the building process. The rest were all volunteers from the community and various student groups.

The *Seneca Chief* is seventy-three feet in length with a beam (width) of twelve feet six inches. It weighs in at about forty tons. The interior cabin of the boat is completely authentic, and uses cabinet-grade hardwood to resemble the appearance of the vessel in the 1820s. The BMC even used its own forge to produce all the bolts used in the keel and rib structure of the boat. Even the boatbuilding tools were produced in this forge, thus contributing to the absolute authenticity of the vessel.

Note that students of the history of early New York and the Finger Lakes region may have encountered references to another vessel named *Seneca Chief*, which navigated the waters of Seneca Lake during the same era. That boat was a steamship constructed in Geneva, New York, from December 1827 through May 1828 and was not related to the Erie Canal boat *Seneca Chief* in any way. That vessel was used for moving both passengers and cargo on Seneca Lake until its final demise in 1848. It was sunk by explosives as part of Geneva's Fourth of July celebration.

ACTIVITIES LEADING TO THE BICENTENNIAL VOYAGE

The inauguration of the *Seneca Chief* took place on May 25, 2024, at the Commercial Slip at Canalside, Buffalo. Its schedule for the rest of 2024 into 2025 consists of a few appearances at local-area festivals and other events, followed by a series of sea trial sailings to cities in western New York. (These events will already be completed by the time this book is released.)

In 2025, *Seneca Chief* will depart from Buffalo en route to New York Harbor in celebration of Governor Clinton's 1825 inaugural sailing. The schedule for this voyage is being prepared and will be publicized in the near future. However, communities all along the Erie Canal and Hudson River will have the opportunity to observe the vessel, which will make numerous stops along the route. Boaters on the Erie Canal (if traveling at the same time) will be able to view the boat as it journeys across the state. Visit https://buffalomaritimecenter.org for details on locations and dates.

ERIE COUNTY

ELLICOTT ISLAND BARK PARK

Address: 10 Creekside Drive, North Tonawanda, NY, 14120.

Park Hours: Summer hours are 7 a.m.–9 p.m., and the park closes at dusk in the winter (Labor Day through Memorial Day).

Note: This park usually closes for a month in early spring to clean up the downed branches and other damage caused by the winter weather. This is an annual cleanup operation that gets the park ready for its busy summer season.

Description: This bark park has literally gone to the dogs! It is a good-sized island (over five hundred meters long) that serves Erie County as a park dedicated to

This castle on the shoreline of Ellicott Island Bark Park is a fitting tribute to man's best friend.
Photo by Larry Weill

providing our canine friends with a place to run off-leash and have fun. There is no need for a fence around this tract of land as it is completely surrounded by the waters of the canal. Access is gained solely by way of a double-gated bridge, so that Fido cannot escape the grounds.

Services: This park offers services to the poochies and their owners alike. For the humans, there are shelters to block the sun and the rain. There are nice, clean restrooms available for public use, and also a small library in case you'd like to catch up on some light reading while the dog is playing.

Rules for canines and humans: Any dogs brought onto the island must be friendly (nonaggressive), and at least four months of age. Dogs over the age of six months must be spayed, and all dogs must be vaccinated and licensed and have a collar with updated tags. Dog owners can bring no more than two dogs onto the island. Owners must also clean up after their pets, and plastic disposal bags are provided both on the island and off.

Other rules for humans include that bicycles are forbidden on the island park, as are glass containers. Children twelve and under must be accompanied and supervised by an adult.

Summary: The feedback from dog owners on this island is superb. People thoroughly enjoy having this park to give their canines a place to run off-leash. It's also a great opportunity to meet other dog owners and socialize your pet. The park is an easy-on-easy-off from the Empire State Trail. The local canine population has given this park two "paws up!"

DOCKSIDE BAR & GRILL

Phone/Address: (716) 693-3600/153 Sweeney Street, North Tonawanda, NY 14120.

Days/Hours: Closed on Monday, Tuesday through Thursday 3 p.m.–midnight, Friday and Saturday noon–1 a.m., Sunday noon–11 p.m. (hours change seasonally).

Reservations accepted? Yes, but only from October 1 through April 30.

Restaurant size: This is a large restaurant with about seventy tables, including those inside, outside (on the deck), and upstairs.

Outdoor seating: Yes.

Dockside Bar & Grill, North Tonawanda, New York.
PHOTO BY LARRY WEILL

Menu items: Lots of appetizers, salads, handheld sandwiches (including loaded steak!), several chicken dishes, turkey bacon wings and tenders, seven different burgers, and a fish fry. The larger entrées include jambalaya, twin filets mignons, prime rib, and meat loaf.

Price range: Most of the smaller dishes on the menu are $15–$20 while many of the entrées are priced between $25 and $30.

Most popular menu item: The fresh seafood and the handcrafted burgers.

Entertainment: No.

Liquor license: Yes.

Description: Dockside Bar & Grill is a large and beautiful spot for many reasons. It is located right next to the dock in North Tonawanda (next to the bridge over Main Street) so boaters can tie up and climb right into the restaurant. It is literally right there. It's been a local favorite for eleven years now, and the owner keeps finding new ways to make improvements.

The entire place is decorated in a nautical theme, with models of sailing ships over the bar and lots of naval mementoes on display throughout the bar-room. For those who wish to sit outside on the deck without worrying about the weather, they have installed retractable awnings that can be rolled out at a moment's notice if needed.

Their extensive list of eight appetizers offers something for every taste bud, and their fish fry is available seven days a week.

The bar also has twenty-four beers on tap at any given time, which compliments their selection of sixteen featured bourbons and eight featured cocktails. So what's not to love!

PRESCOTT'S PROVISIONS

Phone/Address: (716) 525-1260/40 E. Niagara Street, Tonawanda, NY 14150.

Days/Hours: Closed on Sunday and Monday, Tuesday through Saturday 5 p.m.–10 p.m.

Reservations accepted? Yes.

Restaurant size: Fifty-six tables, including those on the front and side patios.

Outdoor seating: Yes.

Menu items: Small plates include beets, Berkshire Pork Belly, grilled scallops, beef tartare, octopus, and raw oysters. The larger dishes advertised are the Provisions burger, salmon, Angus prime sirloin, Angus beef tenderloin, and wood-roasted chicken sausage.

Price range: Most of the small plates list for $15–$19 although some (the oysters) are "market price." The larger entrées are generally $40–$50 with the Angus beef tenderloin at $58.

Most popular menu item: Entrées cooked in the wood-fired oven are all popular.

Entertainment: No.

Liquor license: Yes.

Description: Prescott's Provisions is located directly across the street from the canal, with a picturesque Erie Canal buoy boat parked on the grass in front of the building. It is a relatively large restaurant with two patio decks to augment their regular indoor tables. The front deck has a beautiful view over the canal, and the

Prescott's Provisions in Tonawanda, New York.
PHOTO BY LARRY WEILL

outside tables have a retractable awning to fend off the raindrops. The front deck also has roll-down windows to provide access to the fresh air in warmer months.

This restaurant offers some nice touches that are not often found in the local restaurant scene. For those diners who are oenophiles, they have an extensive wine cellar that boasts a five-thousand-bottle collection. Diners in the main dining room have a great view of the wood-fired oven and can watch their meals being cooked from their seats. The restaurant uses an Argentinian-style grill, which is also on display in the open kitchen. It uses wood or charcoal but never propane and operates at adjustable heights so the heat can be perfectly adjusted and controlled at all times.

Prescott's is proud of the fact that their menu changes almost every week, with new and exciting items appearing throughout the year. They are more meat-based in the winter and then shift to a greater emphasis on seafood in the summer. It is all superbly prepared for your dining pleasure.

ERIE COUNTY • 5

REMINGTON TAVERN & SEAFOOD EXCHANGE

Phone/Address: (716) 362-2802/184 Sweeney Street, North Tonawanda, NY 14120.

Days/Hours: Monday through Thursday 4 p.m.–10 p.m., Friday and Saturday 4 p.m.–11 p.m., Sunday closed (but open Sundays in summer).

Reservations accepted? Yes.

Restaurant size: about thirty-five tables, with lots of bar seating.

Outdoor seating: Yes.

Menu items: This restaurant is all about the fresh seafood and its imaginative preparation. They have a raw bar that provides superb oysters and clams casino. Their appetizers include lobster bisque, shrimp cocktails, fried calamari, crab cakes, pan-seared scallops, and swordfish Oscar. They also offer steaks and chops, for the "landlubbers" in the crowd.

Price range: The raw bar is priced per piece for oysters and clams. The clams are $22 for twelve pieces while the oysters are $21 for six. Most appetizers range

Remington Tavern & Seafood Exchange in North Tonawanda, New York.
PHOTO BY LARRY WEILL

between $12 and $18. The main entrées are generally between $30 and $40, while the steaks range from $40 to $60.

Most popular menu item: Oysters, served either on the half shell, grilled, or "Rockefeller."

Entertainment: Yes (they have a Beatles cover band on Mondays).

Liquor license: Yes.

Description: This is another lovely restaurant in a historic building along the canal. (The sign carved in stone on the front of the building says "Power House: Buffalo & Niagara Falls Electric Railway, 1895.") It is across from the Main Street bridge and the docks along the canal that allow boaters to tie up and walk across the street to the restaurant.

The entire interior of Remington is beautifully decorated and lit, with lots of artwork and antique accessories that reinforce the historic influence of the building. It is truly a wonderful place to simply sit and enjoy a drink.

I had some extra time to kill in this restaurant, so I ordered appetizers of shrimp cocktail and clams casino. They were superb. With the shrimp cocktail they provide a quantity of cocktail sauce topped with freshly grated horseradish. It was amazing!

JIM'S STEAKOUT

Phone/Address: (716) 695-2000/2952 Niagara Falls Blvd. W., Amherst, NY, 14228.

Days/Hours: Sunday through Thursday 10:30 a.m.–midnight, Friday and Saturday 10:30 a.m.–2 a.m.

Reservations accepted? No.

Restaurant size: Ten tables plus high-top counter seating indoors plus four tables on their front patio.

Outdoor seating: No.

Menu items: Lots of subs, hoagies, and other handheld food items. They also serve tacos, sandwiches, and boneless wings, and several varieties of fries (including poutine, "stinger," Philly, and taco fries).

Price range: Small subs (eight inches) are $11–$13, large subs (twelve inches) are $12–$16, different varieties of French fries range from $4 to $7, as do most individual tacos.

Most popular menu item: They are best known for their most popular dish, the steak hoagie, which is made with certified Angus beef (also available with grilled chicken), topped with melted cheese, fried sweet peppers, onions, mushrooms, lettuce, and tomato, plus Jim's secret sauce, all on a toasted Italian bomber roll.

Entertainment: No.

Liquor license: No.

Jim's SteakOut in Amherst, New York.
PHOTO BY LARRY WEILL

Description: Jim's SteakOut is part of a larger chain, but it is so convenient to the Empire State Trail (and the nearby Bark Park) that it's been included in this book. The restaurant is large and has a friendly staff. The portions are large (in case you've worked up a big appetite on the trail), and the prices are low.

The folks at Jim's SteakOut like to point out that everything on the menu is made fresh, and nothing is premade. They say that people can taste the difference, which is what brings their customers back over and over again.

The outdoor tables (located on their front brick patio) are also attractive, especially if you have your dog along with you.

WEST CANAL MARINA WATERFRONT PARK

Phone/Address: (716) 694-4630/4070 Tonawanda Creek Road, North Tonawanda, NY, 14120.

Park Hours: The park is open seven days a week from 7 a.m. to 9 p.m. from Memorial Day through the end of September.

West Canal Marina Waterfront Park, North Tonawanda, New York.
PHOTO BY LARRY WEILL

Note: Most marinas are not covered in this book. However, this facility is quite large and scenic, and it offers many services to the boating community.

Description: This marina is located in the town of Pendleton on the north side of the canal. It is a spacious park spread across twenty-seven acres of canal-side land.

This site can be used by boaters as well as families looking for a scenic picnic setting. The boat docks can be used for boats to tie up or for fishing.

Services: There are five shelters at this park of different sizes (with or without electricity) that can be rented for events. Each of these shelters has its own charcoal grill. Restrooms are also available for public use. There are four boat launch ramps with ample room to drive up and unload boats.

Park Rules: No glass containers are permitted inside the park. If you are bringing along a system to play music, it cannot interfere with other park users. Visitors are not permitted to set up inflatable slides, "bounce houses," dunk tanks, or other amusement devices in the park. Also prohibited are open fires, fireworks, and firearms.

All animals must be kept under control on a leash at all times. Owners are responsible for cleaning up after their pets and disposing of any waste.

Boaters who are staying at the marina overnight must stay within the immediate area of their boats outside of the park's operating hours. All boaters docking, mooring, or anchoring at the marina must record their arrival and departure at the park kiosk. Boaters may stay at the marina for a maximum of three uninterrupted days. They may return after a minimum of five consecutive days since their previous stay.

HERSCHELL CARROUSEL FACTORY MUSEUM

Address: 180 Thompson Street, North Tonawanda, NY, 14120.

Museum Hours: Wednesday through Saturday 10 a.m.–4 p.m., Sunday noon–4 p.m. Hours may change from year to year, so check online to confirm current information.

Seasonal: The museum is open from April 1 through December 31

Description: First of all, this attraction bends the rules a bit to be included in this book. But it is definitely worth the effort. The Carrousel Museum is not located directly on the Erie Canal. Instead, it sits on Tonawanda Creek about one thousand yards before it merges with the canal. But this facility is an incredible pleasure to see, fascinating to tour, and a genuine piece of local history preserved in all its original glory.

Many people do not realize that North Tonawanda is one of the largest cities in the United States for producing carousels. At one time there were four companies producing these rides, with the Herschell brand in production from the mid-1800s until it ceased production in the 1930s. Of all the carousel companies in the city, Herschell is the only one that maintains a museum inside its original buildings.

There are too many features and fun things to do in this museum to describe them all on one page, but I'll do the best I can. First, the museum is organized to allow each visitor and group to take a self-guided tour of the entire facility. From the time you enter the front door, you are directed through the labyrinth of rooms, starting with the woodshop, the master carvers' shop, the carvings and pattern shop, the paint room and Phillip Lockman collection, and the machine

Herschell Carrousel Factory Museum in North Tonawanda, New York.
PHOTO BY LARRY WEILL

shop (currently the Jeanette E. Jones Children's Gallery). There are stories and works of art associated with each of these rooms along the tour route.

Each ticket purchased includes a ride on the 1916 "#1 Special Carrousel," music from historic band organs, and a visit to Kiddieland. Each stop along the route provides a look back into history, including descriptions of how the rough sections of raw timber were planed into smooth boards and then glued together to form blocks of wood that could be carved into carousel animals.

As you tour the building, keep your eyes open for items on the Scavenger Hunt list so you can win a free prize from the gift shop!

Entrance Fees: $12 for adults, $9 for seniors (sixty-five and over) and students (with valid ID), $6 for children ages two to sixteen, children under two are free.

NIAGARA COUNTY

THE SHIP BAR & GRILL

Phone/Address: (716) 210-3020 / 5612 Tonawanda Creek Road, Lockport, NY 14094.

Days/Hours: Monday through Thursday 11 a.m.–midnight, Friday and Saturday 11 a.m.–2 a.m.

Reservations accepted? Yes (highly recommended on Friday and Saturday).

Restaurant size: Twenty-two tables indoors plus twenty more outside.

Outdoor seating: Yes.

Menu items: Wraps, salads, fish fry (three different) on Fridays, and a choice of fifteen different sandwiches, including burgers and chicken or beef on weck, as well as wings. The appetizers include clams casino, artichoke dip, onion rings, pizza logs, and fried ravioli.

Price range: Almost everything on the menu is listed at $15–$20.

Most popular menu item: Fish fry, plus everyone loves coming in on Thursdays for fifty-cent wing night.

Entertainment: Yes (live music at least two or three times every week during the summer and usually once or twice each week in the winter).

Liquor license: Yes.

Description: The Ship Bar & Grill feels like it's in Tonawanda, but it's actually built on a tiny sliver of Lockport. It is a unique and historical site, and is the only establishment of its kind located on the point where Tonawanda Creek meets the Erie Canal.

This bar/restaurant is a very friendly and relaxed place to come and just enjoy yourself. Management wants their customers to feel at home, and look at it more as a meeting place than a restaurant. They prepare steamed clams on the deck in the summer, and also host a lot of private parties and events in their large rooms and outdoor spaces.

The Ship Bar & Grill, Lockport, New York.
PHOTO BY LARRY WEILL

As one of their managers said, "Here you'll find the local laborers, office people, lawyers, blue collar and white collar and no collar all hanging out together. It's just the way we want to be."

By the way, be prepared to eat lots of chicken wings if you stop by on a Thursday. They cook over four thousand of them every wing night, to go along with their beef on weck and certified prime beef. Don't forget to bring along your appetite!

UNCLE G'S ICE CREAM

Phone/Address: (716) 210-3547 / 7030 Washington St., Pendleton (Lockport), NY 14094.

Days/Hours: Typically noon–9 p.m., but they do vary in spring and fall.

Reservations accepted? No.

Uncle G's Ice Cream in Pendleton, New York.
PHOTO BY LARRY WEILL

Restaurant size: Five tables inside, nine tables on the front yard, seven tables on the large covered deck.

Outdoor seating: Yes.

Menu items: In addition to the ice cream, you can get food items here as well, including hot dogs, burgers, salads, and subs. But make no mistake, the ice cream steals the show here, and it is available in many forms. They have soft-serve as well as scoop flavors, milkshakes, sundaes, and gluten/dairy-free varieties. Their unique signature sundaes include their famous "Pie Sundaes" (apple, strawberry/rhubarb, or cherry), which is a warm piece of pie with custard, whip, and cherry! The apple comes with caramel and pecans too. There is also a "Volcano Sundae." Oh, and let's not forget the "pup cups" for the family poochie. Wag that tail!

Price range: Their premium hard ice cream flavors are available in cones in four sizes from $3.25 to $5.65. Prices on soft custard cones are almost the same price. Sundaes range from $4.65 to $6.50, and milkshakes range from $4.25 for a small to $10.95 for a jumbo! Almost everything else on the menu falls within the same price range ($4.25 to $10.00).

Most popular menu item: The Peanut Butter Lover's Sundae, and anything with peanut butter.

Entertainment: No.

Liquor license: No.

Description: This place couldn't possibly be closer to the Canalway Trail. (If you were on the trail and turned sideways, then did a somersault, you'd be on their steps—literally!) This place is popular for its sixty (yes, sixty!) flavors of Perry's hard ice cream. They serve Upstate soft ice cream as well, and both are popular. They also serve great burgers, hot dogs, and other lunchtime favorites.

The bikers arrive in droves, especially during the major events that cross the state in midsummer. They've had over five hundred bikes stop there at once, as they are an official stop on the bike tour. Dogs are welcome here too, and they will gladly help you finish your cone. This place is an integral part of the community and supports local businesses at every opportunity.

STOOGES

Phone/Address: (716) 434-1100 / 2 Pine Street, Lockport, NY 14094

Days/Hours: Wednesday and Thursday noon–8 p.m., Friday and Saturday noon–7 p.m., Sunday 9 a.m.–7 p.m., closed on Monday and Tuesday.

Reservations accepted? Yes, for parties of 10 or more.

Restaurant size: Sixteen tables plus bar seating. There is also a party room that can be rented for large groups.

Outdoor seating: No.

Menu items: Stuffed burgers, chicken and sausage burgers, wraps, sandwiches, mac and cheese, wings, salads, and more. They even have a stuffed burger called the "Larry," which is stuffed with peanut butter, fresh jalapeños, a fresh jalapeño cream cheese, pepper berry jam, and bacon.

Price range: The stuffed burgers run between $20 and $24, salads are $12–$13, wings go for $13–$16 for a plate of ten.

Most popular menu item: Their large stuffed burgers, especially their "Stinger," which contains medium chicken fingers, shaved ribeye, provolone and blue cheeses, topped with lettuce and tomato.

Entertainment: No.

Liquor license: Yes.

Description: Stooges is an extremely cool restaurant built into a historic building that used to function as Brockport's old town hall. It sits on the bridge that spans the canal, so you couldn't get much closer to the water than that. This scenic restaurant serves lunches and dinners, but also offers breakfast on Sundays, when it opens early (9 a.m.) It also features a number of unique items on the

Stooges, in the old Town Hall building in Lockport, New York.
PHOTO BY LARRY WEILL

menu, including some unusual appetizers such as fried pickles and deep-fried cheese ravioli. My favorite from this list is the "Larry" stuffed burger. (Being a Larry myself, I couldn't help this.) The "Larry" is stuffed with peanut butter, fresh jalapeños, a fresh jalapeño cream cheese, pepper berry jam, and bacon. Wow! Try to top that!

To help wash down the burgers, Stooges also has a variety of pilsners, ales, wheat beers, Kölsches, and lagers, along with porters, stouts, and ciders. They even have champagne on tap, so you won't go thirsty.

LOCKPORT'S UPSIDE-DOWN TRAIN TRESTLE

Location: Downtown Lockport. This is the train bridge crossing the canal at Clinton Street, west of Lock 34/35.

Description: The "upside-down train trestle" is one attraction on the Erie Canal that you will see whether you want to or not. Whether you are hiking or biking

The "Upside-Down Train Bridge" viewed from Pine Street in Lockport, New York.
PHOTO BY LARRY WEILL

on the canal path or sailing your boat down the canal, you will pass directly under this historic metal span. You have no choice.

History: This unusual bridge was built over the Erie Canal in Brockport in 1902. The design of the bridge is an inverted Howe truss. This means the truss itself consists of chords, vertical members, and diagonal members. The vertical members are in tension and the diagonal members are in compression. This design was invented by William Howe in 1840, and the concept was used to construct bridges until the late 1800s. This design was also used in many of the covered bridges throughout the eastern United States.

To this day there remains some disagreement over the construction of this bridge, and why it appears to have been built upside down. There are some who espouse the viewpoint that the railroad companies did this intentionally to minimize the clearance beneath the bridge, thus restricting the size of boats that could pass with their cargo. After all, the commercial traffic on the waterway was in direct competition with the railway, and some thought it might be an effective restriction on large canalboats. However this argument can be easily dismissed since the "upside-down train bridge" still affords much more clearance than many of the nearby lift bridges.

The actual reason for the upside-down construction is that it was a cost-saving method that permitted the builders to design and build a narrower bridge, thus saving on materials and overall expenses. It had nothing to do with attempting to restrict boats with tall masts from sailing on the canal.

Summary: The bridge is still in use today, supporting a single train track. It is a fun and fascinating sight in a town that is filled with canal folklore. Even if you don't plan to stop and take pictures, you will see it as you go by. Just remember as you hike, bike, or boat past Clinton Street to look up.

LOCKPORT CAVE AND NIAGARA ZIPPER

Note: The Lockport Cave and the Niagara Zipper (a zipline spanning the Erie Canal) are two separate attractions located near the Erie Canal in Lockport. As of this writing, both are temporarily closed with hopes of reopening sometime in the future. Because of their popularity in past years they have been included in this book.

Phone/Address: The Lockport Cave and the Niagara Zipper share a common ticket office, which is located at 5 Gooding Street, Lockport, NY 14094. It is right next to the Pine Street Bridge. The office phone number is (716) 438-0174.

Websites:

Lockport Cave: https://lockportcave.com

Niagara Zipper: https://ridetheniagarazipper.com

Description: There is some confusion regarding the "cave" in Lockport Cave. There are actually two underground formations beneath the canal area in Lockport: a naturally formed series of limestone caves and a man-made tunnel system. The natural cave system is largely unexplored and was sealed off in 1886, making it inaccessible to the public. The "cave" used for the Lockport Cave tour is really a tunnel constructed between 1858 and 1900. It was an ingenious way of providing unlimited, pressurized freshwater to local industries to manufacture a variety of commercial products. The tour through these tunnels guided visitors through the dark subterranean realm of these eerie (and Erie!) hidden routes. The tours are not wheelchair accessible and do involve ascending several dozen stairs.

The Niagara Zipline is an exciting attraction that includes a series of four lines that traverse the Erie Canal, each spanning a different distance ranging from six hundred to nine hundred feet. To participate in this event, riders must meet a number of requirements, including specific ranges in height/weight, footwear, and health qualifications (no pregnancies or injuries). Riders will be screened and measured before riding. All riding/safety gear (helmet, body harness, and zip line trolley) will be provided. Rides include trips both across the canal and back.

Reservations and restrictions: In the past, reservations were available (and recommended) on the respective websites listed above. No information is currently available about either of these attractions or their future operations. But they have received favorable reviews, and they are both located directly adjacent to both the Erie Canal and the Canalway Trail. It is highly recommended that you call their phone or access their website to check for availability as well as to review their rules and restrictions.

TOM'S DINER

Phone/Address: (716) 439-4283 / 11 Main Street, Lockport, NY 14094

Days/Hours: Every day from 7 a.m. to 2 p.m.

Reservations accepted? No.

Restaurant size: Thirteen tables plus counter seating.

Outdoor seating: No.

Menu items: Breakfasts included a large listing of omelets, biscuits and gravy, French toast and pancakes, waffles, along with bacon, sausage, and corned beef hash. The lunch menu lists sandwiches, salads, "melts," wraps, paninis, burgers, hot dogs, and hoagies.

Price range: Most breakfasts range between $10 and $14, while most lunches are $11–$15.

Most popular menu item: Tom's Diner boasts that they have "the best bacon around." Their "Tom's Ultimate Breakfast" is also very popular.

Entertainment: No.

Liquor license: No.

Description: Tom's Diner has been in operation in Lockport since 2002, so the residents of this canal-side town are very comfortable with its menu and food.

Tom's Diner on Main Street in Lockport, New York.
PHOTO BY LARRY WEILL

The owner mentioned that people are invited to "step inside and come back in time." The walls are covered in murals depicting the Lockport street scenes of an earlier day. Other wall art provides old depictions of the members of the Rolling Stones, "the Fonz" (from *Happy Days*), and lots more.

In addition to the standard breakfast items, the restaurant also advertises a "Tom's Ultimate Breakfast" plate. This morning feast includes three eggs, two choices of meat, toast, home fries, and either pancakes or French toast, all for $16.95.

Although Tom's Diner is only open for breakfast and lunch, they also offer dinner to go, especially for major holidays. "We do a lot of holiday dinners for Thanksgiving, Christmas, Easter, and St. Patty's Day," said the owner. Of those, Thanksgiving is probably the most popular. Everyone wants the traditional Thanksgiving dinner, but not everyone wants to cook.

Tom's Diner is definitely a staple in Lockport's downtown dining scene. It is a great combination of superb food with a hometown feel (including the atmosphere with the customers) that has kept people coming back for generations.

PAPA LEO'S PIZZERIA

Phone/Address: (716) 434-4222 / 36 Main Street, Lockport, NY 14094

Days/Hours: Sunday through Thursday 11 a.m.–9 p.m. Friday and Saturday 11 a.m.–10 p.m.

Reservations accepted? No.

Restaurant size: Fifteen tables.

Outdoor seating: No.

Menu items: This is primarily a pizzeria, but it also serves wings, subs, burritos, chicken fingers, burgers, salads, and seafood. They also offer a bunch of specials, including some large package deals that appear to be targeted toward parties and other large groups.

Price range: Subs are priced from $10 to $14, while salads are $9–$11. Meanwhile the basic cheese pizzas are $12.29 for a small (twelve inches), and $17.99 for an extra-large (sixteen inches). Half-tray pizzas are $19.29, while the full party trays are $28.39. Specialty pizzas (with all kinds of toppings) are $19 for a medium and $24 for an extra-large.

Most popular menu item: Their standard pizza and wings, plus their Philly Cheesesteak subs are also very popular.

Entertainment: No.

Liquor license: No.

Description: Papa Leo's has enjoyed a long tenure in Lockport because of its superior product. The pizza is always "top shelf," but great pizza is always recognized quickly and remains in people's minds. Papa Leo's has been in business for thirty years, and that is not an accident.

In addition to the superior quality of their pizza and other menu items, Papa Leo's is also known by the locals as being a nice, clean, and quiet place to enjoy a meal. Many people either pick up their pizzas or have them delivered, but a lot of town residents enjoy the atmosphere of "dining in" at this long-standing Lockport staple. It's just a great place to enjoy the pizza and be seen.

Papa Leo's is also known for their wings, but even those come with a choice of options. If you do not want to worry about eating around the bones, they offer

Papa Leo's Pizzeria on Main Street in Lockport, New York.
PHOTO BY LARRY WEILL

a choice of regular wings (with bones), or boneless. You pick. Either way, they both come with your choice of sauces.

Don't feel like waiting for your food? Not a problem. Papa Leo's offers the option to order online, so your pizza will be ready when you arrive. You can even order from your boat!

CHENEZ'S GOURMET POPCORN

Phone/Address: (716) 438-8141 / 21 Main Street, Lockport, NY 14094

Days/Hours: Tuesday through Saturday 10 a.m.–7 p.m., Sunday 10 a.m.–5 p.m., closed on Monday. (Note: These are summer hours.)

Reservations accepted? No. (There are no dining options at this store.)

Food items: Lots and lots and lots of popcorn! There are also different candies and soft drinks available.

Price range: Small bags of plain popcorn start at $4 and increase in price with the varieties selected. Large bags run from $15 to $23.

Most popular menu item: Peanut Butter Cup popcorn.

Entertainment: No.

Liquor license: No.

Description: Chenez's Gourmet Popcorn is such a cool and different place. Although it is definitely "food," it is not part of the Lockport restaurant scene. Instead it is a store that sells a huge variety of popcorn flavors, including many that you've never experienced in your life.

The owner of this shop, which is located right on top of the canal, is passionate about the art of producing world-beating popcorn. He got his start while attending a high school baseball tournament in Pennsylvania in 2016 with his son and family. It was there that he sampled some homemade "craft" popcorn, which got him thinking about trying to replicate and improve on that product.

Chenez's Gourmet Popcorn on Main Street in Lockport, New York.
Photo by Larry Weill

Making a long story short, he began by making caramel popcorn for his friends, who all clamored for more. After bursting onto the scene at festivals and other public events, he opened his first shop in Lockport in 2019, followed by a second store in 2020, with a third store coming in the near future.

Chenez's Gourmet popcorn has now expanded to forty-four flavors, including Birthday Cake, "Shout Mix" (for Buffalo Bills fans), Garlic Parm, Fruit Medley, PB&J, Smores, Cocomallow, Buffalo & Cheddar, and Cookies & Crème. They are all amazing, and all you need to do to become hooked is to try a small sample. (I made that mistake today. Yum!) I highly recommend stopping at their store on Main Street and giving it a try. Your fellow boat crew members will thank you.

STEAMWORKS COFFEE

Phone/Address: (716) 727-0701 / 51 Canal Street, Lockport, NY 14094

Days/Hours: Monday through Friday 7 a.m.–6 p.m., Saturday and Sunday 8 a.m.–6 p.m.

Reservations accepted? No.

Restaurant size: Four tables.

Outdoor seating: No.

Menu items: Home-ground and roasted coffees, espressos, and teas. Also a great selection of baked goods to go with the hot beverages, including muffins, biscotti, scones, and cinnamon rolls.

Price range: Teas around are around $6, while espressos cost between $4 and $6. Most coffee drinks range between $2 and $6.

Most popular menu item: Cold-brewed coffee drinks and a cinnamon roll.

Entertainment: No.

Liquor license: No.

Description: Steamworks Coffee is rightfully proud of their coffee products since they grind and roast all their own coffees in-house. It is a labor of love for those who enjoy putting a quality product on the shelf for their customers.

This is a quiet store that boasts a premium cup of coffee and the best of bakery products to go with it. Located right next to the canal, they receive a great many visitors coming off the water and canal path for a cup of their favorite joe. Everyone knows where the best coffee resides in Lockport, and this is it.

Steamworks Coffee, Lockport, New York.
PHOTO BY LARRY WEILL

They offer a plethora of choices for almost everything. Their espressos include double-shot, Gibraltar, cappuccino, Americano, and latte. If you prefer "plain" coffee, their menu board lists Ethiopian, Columbian, Peru Las Damas, Bourbon (Brazil), Sumatra, Mexico (decaf), and Uganda AA.

Stop in and visit the good people in this wonderful coffee shop. You are guaranteed to walk out satisfied (and very awake)!

LAKE EFFECT ARTISAN ICE CREAM

Phone/Address: (716) 201-1643 / 79 Canal Street, Lockport, NY 14094

Days/Hours: Monday through Friday 4 p.m.–9 p.m., Saturday and Sunday 11 a.m.–9 p.m.

Reservations accepted? No.

Restaurant size: Six tables.

Lake Effect Artisan Ice Cream in Lockport, New York.

Outdoor seating: Yes, in summer.

Menu items: This local ice cream shop has lots and lots of flavors, which are available in cones, cups, and other containers. The flavors include frozen hot chocolate, "Big Wayne's Cake Batter," loganberry, "Extra Cookies Extra Cream," "Pure Coconut," "Extra Vanilla," and tons more. (How about "London Fog" and "Revolution Coffee"?)

Price range: Ice cream in a bowl is $4.00 for 1 scoop, $4.50 for two scoops and $5.00 for three scoops. Their menu lists a choice of thirteen different toppings, each is $0.75. Pints of ice cream go for $5.75, milkshakes are $5.00 for regular or $5.75 for large. Ice cream cakes are available for $29–$43 depending on size and specialty. Lots more is on the menu, so stop in to check it out.

Most popular menu item: Salty caramel, peanut butter, and black raspberry truffle.

Entertainment: No (although "Rock the Locks" concerts are held outside in the summer).

Liquor license: No.

Description: The owners here are fond of saying, "It's never too cold for ice cream," and they are quite right. They are open in winter as well as summer, although their winter hours are somewhat limited.

Lake Effect is known in Western New York for creating flavors that are unique and cannot be found anywhere else. They sell a huge array of sauces, syrups, popcorn, and candles that are sourced from small local businesses. (Please don't try to eat the candles!)

This company is also fantastic in that it is a major "player" in community affairs. It sponsors patients in local children's hospitals, and also supports local sports teams across the area. That's just the kind of people who own this wonderful ice cream store.

This store, which is right next to the canal, should be on your "must visit" list. It is a bike-friendly business, for those biking the Canalway Trail, and it's worth the stop.

ERIE CANAL DISCOVERY CENTER AND LOCKPORT VISITOR CENTER

Phone/Address: (716) 439-0431 / 24 Church Street, Lockport, NY 14094.

Seasonal: This attraction is open year-round. However, it is open fewer days and hours during the offseason.

Days/Hours: Summer (from May 1 to October 31), open 9 a.m.–5 p.m., 7 days a week. Winter (from November 1 to April 30), open on Friday and Saturday 10 a.m.–3 p.m.

Admission: $6 for adults, $5 for seniors, veterans, and AAA members. children (under 18) are free.

History: The building that houses the Erie Canal Discover Center and Lockport Visitor Center is a piece of history in its own right. It was built in 1843 from left-over canal stones, which were plentiful at the time. It served as the Universalist Church in the community, which explains the appearance of the building both inside and out. It was later acquired by the Presbyterian Church across the street and used as a social hall. It has served in its current role for over twenty years.

Erie Canal Discovery Center and Lockport Visitor Center, Lockport, New York.
PHOTO BY LARRY WEILL

Dual role: The building today serves in two capacities. It is both the Erie Canal Discovery Center and the Lockport Visitor Center. The majority of the rooms are dedicated to the history, creation, and operation of the Erie Canal. However, on the lower level (gift shop), the City of Lockport maintains a small area where information on local sites and attractions is available. A staff member from Lockport is sometimes on duty to answer questions from visitors.

Exhibits: The Erie Canal Discovery Center and Lockport Visitor Center make up a wonderful facility filled with educational and historic exhibits and interactive displays. Visitors are first led to the small theater room on the second floor where they watch a fifteen-minute presentation about the construction of the Erie Canal. Local challenges including the "Flight of Five" locks and the massive "deep cutting" through bedrock are explained in the film.

After viewing the movie, visitors are free to roam through the exhibits, some of which provide guests the opportunity to try their hands at operating a lock and maneuvering a boat through the lock's rising or lowering water levels. Other displays explain the backgrounds of people important to the construction of the Erie Canal, from technical innovators to the laborers who risked their lives excavating the ditch and removing the countless tons of rock and rubble.

The bottom floor of the building contains a nice gift shop where visitors can purchase canal-related souvenirs. The City of Lockport also has a stand with free information in this room.

Access: This building is located "within a stone's throw" of the canal and bike trail, next to Locks 34 and 35. It is an easy-on-easy-off for canal travelers and within a short walk of several restaurants and services. Restrooms are also available to the public at this facility.

"FLIGHT OF FIVE" STAIRCASE LOCKS

Location: Downtown Lockport, on the Erie Canal, beneath the Pine Street Bridge.

Description: The city of Lockport is perhaps the most historic and scenic community in Upstate New York, and the Erie Canal forms an integral and key part of that history. One of the major engineering challenges of the original construction was how to raise the canal up sixty feet to meet the elevation of the Niagara Escarpment.

The solution to this incredible challenge was the construction of a series of five staircase locks, (numbered 67–71), which were completed in 1825. The locks were narrow, so two sets were built to accommodate eastbound and westbound traffic.

One set of these locks is still in place today, and can be viewed and toured from the middle of Lockport. A later upgrade to the canal replaced the other series of staircase locks with the modern Lock 34 and 35, which are still in use today.

A partial view (looking northeast) of the "Flight of Five" locks on the Erie Canal in Lockport, New York.
Photo by Larry Weill

Anyone visiting this site today will appreciate the sheer magnitude of manual labor required to excavate these canals. It has been estimated that as many as two thousand men worked on this project at any one time. Many tools and devices were invented for the sole purpose of digging rock, using explosive charges, and lifting rock from the blast sites out of the canal ditch.

If you decide to visit this amazing site, there are tours that will guide you through the most pertinent sections of the route. There is also a paved ramp that you can walk instead of descending the stone staircases. This ramp was part of the original towpath on which teams of horses and mules used to pull boats on the canal. In either case, please note that the ramp is quite steep, and pushing a wheelchair up this incline will be a strenuous task. Also be advised that the stone staircases are also very steep, and each step is much higher than found in modern-day construction. Persons with mobility issues may have trouble in climbing or descending these stairs.

An excellent model of the staircase locks is on display inside the Lockport Locks District Museum, located at the bottom of the locks.

CANAL BUOY TENDER BOAT 110

Location: In Lockport, at the corner of South Transit Street and West Genesee Street, right next to the Walgreens parking lot.

Note: This is a busy intersection with a lot of car traffic. Please be cautious when crossing to view the boat.

Description: This triangular patch of brick-covered surface is too small to call a park. However, it does serve to display a proud piece of canal history in the form of a canal buoy boat. These vessels were utilized along the canal to refill the lanterns that sat upon the navigational buoys. At one time there were over 150 of these boats in service. although not all of them remain today.

Not all these boats are retired today. Some are still used for the purposes of conducting general errands, performing maintenance work, and taking channel soundings. Regardless, they are still a colorful and picturesque part of the local canal history.

Canal buoy tender boat 110, on display near the canal in Lockport, New York.
PHOTO BY LARRY WEILL

LOCKPORT LOCKS DISTRICT MUSEUM

Location: In Lockport, on the lower canal level beneath the "Flight of Five" staircase locks.

Description: This museum is an interactive look back into the creation and history of the Erie Canal. It contains not only antique artifacts of the canal's operations, but also several displays and models that demonstrate how locks work and how boats move through the waterway.

For those who would rather listen than read, there are several pushbutton displays that will read and demonstrate various phases of the operations. Other displays inside the building outline the history of the construction, including fascinating timelines of the three main stages of development from 1825 to the present.

There is a paved ramp that you can walk instead of descending the stone staircases. But please note that the ramp is quite steep, and pushing a wheelchair up this incline will be a strenuous task. Be advised that the stone staircases are also

Lockport Locks District Museum in Lockport, New York.
PHOTO BY LARRY WEILL

very steep, and each step is much higher than what is found in modern-day construction. Persons with mobility issues may have trouble climbing or descending these stairs.

Days/Hours: The museum is open seven days a week, from 8 a.m. to 5 p.m. during the summer months. It is also open limited hours during the offseason. Check online to determine availability during your visit.

Admission: Admission is free. Donations are always welcome.

CANAL TENDERS TRIBUTE STATUES

Location: On the set of stairs adjacent to the "Flight of Five" staircase locks in Lockport. These statues can be observed looking down from the Pine Steet bridge, or accessed directly from the stairs descending the locks en route to the museum.

Bronze statues of canal tenders, located at the staircase locks in Lockport, New York.
Photo by Larry Weill

Background: The artist who sculpted these works was Susan Geissler, a native of Youngstown, New York. She is a highly regarded sculptor of human figures, with examples of her artwork on display in thirteen states. This series of figures at the Lockport section of the canal is the largest display of bronze sculptures in Western New York.

History: This artwork is modeled on an 1897 photograph of canal tenders taken by F. B. Clench, a noted photographer of the day. There were twenty tenders employed at this location during the 1897 season. The photograph included twelve of those workers, plus the image of Bessie Wagoner, who was the daughter of Fred J. Wagoner. She was the only female in the photograph (and also the only female sculpted with the others), although no one knows why she was at the canal on that day.

Completion and dedication: The series of bronze sculptures took four years of hard work by Geissler, along with research from a dedicated team of local historians. The dedication of the final set of figures took place on September 16, 2023.

It was attended by more than seventy descendants of the original lock tenders in the 1897 photograph. This will forever remain an indelible part of Lockport's history, and that of the Erie Canal.

Visitation: If you are hiking, biking, or boating the canal, this is something you will see as you transit through the area. You should definitely take a few moments as you pass through to stop and visit. There is no admission fee, and it takes very little time. Just do it!

LOCKPORT LOCKS & ERIE CANAL CRUISES

Phone/Address: (716) 433-6155 / 210 Market Street, Lockport, NY 14094.

Seasonal: This attraction is open from mid-May through Columbus Day/Indigenous Peoples' Day (mid-October).

Hours: The cruise boats generally make three cruises/day, at 10 a.m., 12:30 p.m., and 3 p.m.

Admission: $24.50 for adults and $10–$11 for children. Tickets are purchased online or on-site.

Background: The owners of Lockport Locks & Erie Canal Cruises, Mike and Sharon Murphy, founded the company in May 1987. They started the company with three employees and a pair of pontoon boats capable of carrying eighteen passengers. Through their stewardship and love of the Erie Canal and community, they have grown the business into a flourishing cruise company with three large and beautiful boats that can provide visitors with a memorable canal experience.

The cruises: Their fleet of three cruise boats includes a craft that served as a whale watcher (holds 125 passengers) and a paddle wheel boat (which holds 150 passengers) that came from the St. Lawrence Seaway. The paddle wheel boat, named the *Lockview VI*, is the only paddleboat on the Erie Canal. Their third boat, *Lockview IV*, is an island waterway craft designed for river, canal, and small lake tours. It has a capacity of 48 passengers.

Passengers do not get to select which boat they will ride for their tour. This selection is made by the cruise director based on the number of passengers on the tour.

The cruises are fully narrated by the boat captains, each of whom is fully versed in the history and operation of the Erie Canal. Round trips are approximately

The *Lockview VI* departing on an Erie Canal cruise.

two hours in length and transport passengers past drydocks, lift bridges, locks from modern and past times, and the famous "upside-down train trestle."

Note: Lockport Locks & Canal Cruises does not maintain a daily kitchen staff. Meals and cocktail parties must be prearranged and are for groups and charters only. Groups interested in dining/bar/event service must arrange this ahead of time.

Other facilities: The company also operates a beautiful banquet facility that is located right at the pier on Market Street. They offer lunches to many organizations, including senior citizens' groups and schools. They also provide banquet services for special occasions, including weddings, showers, funerals, and more.

Bikers on the Canalway Trail are always welcome. Bikers lock their bikes to the fence in front of the building. For bikers who are cycling the entire canal (west-to-east) in July, this is the first stop on the weeklong journey.

CANALSIDE INN

Phone/Address: (716) 772-7733 / 4431 Main Street, Gasport, NY 14067

Days/Hours: Monday through Saturday, 11 a.m.–midnight, Sunday noon–6 p.m.

Reservations accepted? No.

Restaurant size: Fifteen tables.

Outdoor seating: No.

Menu items: Beef on weck, beef with cheddar, smoked ham, chicken wings, chicken tenders, shrimp, scallops, and a seafood platter.

Price range: Most lunches are between $11 and $14, while the seafood entrées range from $15 to $20, and the seafood platter is $28.

Most popular menu item: Roast beef and chicken wings.

Canalside Inn in Gasport, New York.
PHOTO BY LARRY WEILL

Entertainment: No.

Liquor license: Yes.

Description: The Canalside Inn is a very casual and comforting pub that sits close to the Gasport lift bridge on the canal. From the moment you walk in the door you will feel like you are among friends. (Everyone inside this place knows everyone else, as the entire town of Gasport has fewer than two thousand residents.)

This pub has a unique approach to food, and concentrates on fare that is popular in western New York. Folks who eat here love the beef on weck, which is piled high on the roll and just dripping with flavor. The menu features meals that can be either lunch or dinner, and they are happy to prepare meals to go, in case you don't have time to dine in.

The Canalside Inn is a family-run establishment, and they consider it to be half restaurant and half bar. This is another location that is easy to reach from either the canal or the walkway, since it sits on the corner adjacent to the bridge.

Even if you're not hiking, biking, or boating on the canal, it's easy to find parking right along the street. So come on in, especially if you're a Buffalo Bills fan.

PONY'S IRISH PUB

Phone/Address: (716) 735-9989 / 23 Main Street, Middleport, NY 14105

Days/Hours: Tuesday and Wednesday 3 p.m.–9 p.m., Thursday 3 p.m.–10 p.m., Friday and Saturday noon–midnight, Sunday noon–7 p.m., closed on Monday.

Reservations accepted? No.

Restaurant size: Approximately twenty-one tables inside, plus bar seating.

Outdoor seating: No.

Menu items: Lots of grilled foods, plus seafood, fish fries, mussels, clam strips, shrimp, and quarter-pound Angus burgers, with many dishes served with their special homemade sauces.

Price range: Lunches $7–$12, dinner $15–$20.

Most popular menu item: Breaded chicken wings,

Entertainment: Yes (live bands on weekends in the summer).

Liquor license: Yes.

Description: At the time of my visit, the entire restaurant was shut down and in the middle of an extensive remodeling project. I got to meet the owners, who are charming people excited about bringing a new, upgraded restaurant to the community.

This restaurant has a large menu with more seafood than usual for its location in western New York. They are proud of the special sauces they produce, all homemade, served with many of the dishes.

Pony's is currently the only bar in Middleport and has an outstanding reputation for its food as well as

Pony's Irish Pub in Middleport, New York.
PHOTO BY LARRY WEILL

its drink. It is close by the canal, so it receives a large number of bikers who stop in while cycling through the town.

This place is also famous for its breaded wings, which stand out from most "conventional" chicken wings. By the way, Pony's Famous Sauce is available in mild, medium, and hot (for those brave souls who are up to it!).

VILLAGE PIZZERIA

Phone/Address: (716) 735-7621 / 4 State Street, Middleport, NY 14105

Days/Hours: Tuesday and Wednesday, 4 p.m.–8 p.m., Thursday 11 a.m.–8 p.m., Friday 11 a.m.–10 p.m., Saturday 3 p.m.–10 p.m., Sunday 3 p.m.–8 p.m.

Reservations accepted? No.

Restaurant size: Six tables.

Outdoor seating: No.

Village Pizzeria in Middleport, New York.
PHOTO BY LARRY WEILL

Menu items: Lots of varieties of pizza (of course), chicken wings, subs and "specialty" subs (including chicken Parmesan, bacon cheeseburger, and chicken cordon bleu), wraps, nachos, and salads. They even offer six different seafood dishes.

Price range: Most subs are between $10 and $13, while the pizzas are $17–$20.

Most popular menu item: Steak hoagies, and the pizza of the month.

Entertainment: No.

Liquor license: No.

Description: This local pizzeria is another one of those establishments that is within the very shadow of the canal lift bridge. It is very much part of the scene in the Middleport community.

The Village Pizzeria offers a very large menu for a restaurant that features only one main dish (pizza). Those other options include lots of wings and subs for those who aren't in the mood for pizza that day.

Their pizza come in a variety of sizes, including "personal" (eight inches), small (twelve inches), large (sixteen inches), extra large (eighteen inches), and a "Tortizza" that is made with a cracker-thin crust. They offer a ton of different toppings, to satisfy the cravings of every pizza lover.

Still haven't heard something that tickles your taste buds? How about a Pickle Pizza (made with sliced dill pickles), or a Cherry Cheesecake Pizza? Yes, you heard that right! It's made with a cheesecake-layered crust topped with cherry pie filling, which is then baked and topped with crushed graham crackers. It's also available with apple, strawberry, or blueberry filling instead of cherry. After a slice of this, who needs dessert? Bring a slice back to your boat!

ORLEANS COUNTY

FITZGIBBONS PUBLIC HOUSE

Phone/Address: (585) 318-4024 / 429 Main Street, Medina, NY 14103.

Days/Hours: Wednesday and Thursday noon–10 p.m., Friday and Saturday noon–midnight, closed on Sunday, Monday, and Tuesday.

Reservations accepted? Yes (for parties of five or more).

Restaurant size: Lots of tables and bar stools to seat approximately one hundred people.

Outdoor seating: Very limited.

Menu items: Reuben sandwiches, half-pound steakburgers, lots of Celtic specialties including shepherd's pie, bangers and mash, and Guinness stew. Also offered are various salads, wraps, burgers, and sandwiches.

Price range: Most items on the menu range from $13 to $17.

Most popular menu item: Shepherd's pie, Guinness stew, and bangers and mash.

Entertainment: Yes (live bands on weekends, Celtic music, and cover bands).

Liquor license: Yes.

Description: Before we talk about the food here, we have to mention the interior of this Medina restaurant/pub. It is absolutely beautiful, constructed with dark wood paneling and lots of artistic touches. The building has been in place since the 1800s, which contributes to its old-world feel. The craftsmanship is simply beautiful, and dining here is a real treat even before the food and drink arrives at your table.

Many of the ingredients at the Irish-themed pub are imported from the old country, and the taste of the dishes reflects that dedication to authenticity. I decided to have lunch in this restaurant, and was amazed at the flavor they were able to pack into a simple bowl of soup. (As I recall, I had a steak and potato soup.) Wow!

Fitzgibbons Public House in Medina, New York.
PHOTO BY LARRY WEILL

Fitzgibbons maintains a great variety of choice Irish brews, including Guinness stout, Kilkenny, Harp, and Black Marble stout. A full selection of American brews is also available on tap.

The atmosphere inside Fitzgibbons was also very pleasant, with a continuous stream of Irish/Celtic music playing in the background. The prices on food and drink are quite reasonable, making this a convenient place to hop off the canal path for a wonderful lunch or dinner.

ZAMBISTRO

Phone/Address: (585) 798-2433 / 408 Main Street, Medina, NY 14103.

Days/Hours: Monday through Thursday 11 a.m.–9 p.m., Friday and Saturday 11 a.m.–10 p.m., Sunday 10 a.m.–2 p.m.

Reservations accepted? Yes.

Zambistro in Medina, New York.
PHOTO BY LARRY WEILL

Restaurant size: About twenty-eight tables, including the bar area and the side room.

Outdoor seating: Yes. An additional nine tables plus bar stool seating is available on the rooftop (summertime only).

Menu items: Lots of great menu selections are available on both the lunch and dinner menus. Lunch has lots of salads and flatbread pizzas, calamari, a charcuterie board, burgers, and sandwiches. Dinners include a host of tasty choices including some great appetizers, several steaks, seafood, lobster pasta, and Spanish seafood risotto.

Price range: Items on the lunch menu are mainly from $15 to $20, and the dinners range from $30 to $40, with some of the higher-end steaks costing more.

Most popular menu item: Chicken cutlets and the steak tips.

Entertainment: Yes (live music on random nights).

Liquor license: Yes.

Description: Zambistro is a bit of a change from most places in the town of Medina because it is definitely classified as a "fine dining" establishment rather than "pub fare." The interior of the restaurant is very classy (including the white tablecloths), and the food that is served there matches the decor. Very tasteful.

The main dining room in this restaurant is probably the "classiest" place to sit, although the bar area is also very nice. The bar is known for mixing up superb cocktails, which can be enjoyed either with dinner or while relaxing at the bar.

Most of the menu has an Italian influence, although there are great-looking burgers to go along with the variety of steaks. And yes, you can even get mac and cheese if so inclined.

Other nice touches at Zambistro include a Sunday brunch, rooftop dining, and even an "igloo dining experience" on the downstairs patio or on the rooftop. (Days and times are limited, with reservations costing an extra fee.) It's a great experience with a great view. Check it out!

CULVERT ROAD TUNNEL

Location: The Culvert Road Tunnel is built beneath the Erie Canal on Culvert Road in the town of Medina.

Description: As pointed out on the sign next to the tunnel entrance, this is the only location along the entire length of the Erie Canal where a tunnel passes beneath the canal from one side to the other.

There are warning signs on either side of the tunnel stating that the maximum height of the overhead is seven feet six inches. This not only precludes all commercial tractor-trailers, but it is also too low for many smaller trucks and any vehicle carrying roof-mounted cargo.

The entire tunnel is only one lane wide, so cars must be careful when entering to ensure there are no vehicles coming from the other direction. There are sidewalks on either side of the roadway, although most people probably do not choose to walk through this underpass. If you are hesitant to drive (or walk) through the tunnel, there are nearby bridges that will avoid this passage.

Another disadvantage of walking through the tunnel is that it is very damp inside. The stone masonry is over two hundred years old, and has many leaks

Culvert Road Tunnel in Medina, New York.
PHOTO BY LARRY WEILL

throughout the structure. Supposedly, there are icicles that hang from the tunnel ceiling in winter months, also due to the dripping stones.

A sign outside the tunnel proudly proclaims this to be the only tunnel beneath the Erie Canal and also announces its inclusion in *Ripley's Believe It or Not!*

THE RISEN CAFE

Phone/Address: (585) 283-4038 / 469 E. State Street, Albion, NY 14534.

Days/Hours: 9 a.m.–3 p.m. every day, except closed on Sunday.

Reservations accepted? Yes (for large groups).

Restaurant size: Approximately ten tables inside, plus counter seating.

Outdoor seating: No.

The Risen Cafe, Albion, New York.
PHOTO BY LARRY WEILL

Menu items: Breakfast sandwiches, lots of egg dishes and omelets, and French toast. Lunch and dinner dishes include sandwiches, burgers, and wraps. Almost everything on the menu is $10 or less.

Price range: $6–$10.

Most popular menu item: Breakfast plates and burgers.

Entertainment: Yes (open mic night every third Friday of the month).

Liquor license: No. All alcohol is strictly prohibited here (please read below).

Description: The Risen Cafe is a very cool place because it is based on helping people and providing for those less fortunate. First and foremost, it is basically half café and half church. (The church is in the back half of the building.)

You don't have to be a staunch religious zealot to dine here. Lots of people visit for the good food and the conversation. Seriously, the conversation action is one of the main reasons local residents visit. They'll get a cup of coffee and chat with their friends for hours.

The Risen Cafe is very dedicated to helping those who need a meal or a temporary place to get out of the cold. While visiting, people leave a few extra dollars ($3 or $5 or whatever they can afford). That amount gets written onto a three-by-five card along with a meal description. When a hungry and perhaps homeless visitor stops in for a break, they can pull a card off the line in the back of the dining room and exchange it for a hot meal. This is so amazing; I had never been in a place that offers such a wonderful service.

Almost all the "employees" in this café are volunteers, dedicated to helping the less fortunate. This location is worth a visit for everyone who passes by. It is amazing and very uplifting.

39 PROBLEMS

Phone/Address: (585) 283-4584 / 41 N. Main Street, Albion, NY 14534.

Days/Hours: Wednesday and Thursday 11 a.m.–10 p.m., Friday and Saturday 11 a.m.–midnight, Sunday 11 a.m.–8 p.m.

Reservations accepted? Yes (for parties over six).

Restaurant size: Approximately fifteen tables inside, plus counter seating.

Outdoor seating: No.

Menu items: Lunch includes the whiskey bacon burger, Cuban sandwiches, wraps, and burgers. Dinner entrées on the menu include spaghetti with marinara sauce, mac and cheese, fish fry, chicken Parmesan, and grilled sirloin.

Price range: Salads and sandwiches are mostly $12–$13, dinners range between $14 and $17.

Most popular menu item: Fish fry and the chicken Parmesan.

Entertainment: Yes (live bands on weekends).

Liquor license: Yes.

Description: This is another spot that is more of a pub than a restaurant, but people do come to enjoy the "pub fare." It's good food at a good price in ample portions.

They have numerous recognized beers on tap, including those that are both Irish and American. During the time of my visit, they were serving Guinness stout, Harp lager, Sam Adams, and Steampunk Cider.

39 Problems on Main Street, Albion, New York.
PHOTO BY LARRY WEILL

A selection of special drinks is posted on most days at 39 Problems, which (on my visit) were the Love Potion and the Captain in Paradise.

HOLLEY CANAL FALLS

Location: The Holley Canal Falls is a beautiful waterfall located close to downtown Holley. To access these falls from the canal path you will have to cross over the lift bridge, since the falls are on the other side of the canal from the trail. But the view from the falls is very scenic, so take advantage of this stop if you have time.

Note: From the back of the parking lot, a trail departs to the west. This is not the canal trail (Empire State Trail), but the Holley Falls Trail, which merges with the Canal Park Trail and then heads north toward the East Avenue Lift Bridge.

Description: The water flowing down these falls flows out of the canal itself. It tumbles into a collecting pool at the bottom of the slope before draining into

Holley Canal Falls in Holley, New York.
Photo by Larry Weill

Sandy Creek. There is significant water in the falls year-round, including during the hot summer months and when the water is drained from the canal in the winter.

In addition to being such a beautiful spot, it is also very accessible by car. From the middle of town, follow Frisbee Terrace to Holley Falls Park Road, which ends in a parking lot directly in front of the falls. There is a lovely small park with picnic tables for the public's use, and several trails cross the property

These falls are often used as a backdrop for wedding or graduation pictures. They can be photographed from either side of the bottom pool, and the arched foot bridge over Sandy Creek is also used to pose memorable photos.

One point to note here is that the Holley Canal Park and Falls are on the opposite side of the Erie Canal from the canal trail. To access the site you will need to cross over the lift bridge before descending to the park. Some of this ground can get a bit muddy during rainy periods, so waterproof footwear or boots are recommended.

MONROE COUNTY

JAVA JUNCTION COFFEE ROASTERS & BAKERY

Phone/Address: (585) 637-9330 / 56 Main Street S., Brockport, NY 14559.

Days/Hours: Monday through Sunday 7 a.m.–4 p.m.

Reservations accepted? Yes.

Restaurant size: Sufficient table seating inside the main dining room to handle hikers and bikers coming in off the canal, plus tables on the front sidewalk in the summer months.

Outdoor seating: Yes.

Menu items: *Great* coffees, which are roasted on the premises and brewed to bring customers the very best in flavor. Additionally, breakfast and lunch items are continuously prepared in the kitchen for those who want a great morning meal. Breakfasts feature pancakes and lots of bagel specials. Meanwhile, lunches offer soups, salads, paninis, sandwiches, and Black Angus burgers.

Price range: Prices on breakfast dishes range around $7 or less. Coffee drinks range anywhere from $2 to $6 depending on size and variety, with smoothies listing up to $7.

Most popular menu item: Visitors to Java Junction tend to favor their coffees and scones.

Entertainment: No.

Liquor license: No.

Description: Visitors to the Union Street Coffee House enjoy the attention that the owners have provided to the quality of the coffee since opening in 1993. (The shop has been in the same location since 1995.) As soon as you walk in the door you are hit with the aroma of ground coffee beans, which are roasted on-site and ground for purchase in the coffee bins in the front room.

The restaurant is a local favorite with the hordes of bikers and canal path hikers who make a special trip from the canal into the shop for a cup of their favorite brewed beverages. The restaurant has also been a "fan favorite" with the locals for all those years, with many of those patrons having enjoyed the warm

Java Junction Coffee Roasters & Bakery on Main Street in Brockport, New York.
PHOTO BY LARRY WEILL

(and wonderfully scented!) interior for decades. It is a mainstay of downtown Brockport.

CUSTOM HOUSE BAR & GRILL

Phone/Address: (585) 391-3017 / 1 Main Street S., Brockport, NY 14559.

Days/Hours: Hours vary not only by day of the week but also by season. Check their website online to determine current hours.

Reservations accepted? Yes (for large groups).

Restaurant size: There are about twenty tables between the upper and lower levels, plus bar seating.

Outdoor seating: Yes.

Custom House Bar & Grill, Brockport, New York.
PHOTO BY LARRY WEILL

Menu items: This restaurant serves brunch, lunch, and dinner. The menu is large and includes sandwiches, salads, tacos (five different varieties!), an assortment of burgers, wings, poutine, and more. They also list some great-looking desserts including a cookie skillet, which is a chocolate chip cookie cooked in a hot skillet with vanilla ice cream.

Price range: Prices on lunch dishes range between $12 and $20.

Most popular menu item: Shrimp tacos. Patrons also file in for their extensive collection of fine bourbons. (There are forty-eight brands on their bourbon menu!)

Entertainment: Yes, including trivia contests, live music, and karaoke. So start singing!

Liquor license: Yes.

Description: The Custom House Bar & Grill is a large establishment tucked into the edge of the canal bridge in the middle of town. It is probably best described as a place to find relaxed, casual dining in an attractive barroom setting. The upstairs room looks quite extensive, but the place starts filling in from the large barroom downstairs. Downstairs also appears to be a bit louder and more action-packed. But guests can sit wherever they choose, and it is all very attractive.

In addition to all the good food, customers show up for their extensive menu of fine bourbons, which is probably the bar's greatest claim to fame. They also serve a large array of beers, including lagers, Pilsners, cream ales, ambers, and brown ales, not to mention several hard ciders.

While visiting, I tried a bowl of a wonderful spicy tomato soup, accompanied by thick slices of cheese-covered toast, which was wonderful.

COLEEN'S KITCHEN

Phone/Address: (585) 637-0490 / 42 Main Street S., Brockport, NY 14559.

Days/Hours: 7 a.m.–noon, Monday through Saturday. (Closed Sundays.)

Reservations accepted? Yes.

Restaurant size: This restaurant has five tables and ample counter seating. (About twenty-two maximum seating.)

Outdoor seating: No.

Menu items: Lots of breakfast sandwiches, including eggs with different cheeses, bacon, turkey, and steak. Corned beef hash is also on the menu along with combination platters and challah French toast. All the breads and bagels are homemade.

Price range: Most breakfast sandwiches are between $6 and $9, with complete breakfasts averaging between $13 and $17.

Most popular menu item: Breakfast sandwiches and French toast.

Entertainment: No.

Liquor license: No.

Description: Make no mistake about it: this is Coleen's restaurant, and she runs it the way she thinks a restaurant should be run. Her "Rules to Eat By" are on

Coleen's Kitchen, Brockport, New York.
PHOTO BY LARRY WEILL

display on the tables and counter for all to see. Coleen has run this restaurant for twenty-three years, and she has mastered the art of providing a top-notch breakfast with little or no assistance from other service personnel.

In her time at this establishment Coleen has built up a loyal following. She specializes in only one meal, which is breakfast. The tables and booths in this place are always crowded to start the day, so be ready to arrive early to ensure seating.

Coleen pointed out there are really only five tables along the left wall of the restaurant instead of six. The sixth (rear) table is her "office" where she does her paperwork and other administrative work. She did say, however, that her husband sits at that table while in the restaurant, but that is one of her unwritten rules.

In summary, Coleen's Kitchen is a great place to visit from the canal if you are looking for a flavorful hot breakfast to start your day.

BARBER'S GRILL & TAPROOM

Phone/Address: (585) 637-2989 / 22 Main Street S., Brockport, NY 14559.

Days/Hours: Open daily from 11 a.m. until 2 a.m. Only closed on Christmas Day!

Reservations accepted? No.

Restaurant size: Has five to six tables plus lots of bar stools at the bar.

Outdoor seating: Yes.

Menu items: The menu here is large, with a full lineup of appetizers and "share-ables" including "macho nachos," poutine, loaded waffle fries, and more. They also list a dozen different burgers, a variety of chicken dishes, salads, and of course wings and tenders. But the biggest category on their menu is reserved for their iconic dish "The Balboa." This is the sandwich/meal that made Barber's famous and has kept their customers coming back for almost a hundred years.

Barber's Grill & Taproom, Brockport, New York.
PHOTO BY LARRY WEILL

Price range: Most dishes between $12 and $18.

Most popular menu item: The Balboa, because there is no place else that makes it! This is a massive sandwich made with a French baguette, and then your choice of ribs, ham, capicola, or more. It is prepared with all the fixings (grilled onions, peppers, mushrooms, and cheese) and toasted with garlic on the grill.

Entertainment: No.

Liquor license: Yes.

Description: Barber's Grill & Taproom is an amazing pub that has stood the test of time for almost one hundred years. Built in 1929, it continues to enjoy a high level of success because of its hearty food and drink, especially focused on the Balboa. This bar has the reputation of being "the bar" in town for atmosphere and late-night food. Barber's menu sums up their iconic Balboa as follows: "Half is a meal, full is a challenge." Believe it!

Looking around the bar one can only feel the history of the place speaking to you. The grill where the Balboas are pressed has been there since at least the 1940s. There are beer taps on the bar that probably pre-date the grill. Over ninety years in business and still going strong! Give it a try if you are on the canal in Brockport. Even the kids are welcome until 9 p.m.

58 MAIN BBQ & BREW

Phone/Address: (585) 637-2383 / 58 N. Main Street, Brockport, NY 14559.

Days/Hours: Open daily from 11 a.m. until 10 p.m. Sunday through Thursday, 11 a.m.–1 a.m. on Friday and Saturday.

Reservations accepted? Yes.

Restaurant size: Has thirty-five to forty tables located in their two large rooms, plus lots of bar stool seating.

Outdoor seating: Yes.

Menu items: Lots of great barbecue selections, plus an array of popular selections that include brisket on weck, pulled pork egg rolls, Cubano sandwiches (pulled pork and smoked ham with Swiss cheese and pickles), steaks, and even seafood and main course salads.

58 Main BBQ & Brew in Brockport, New York.
PHOTO BY LARRY WEILL

Price range: Most dishes between $12 and $22, with some entrées (mainly seafood) higher.

Most popular menu item: Smoked, fried, grilled chicken wings. You are guaranteed to drool if you read how they are prepared on the menu!

Entertainment: Yes. They have live bands on Thursday and some Fridays in summer.

Liquor license: Yes.

Description: This barbecue joint and bar is a really fantastic place that is one of the few restaurants north of the Brockport canal bridge. It serves lunches and dinners, and is unique in its focus on tempting barbecue dishes with all the sides.

Customers describe this place as a "relaxing spot where you get to enjoy great food and you also know all the bartenders, as they all become your friends."

Also known as a great sports bar, 58 Main BBQ & Brew embraces the Buffalo Bills. The bar really fills up in advance of games in Orchard Park, and a large contingent of "Bills Mafia" keeps the place rocking throughout.

This bar has lots of seating, including a very large front room that is available to cater parties. If you return from your hiking/biking/boating tour on the canal and decide to cater an office party, retirement party, or other event, 58 Main BBQ & Brew will provide your group with a great setting and a memorable event.

CLUTCH ON THE CANAL

Phone/Address: (585) 617-3477 / 94 S. Union Street, Spencerport, NY 14559.

Days/Hours: Monday and Wednesday 4 p.m.–12 a.m., Tuesday and Thursday 11 a.m.–12 a.m., Friday and Saturday 11 a.m.–2 a.m., Sunday 11 a.m.–12 a.m.

Reservations accepted? Yes.

Restaurant size: About thirty tables between upstairs and downstairs, plus numerous stool seats at the bar.

Outdoor seating: About ten tables on back patio.

Menu items: Very varied menu including quesadillas, wraps, soups, salads, mac and cheese, and the "Clutch Platter," which includes two smash patties with cheese, macaroni salad, tater tots, onion, hot sauce, and pepper relish. Also, on Fridays, check out their fish fry. The Sunday brunch is a new addition, with menu items including blueberry biscuits, "Central Perk Toast," steak and eggs, French toast, and more.

Price range: Sunday brunch items are mostly between $13 and $17, while most selections on their regular menu are in the $15–$20 range.

Most popular menu item: The smashburger and their Nashville hot chicken sandwich are very popular.

Entertainment: Yes.

Liquor license: Yes.

Description: Clutch on the Canal is a very popular bar/restaurant that sits on Union Steet very close to the canal bridge. It is the sports bar in the town, which is one of the reasons it is such a popular spot.

Clutch on the Canal, Spencerport, New York.
PHOTO BY LARRY WEILL

The inside of the restaurant resembles an old-fashioned New York City pub, and includes a beautiful curving staircase that leads to upstairs seating. The entire place is backlit from windows on the rear wall, which looks out on the canal as well as on their back patio.

The owner of the establishment is proud of saying that they do not serve ordinary bar food. Their burgers and other food (and drink) items are handcrafted to stand out from the rest. People come to Clutch on the Canal for good food, good drink, and good times.

UNION STREET COFFEE HOUSE

Phone/Address: (585) 617-4912 / 123 S. Union Street, Spencerport, NY 14559.

Days/Hours: Monday through Friday 7:30 a.m.–5 p.m., Saturday 8 a.m.–5 p.m., Sunday 9 a.m.–2 p.m.

62 • THE ERIE CANAL TRAVELER'S GUIDE

Union Street Coffee House on S. Union Street in Spencerport, New York.
PHOTO BY LARRY WEILL

Reservations accepted? No.

Restaurant size: About seven or eight tables plus those located outdoors.

Outdoor seating: Yes.

Menu items: Every kind of coffee, latte, cappuccino, chai, and tea you would expect to find in a cozy coffee shop. But here you will also find a menu loaded with great breakfast and brunch items, including breakfast sandwiches, a bacon and eggs "slam," three-cheese wraps, and spanakopita. Many lunch dishes are also listed, including salads, chipotle chicken, grilled cheese paninis, and the classic BLT wraps.

Price range: Breakfast items generally range from $6 to $8, while lunch dishes are generally between $9 and $11.

Most popular menu item: The Southwestern breakfast sandwich is very popular at Union Street Coffee House, while the favorite drinks are the chai or the Jamaican Me Crazy drip coffee.

Entertainment: No.

Liquor license: No.

Description: The Union Street Coffee House is a great place to stop and take the load off your feet in the morning or afternoon. The inside is light and airy, and the wonderful smell of coffee and good things baking will have you longing for that first sip of java.

Another nice feature of this coffeehouse is that it is so close to the canal that you can detour in for a hot drink without taking you more than a few steps out of your way. Whether you are hiking or biking along the canal path, it's a great stop to get a great cup of caffeine.

Lastly, the Union Street Coffee House menu has some truly unique and tempting menu items that would easily pass as dessert, even for breakfast. When was the last time you enjoyed a peanut butter and banana wrap? If the answer is "never," then you definitely need to stop in and give one a try!

MCCOLLEY'S

Phone/Address: (585) 617-4279 / 89 S. Union Street, Spencerport, NY 14559.

Days/Hours: Monday through Thursday 11:30 a.m.–9 p.m., Friday and Saturday 11:30 a.m.–10 p.m., Sunday noon–8 p.m.

Reservations accepted? Yes (most nights).

Restaurant size: Can accommodate one hundred people inside, plus many more at the outside tables in the alley (summers only).

Outdoor seating: Yes.

Menu items: Great Irish lunch and dinner items including corned beef Reubens, Guinness chutney roast beef melt, Guinness Harp burgers, bangers and mash, and shepherd's pie.

Price range: Most of the entrée items fall into the $15–$20 range.

Most popular menu item: Corned beef Reubens, and the Friday fish fry (salt and vinegar). Also popular is the lobster bisque on Fridays.

Entertainment: Yes. Every Saturday is live entertainment, plus "Open Mic" night on Thursdays.

Liquor license: Yes.

Description: McColley's is an extremely popular establishment in Spencerport, featuring an Irish theme and similarly patterned food and drink items. The bar always offers Guinness stout, Smithwick's, and a revolving selection of different popular Irish brews.

Another amazing feature about McColley's is the "hidden size" of the establishment. As you walk back from the front barroom, you enter another dining room. Then another. Then another! It just seems to keep on going, which is why it seats so many people indoors. In the warmer seasons, the alleyway outside the pub is blocked off to accommodate many more tables, so the capacity is very

McColley's on South Main Street in Spencerport, New York.
PHOTO BY LARRY WEILL

high. (But getting a seat on St. Patty's Day is still a challenge.)

The employees of this establishment describe it as "an Irish pub with a lot of American mixed in." But you can always wear your green inside, especially on St. Patty's Day!

TEXAS BAR-B-Q

Phone/Address: (585) 476-3179 / 122 S. Union Street, Spencerport, NY 14559.

Days/Hours: Monday through Thursday 11 a.m.–8 p.m., Friday 11 a.m.–9 p.m., Saturday noon–9 p.m., Sunday 1 p.m.–8 p.m.

Reservations accepted? No.

Restaurant size: Ten tables in the dining room.

Outdoor seating: Yes.

Texas Bar-B-Q on Union Street in Spencerport, New York.

Menu items: Lots and lots of barbecue. Their sandwiches include pulled pork, barbecue chicken, chopped or sliced brisket, crispy chicken, or beer-battered haddock. They also list salads, smoked brisket chili, ribs, wings, and meat platters with one, two, or three different meats.

Price range: Sandwiches range from $7 to $14 depending on the variety and the number of side orders. Chili bowls vary widely from $6 to $21 depending on the size. Ribs are $15 for a half rack and $29 for a full rack. The also have larger family platters up to $70 for the "Ultimate Rib Smacker" which includes two full racks of ribs and four side orders, plus corn bread.

Most popular menu item: Pulled pork.

Entertainment: No.

Liquor license: No.

Description: Texas Bar-B-Q in Spencerport is all about the wonderful bar-bequed meats served in their special sauces. It's easy to sniff the barbecue scents as you pull your car into their parking lot, and it may even be detectable from the canal!

This restaurant is known for its casual atmosphere and their specialization in ribs, chicken, and homemade side orders. Those sides include French fries, fried okra, onion pedals, fried pickles, fried medley, and fried cheese curd. All of these are available for $4–$7, and many of the platters are ordered with one or two each. They also serve up home-baked corn bread, which can be ordered by the piece for $1.50 or a dozen pieces for $12.00.

This restaurant has been a staple in the Spencerport community for the past twenty years. They also operate a catering service to take care of private events.

SPENCERPORT DEPOT & CANAL MUSEUM

Phone/Address: (585) 352-0942 / 16 East Avenue, Spencerport, NY 14559. The museum is located directly next to the canal.

Months of Operation: This is a seasonal museum that is only open during the months of May through October.

Hours: These may vary depending on the availability of volunteers and other factors. Call the number above to inquire about the day of your visit.

Background: The building that is today the Spencerport Depot & Canal Museum has been moved several times over its storied history. It was originally the Spencerport Trolley Station, which was built in 1906 as part of the Rochester, Lockport and Buffalo Railroad. Rail service commenced in 1908, and ran until its closure in 1931.

The building was moved in the 1930s with the intention of converting it into a house. After numerous changes, it was finally moved to its current location next to the canal in May 2005. It opened its doors in 2007 to serve as a museum, visitor center, and lending library.

Museum Focus: The Museum "houses exhibits and displays about the Erie Canal, Transportation, Communication and Local History." There is a lot to see inside the exhibit room, so make sure to leave at least an hour to gain a great understanding of the Erie Canal and the town of Spencerport.

Services: The Spencerport Depot & Canal Museum provides some superb services for boaters as well as visitors who are traveling along the canal path. In the

Spencerport Depot & Canal Museum, Spencerport, New York.
PHOTO BY LARRY WEILL

lower level of the building there are restroom facilities for anyone traveling along the canal. These include showers for boaters who may be staying overnight.

For boaters, there are also dock spaces that are available on a first come, first served basis. Boats are limited to use of the dock spaces for forty-eight continuous hours in any seven-day period. There is also free water and electrical hookup available at the docks. They even have Wi-Fi access at the dock. The password is available from the museum staff or from the dockmaster. (Once again, please consider making a donation to the museum for the use of these facilities.)

Fees: The museum does not charge an admission fee. However, the facility is a nonprofit organization that is largely funded by visitor donations, which are greatly appreciated, so please consider helping out if you can.

GREECE CANAL PARK

Address: 241 Elmgrove Road, Rochester, NY 14626.

Note: This book does not include most town and county parks. This park is only covered due to the presence of the fenced-in dog park.

Months of Operation: This park is accessible year-round.

Hours: Open from 7 a.m. to dusk, although the park reserves the right to close periodically for cleaning and maintenance.

Fees: Before entering any dog park in Monroe County you are required to register and pay a user fee, which is $24. The application for entering this facility can be found online at https://webapps.monroecounty.gov/mcparks/reserve/dogs.

Background: Monroe County now owns and operates seven dog parks for the use of county residents and their dogs. The intent is to give dogs a safe and enclosed place to run off-leash and interact with other dogs. Greece Canal Park

Dog "Bark Park" inside Greece Canal Park, Rochester, New York.
Photo by Larry Weill

is the only dog park in Monroe County that is adjacent to the Erie Canal, thus providing canal travelers with a safe and convenient facility to exercise their dogs.

The dog park is only a small part of Greece Canal Park, which is a very large facility spread over 577 acres. The park also contains softball and soccer fields, pickleball and tennis courts, playgrounds, and lots of open ground. There are two public restrooms inside the park, but neither is located near the dog park. Access to the park is via a stairway from the canal.

The gate used to enter the bark park has a cipher lock. You will be provided with a code to enter this area when your pass is granted. There is also a large area that is specifically reserved for use by small dogs.

The dog park is a great recreational area for animals to run in a safe, fenced-in area. The ground surface is small, crushed rock that is safe for pets. There are numerous obstacles positioned for dogs to run around and through inside the fence. It even includes a pair of nonfunctional fire hydrants, because what dog can resist using a fire hydrant?

Rules: Monroe County dog "bark parks" are unsupervised. Park users assume all risks when inside the park. Dogs must have a standard dog license from the City of Rochester, and must also be vaccinated for rabies. All dog owners who apply for access to the bark park will receive a tag that must be worn by the dog on every visit. All dogs must be accompanied by an owner or authorized person. Dogs must be on a leash once they exit the enclosed bark park. Please clean up and remove any "dog deposits" left by your canine companion.

EZZY'S RESTAURANT

Phone/Address: (585) 436-9340 / 885 Buffalo Road, Rochester, NY 14624.

Days/Hours: Monday, Wednesday, Thursday, and Friday 7 a.m.–8 p.m., Tuesday, Saturday, and Sunday 7 a.m.–2 p.m.

Reservations accepted? No.

Restaurant size: Thirty-three tables (seating 115 people).

Outdoor seating: No.

Menu items: The breakfast menu features a lot of omelets, breakfast sandwiches, French toast, pancakes, and waffles, along with side orders of bacon, sausage, Canadian bacon, and five varieties of frittatas. Lunch and dinner include lots

Ezzy's Restaurant in Rochester, New York.
PHOTO BY LARRY WEILL

of great appetizers, salads, soups, sandwiches, cold plates, and more. The dinner entrées offer fourteen different Italian dishes (i.e., eggplant Parmesan, gnocchi, breaded veal Parmesan, and artichokes French), plus thirteen seafood dishes.

Price range: Most breakfast dishes are $7–$12, while the soups and salads range between $3 and $9. Most dinners are $15–$20, although some items (i.e., lobster tail) are "market price."

Most popular menu item: Fish fry and chicken French.

Entertainment: No.

Liquor license: No

Description: Ezzy's Restaurant is very much a family business that has earned a devoted following from the local community. According to the owners, about 90 percent of their breakfast customers are "regulars" who think of it as a cozy extension of their home.

This restaurant has specific hours for serving breakfast, which are from 7 a.m. to 11:30 a.m. daily, so make sure to be on time if you want that early-morning omelet.

They also offer their own version of the "everything-on-one plate" meal. Called the Ezzy Plate, it's got two burgers or hot dogs, mac salad, and French fries all for $12.95. Yum!

Also, if you enjoy seafood, Ezzy's lists a lot of great selections under their "Appetizers," including calamari, shrimp cocktail, and clams casino.

Ezzy's is located right down Buffalo Road from the canal, so it's an easy-on-easy-off from the pathway. It's a nice place to get a quick, nutritious meal and a friendly smile.

CAMPI'S

Phone/Address: (585) 235-7205 / 205 Scottsville Road, Rochester, NY 14611.

Days/Hours: Every day from 11 a.m. to 8 p.m., closed on Sunday.

Reservations accepted? No.

Restaurant size: Fifteen tables.

Outdoor seating: No.

Menu items: You'd have an easier time listing items that Campi's doesn't have on their menu than those that they do. On their menu boards are sandwiches, "bombers," "Campi's sloppy plates" (with two burgers or two hot dogs, French fries, and mac salad or baked beans), burgers (up to ¾ lb.), snack plates with fried clams, chicken fingers, fish 'n chips, mozzarella sticks, fish fries, and so much more.

Price range: Most items on the menu are between $7 and $13.

Most popular menu item: The steak bomber.

Entertainment: No.

Liquor license: No.

Description: If you visit Campi's and notice that the building appears to be old, it is. Campi's has been doing business for about one hundred years, and looks much the same as it did many decades ago. The owner informed me that "I am

Campi's on Scottsville Road in Rochester, New York.
PHOTO BY LARRY WEILL

the last of three," meaning that there have only been three owners since the place opened in the early 1920s. He has been there himself for twenty-five years.

Campi's is a nostalgic place where people visit to enjoy their memories of the past. I personally visited this place in the 1970s, and I don't recall that it looks any different on the inside or outside. It still has a pay phone next to the entrance door!

Most people dining here seem to enjoy the submarine sandwiches and other hearty fare, including the gyros. The "sloppy plates" also appear to be rather popular, but that is also a Rochester thing that dates back to "forever."

During my visit, the owner (who also cooks and runs much of the operation) was having a great time chatting with the customers in the dining room. That is also part of the appeal, as he makes you feel like family. It is also a quick on-off the Erie Canal pathway, for those on the go.

KAMARA'S AFRICAN RESTAURANT

Phone/Address: (585) 730-7071 / 2003 Lyell Ave., Rochester, NY 14606.

Days/Hours: Monday–Friday 11 a.m.–10 p.m., Saturday 11 a.m.–midnight, closed on Sunday.

Reservations accepted? Yes.

Restaurant size: Eleven tables, plus seven more in a side room.

Outdoor seating: No.

Menu items: Lots of "platter meals" including jollof rice with chicken, jollof rice with tilapia or red snapper, and more. Also served with fried okra or potato greens. Fufu (a starchy dough) served with various combinations, and lots of selections with fried plantains.

Price range: Most entrées range between $15 and $20, although a few of the seafood selections can list for up to $25.

Kamara's African Restaurant in Rochester, New York.
PHOTO BY LARRY WEILL

Most popular menu item: Jollof rice with chicken, and the plantain fufu or yam fufu with goat pepper soup.

Entertainment: No (although they may have entertainment in the future).

Liquor license: No (although this is being planned as well).

Description: This restaurant is such a great concept that I'm planning on returning there myself for a full dinner. The entire restaurant is African themed, with African artwork and painting on the walls, and giraffe carvings on each of the tables. It is fun and authentic, and the food is wonderful.

The owner started this restaurant in 2017, and has done a superb job of keeping it going and expanding through the tough years of the pandemic. The menu contains many items (i.e., jollof rice and fufu) that are probably new to most casual diners. However the menu explains what each item is and how it is prepared, and the owner is available to answer any questions.

They offer lots of specials on Thursday through Saturday, including beef kabob, grilled chicken, rice bread and banana bread, and suya, which is a traditional smoked meat skewer that originated in Nigeria.

This is a great place to get off the canal and expand your culinary horizons with something new. Give it a try!

EL LATINO RESTAURANT

Phone/Address: (585) 235-3110 or 3116 / 1020 Chili Ave., Rochester, NY 14611.

Days/Hours: Daily from 10 a.m. to 8 p.m., closed on Sunday.

Reservations accepted? No.

Restaurant size: Only four tables, but almost everyone takes food out from this restaurant.

Outdoor seating: No.

Menu items: Various salads with seafood (cod fish, shrimp, or octopus) or chicken, fresh homemade soups, fish and seafood dinners served with rice or tostones (which are twice-fried plantains that are not completely ripe). Other popular entrées on the menu include flank steak, pepper steak, chicken, tripe, ribs, and a variety of chicken and pork dishes that may be served with yellow rice and (sometimes) red beans.

El Latino Restaurant in Rochester, New York.
PHOTO BY LARRY WEILL

Price range: Most dishes range between $12 and $20.

Most popular menu item: Pork and beef dishes, many of which are on display basting in wonderful-looking sauces in their serving area.

Entertainment: No.

Liquor license: No.

Description: El Latino is another unique restaurant that specializes in a very specific cuisine. It's entire menu is focused on the food of the Dominican Republic, which has some of the most flavorful fare in the world.

If you are unfamiliar with Dominican food, you may need to ask for some translations on your first visit. Tostones, mofongo (another plantain dish), and other food items on the menu are probably unknown to many American diners. But they are all worth trying here.

Note: This is one restaurant for which I had to do a small bit of "tape measure stretching," because it is probably a little over 500 feet down Chili Avenue from the Erie Canal. But the dishes on the menu and the incredibly appetizing scents emanating from the kitchen necessitated its inclusion in this book.

The only drawback to this restaurant is that it suffers from its own success, as the lines to pick up orders may extend out the door. This is the price for being that unique and that good.

LABEL 7 NAPA EATERY & BAR

Phone/Address: (585) 267-7500 / 50 State Street, Pittsford, NY 14534.

Days/Hours: Lunch Tuesday–Saturday, 11:30 a.m.–4 p.m., Dinner Tuesday–Thursday, 4 p.m.–9 p.m., Dinner Friday and Saturday, 4 p.m.–10 p.m.

Reservations accepted? Yes.

Reservations recommended? Yes.

Outside view of Label 7 Napa Eatery & Bar in Pittsford, New York.
PHOTO BY LARRY WEILL

Restaurant size: Approximately twenty-five tables inside, including bar area.

Outdoor seating: Yes.

Menu items: Small plates, salads, burgers, sandwiches, wraps. Some vegetarian and vegan selections.

Price range: Small plates $6–$15, most other dishes $14–$22.

Most popular menu item: Chicken and Waffles ("LA Chicken").

Entertainment: Yes (local bands and singers, inside and outside).

Liquor license: Yes.

Description: Label 7 is a long-standing favorite of the Pittsford Canal scene. It is very laid back and casual, and a majority of the customers are locals stopping by for either a meal or a drink. The upstairs bar area is attractively arranged with both tables and bar (stool) seating, while the lower room is designed with a beautiful wood floor, wood tones throughout, and wicker-style chairs.

Another nice feature of this restaurant is that the food is both good and economical. Almost everything on the menu falls into the $15–20 range.

Remember that this restaurant does fill up during peak hours, so reservations are recommended.

DOLCE CUPCAKERY

Phone/Address: (585) 383-0200 / 50 State St., Building R, Pittsford, NY 14534

Days/Hours: Wednesday through Saturday noon–4 p.m. (for walk-in retail), closed on Sunday, Monday, and Tuesday, but catering and custom orders are available seven days a week.

Reservations accepted? No.

Restaurant size: Five tables.

Outdoor seating: Yes (bench seating).

Menu items: Cupcakes and other related goodies! In addition to the standard cupcakes, they also sell cakes, pies, cannoli, Italian cookies, and cake pops (like a lollipop but with a cake on top). In addition to the standard cupcakes, they also sell gluten-free alternatives to many of their popular varieties. Jumbo and mini-versions of the many varieties are also available.

Dolce Cupcakery, Pittsford, New York.
PHOTO BY LARRY WEILL

Price range: Most standard cupcakes are $4.25 each, while the gluten-free and specialty versions are $4.75/each. Vegan standard versions are also $4.75, "minis" are $24./dozen, while specialty and gluten-free minis are $27/dozen. Vegan minis are $27/dozen, jumbos are $8 each, specialty jumbos, gluten-free jumbos, and vegan jumbos are also $8.50 each.

Most popular menu item: The "Signature 5," which are available every day. The most popular additional flavors are the lemon-blueberry cupcakes and carrot cupcakes.

Entertainment: No.

Liquor license: No.

Description: Dolce is, first and foremost, a "cupcakery," where the world's best ingredients are turned into miniature cakes with decorative frostings that will make anyone smile. Lisa, the current owner, was an employee at this establishment over ten years ago when she learned that the previous owner was looking to sell the place. She loved the art of designing and baking world-class cupcakes and decided to buy the cupcakery and make it her own. Since then, it has become a family business, with Lisa's mother, husband, and children all participating in the operations.

Dolce's today makes over eighty-five flavors and varieties of cupcakes in their Pittsford store, which is located in the Northfield Commons (adjacent to Schoen Place).

Warning: The smell inside this store is absolutely amazing! If you walk inside the store, you will end up buying some cupcakes. The smell is overwhelming.

COPPER LEAF BREWING

Phone/Address: (585) 678-1383 / 50 State Street, Building G, Pittsford, NY 14534.

Days/Hours: Monday 4–9 p.m., Tuesday closed, Wednesday 4–9 p.m., Thursday 3–9 p.m., Friday 2–10 p.m., Saturday noon–10 p.m., Sunday 1–8 p.m.

Reservations accepted? Only for large parties, fifteen people or more.

Restaurant size: Only five or six tables inside, plus bar seating, but the inside bar can accommodate a pretty good crowd.

Outdoor seating: Yes (in the summer; approved by the town).

Menu items: At any given time, the brewery has ten to fifteen different beers on tap. Small bags of snacks can be purchased at the bar, and food can be brought in from any of the surrounding restaurants in the area.

Price range: Most of the "taster" size glasses are $3–$5, while the full-size glasses (10 oz.) are $7–$8. "Cans to Go" (32 oz.) are available for $12–$14.

Most popular menu item: Any one of their delicious brews!

Entertainment: Available for private parties and sometimes during festivals.

Liquor license: Obviously!

Description: Copper Leaf Brewing is a "nano-brewery" housed in a small building inside Northfield Commons, at Schoen Place in Pittsford. The business opened its doors in 2021 and has gained a reputation for putting out a wide

Brewing tanks inside Copper Leaf Brewing in Pittsford, New York.
PHOTO BY LARRY WEILL

variety of quality brewed products. These include (in any given week) a selection of lagers, Pilsners, stouts, and more.

Part of the fun of this hometown brewery is that the products served at the bar are all brewed on-premises. Clay Killian concocts masterpieces like Vienna Lager, Flanders Red Ale, and Belgian Dark Strong with Cherries (which was the author's favorite!) Stop in any day but Tuesday, which is when they brew the beers. It's worth the special trip, and it's pet friendly!

NEUTRAL GROUND COFFEEHOUSE

Phone/Address: (585) 348-9303 / 45 Schoen Place, Pittsford, NY 14534.

Days/Hours: Open 8 a.m.–4 p.m., every day of the week.

Reservations accepted? No.

Restaurant size: Fifteen tables plus outdoor tables and seats.

Neutral Ground Coffeehouse, Pittsford, New York.
PHOTO BY LARRY WEILL

Outdoor seating: Yes.

Menu items: First let's talk about the coffee, since this is a coffeehouse. They serve piping hot coffees, double espresso, macchiato, cortado, affogato, latte, cappuccino, and five other tempting hot drinks (including steamed cider). They also serve several drinks that can be made hot or cold, such as matcha latte and chai latte. Their breakfast menu lists nine selections, many of which are breakfast sandwiches served on your choice of sourdough, multigrain, wrap, bagel, or croissant. Several have canal-related names, including The Towpath (a bacon and egg sandwich with Brie and your choice of bacon, ham, or sausage). Others are the Lift Bridge and the Barge Burrito. Yes, they taste as good as they sound and are available all day. The lunch menu is available at 11:00 a.m. and offers nine great salads, sandwiches, and wraps. And don't forget the ice cream, served year-round.

Price range: Most breakfast selections are between $5 and $10, lunches from $9 to $14, coffee and other hot drinks are $3–$5, baked goods are $4–$6, and ice cream/desserts are $5–$9.

Most popular menu item: Cold brew drinks, "The Pittsford" sandwich, and "Sal's Breakfast Chowder" (a creamy chowder made with bacon, egg, potato, cheese, onion, and maple syrup).

Entertainment: No.

Liquor license: No.

Description: There is too much good stuff to say about Neutral Ground to fit on one page, but we'll start with their philosophy, which is to serve super-fresh food that tastes great in an all-inclusive and friendly environment. Everyone is welcome, and their staff will instantly make you feel that way. The restaurant is located so close to the canal and the Canalway Trail that you could literally vault from one to the other.

The restaurant is biker friendly, and also welcomes all dogs, as long as they are friendly and can get along with the "house dogs." (Wag that tail!)

SAM PATCH CANALBOAT (CORN HILL NAVIGATION)

Phone/Address: (585) 662-5748 / 12 Schoen Pl., Pittsford, NY 14534.

Days/Hours: The *Sam Patch* canalboat makes three to five cruise tours per day. Check online to see the times at which the cruises are available each day.

Admission: Varies per day and cruise. Check www.cornhillnav.org for specific prices. Lunches are an additional fee, generally $21/adult and $12/child. Lunches must be purchased twenty-four hours in advance of the departure date/time.

Origin of the Corn Hill Waterfront and Navigation Foundation: It's a long name, but that is the official appellation of the nonprofit organization that owns and operates the *Sam Patch* canalboat. The *Sam Patch* was built in 1991 for the sole purpose of navigating on the Erie Canal (and the Genesee River) to provide the people of Rochester and the surrounding areas with the opportunity to experience the beauty of the waterways through education and enjoyment. The company was organized as a nonprofit 501(c)3 organization and remains so today. A second boat, the *Riverie*, was added in 2023 to expand its capacity.

Sam Patch canalboat in Pittsford, New York.
PHOTO BY LARRY WEILL

Cruises offered and how to get onboard: For the purposes of this article, we'll address only the *Sam Patch* since it operates almost solely on the Erie Canal. The *Sam Patch* carries a maximum of forty passengers, which makes for a safe and highly personalized canal experience. They offer a large variety of cruise options, including Sunset Cruises, Lunch Cruises, and a seventy-five-minute Kids Cruise. Most of these cruises carry the passengers through Erie Canal Lock #32, where they get to experience the change in elevation as the lock raises and lowers the water level.

Other options include the Live Music Sunset Cruise where passengers are entertained by lively musicians while taking in the breathtaking sunset. There is also an Arts & Culture Series cruise, with special guests who give oral presentations in addition to hands-on art classes.

Lunches offer a choice of five salads/sandwiches for adults and two sandwiches for children.

In addition to all the regular cruises listed above, the *Sam Patch* also hosts occasional special voyages with unique and educational topics. They host bird-watching tours at least once a month, with specialists who will help you to spot and discuss some of the interesting species of birds found along the Erie Canal.

There is also a "Juneteenth on *Sam Patch*" cruise that focuses on the Underground Railroad and its interaction with the Erie Canal. (This is held in collaboration with the Erie Canal Museum.)

Note: Some of the special-focus cruises are conducted only once a year. Tickets are limited, and advance reservations/ticketing are highly recommended. The *Sam Patch* is also available for private charters and special occasions. Email www .cornhillnav.org to inquire

ERIE CANAL NATURE PRESERVE AND FROG POND TRAIL

Location: Between the Erie Canal and the Auburn Trail in the Village of Pittsford.

Hours: This trail is open the same hours as the Canalway Trail, from dawn to dusk, seven days a week.

Admission: Free.

Note: This trail would only be of interest to the hikers and bikers on the Canalway Trail. This is a side path from the bike trail on the north side of the canal.

About the trail: The Frog Pond Trail is a wetland and woodlands pathway that cuts between the Erie Canal and the Auburn Trail. The Auburn Trail (which is not as well-known as the Canalway Trail) is an eleven-mile-long path that follows the route of the old Auburn & Rochester Railroad.

History: There are several places of interest along this short and gently graded walking trail. Along the route, hikers will pass by a series of small ponds that were used by the Ward's Natural Science Establishment in the 1970s to breed frogs for scientific use. Although partially covered today with duckweed and other vegetation, they still serve as a breeding ground for frogs and other amphibians.

Of additional historical interest are the support walls that served as a base for the New York Central Railroad. Those walls are still present and very visible at the north end of the Frog Pond Trail.

Educational display signs: Numerous signs have been placed along the trail for the benefit of visitors. Signs appear along the sides of the frog ponds as well as near the remains of the train supports below the Auburn Trail. Some of these

Erie Canal Nature Preserve and Frog Pond Trail, Pittsford, New York.
PHOTO BY LARRY WEILL

displays explain the benefits of "indicator species" such as frogs to determine the environmental health of an ecosystem.

Access: The south end of the Frog Pond Trail is on the north side of the canal, a short distance east of the point where the Canalway Trail crosses beneath Monroe Avenue. It can also be accessed from the northern end, where a simple signpost marks the intersection of the Auburn Trail and the Frog Pond Trail. For reference purposes, the southern end of the Frog Pond Trail is located directly across the Erie Canal from the Talbots store, located at 66 Monroe Avenue in Pittsford.

The entire Frog Pond Trail is very short, no more than a half mile from end to end. It is about ten feet wide and has a gravel surface that is suitable for walking, running, or biking. The trail crosses some wet marshland on a wide, composite bridge that is also simple to navigate. It is a short, relatively level, and easy hike that may be of interest to nature lovers.

VILLAGE COAL TOWER RESTAURANT

Phone/Address: (585) 381-7866 / 9 Schoen Place, Pittsford, NY 14534.

Days/Hours: Monday through Thursday, 8 a.m.–2 p.m., Friday 8 a.m.–8 p.m., Saturday and Sunday 8 a.m.–1 p.m. (breakfast only).

Reservations accepted? No.

Restaurant size: About twenty-two tables, plus counter seating.

Outdoor seating: Yes.

Menu items: Very large variety of choices for breakfast, lunch, and dinner. Includes salads, sandwiches, soups, plus lots of standard main courses like meat loaf and chicken and waffles, and a whole host of side dishes.

Price range: Most of the menu is set within the $9–$14 range, although some of the higher-end seafood selections are listed up to $23.

Village Coal Tower Restaurant in Schoen's Place, Pittsford, New York.
PHOTO BY LARRY WEILL

Most popular menu item: Breakfast items, including eggs Benedict and omelets, and their Friday fish fry.

Entertainment: No.

Liquor license: No.

Description: The Coal Tower requires very little in the way of descriptive terms since it is the only restaurant in the region that incorporates an actual historic coal tower into its architecture. The coal tower itself dates back to the early 1900s when the coal stored inside the round structure was used to provide fuel to the boats operating on the Erie Canal. The restaurant itself was opened in 1967 when the tower was purchased from the Schoen family.

It boasts an ardent patronage of local customers who grew up dining in this establishment. It is open seven days a week, although on some of those days (on weekends) it closes earlier and does not serve dinner.

An important detail to note is that the restaurant does not accept credit cards; it is cash only. (But there is an ATM located inside the main dining room.)

ALADDIN'S NATURAL EATERY

Phone/Address: (585) 264-9000 / 8 Schoen Place, Pittsford, NY 14534.

Days/Hours: Hours of operation are seasonal. Call ahead to request current hours on the day of your visit.

Reservations accepted? No.

Restaurant size: About thirty to forty tables, including upstairs, downstairs, and outside deck seating (which is seasonal).

Outdoor seating: Yes.

Menu items: The menu is described as being Mediterranean, with all dishes prepared from fresh, all-natural ingredients that are free of preservatives. Appetizers include hummus, falafel, dolmas, and spanakopita. They offer a wide variety of soups and salads, along with pita rolls, pockets, and specialties such as a souvlaki plate, moussaka, and a mixed grill. The menu also features a dozen different pasta dishes, which can be customized with different toppings and proteins.

Aladdin's Natural Eatery, Pittsford, New York.

Price range: Most of the menu is set within the $9–$14 range, Some items do trend a bit higher (with the mixed grill set at $20.95), but the entire menu is quite reasonable.

Most popular menu item: The Chicklaki Plate, with chicken on mixed greens salad, mushrooms, and feta, with a pita chip and choice of dressing.

Entertainment: No.

Liquor license: No (but wine and beer are served on-premises).

Description: Open since 1980, Aladdin's Natural Eatery in Pittsford is described on their website as a place that has a "warm atmosphere and serves delicious health dishes." The setting inside is cozy, and everything on the menu is tasty and freshly prepared. Aladdin's has been recognized for being Rochester's best Mediterranean restaurant, and also for the "Best Meal under ten dollars."

Warning: If you do not want to indulge in dessert, avoid sitting on the upper floor in front of their cake display counter. The different desserts contained inside look absolutely stunning, and may be tough to turn down!

AURORA BREWING COMPANY

Phone/Address: (585) 485-0033 / 604 Pittsford-Victor Road, Pittsford, NY 14534.

Days/Hours: Monday through Thursday 2 p.m.–9 p.m., Friday noon–10 p.m., Saturday Noon–10 p.m., Sunday Noon–8 p.m.

Reservations accepted? No.

Restaurant size: About eighteen tables inside and twenty to twenty-five outside.

Outdoor seating: Yes.

Menu items: The menu features a wide variety of continuously rotating craft beers, all brewed locally by Aurora's own brewmasters. These include three "crispy beers," six "hoppy beers," one sour beer, and three bottle pours. The menu also lists three ciders along with five wines that can be purchased either by the glass or by the bottle. The specific names of the beers can be viewed on Aurora's website since the varieties are rotated so frequently. There is no food kitchen yet, but plans are in the works to provide food within the coming year.

Price range: Beers are $7, $8, or $10 for a "full pour," (which can be 12 oz. or 16 oz. depending on the beer). The wines are available by the glass ($10–$13) or by the bottle ($30–$42). The ciders are $7 per serving and the canned cocktails (all New York State products) are $9–$10.

Most popular menu item: The most popular varieties are the sours and the Hazy IPAs.

Entertainment: Yes (live music twice/week, usually on Thursday and Saturday).

Liquor license: Some canned cocktails, wine, and beer.

Aurora Brewing Company, Pittsford, New York.
Photo by Larry Weill

Description: Aurora Brewing Company is a unique pub and brewery that sits right on the edge of the Erie Canal in Pittsford. It has an amazing atmosphere both inside and out. Inside, the pub has small, cozy rooms with dark wood floors and heavy overhead beams to complement the amazing wooden bar. The entire outside of the building is surrounded by attractive seating areas, from the back deck overlooking the canal to the tables positioned beneath the overhead trees.

Between the brewery and the canal, they have constructed a "Tap Shack" that offers the same brews that are on tap at the bar. Boaters can come ashore and grab a great brew without ever having to enter the main building. This pub offers a fantastic environment in both the summer and the winter. Sit in front of the fireplace (with a real wood fire) in the winter, or enjoy sitting beneath the trees and watching the boats sail by in the summer. Each one is a treat

SIMPLY CREPES

Phone/Address: (585) 383-8310 / 7 Schoen Place, Pittsford, NY 14534.

Days/Hours: Sunday and Monday 8 a.m.–8 p.m., Tuesday closed, Wednesday and Thursday 8 a.m.–8 p.m., Friday and Saturday 8 a.m.–9 p.m.

Reservations accepted? Yes.

Restaurant size: About fifteen tables.

Outdoor seating: No.

Menu items: As one might guess from the name of the restaurant, they are best known for their wide variety of crepes, which are individually prepared and served piping hot. But they also serve breakfast sandwiches, fondues, burgers, breakfast tacos, wings, soups, salads, and more. Another perk is that they will brew you a barista-prepared cup of coffee that will compete with any coffee shop.

Price range: Most of the crepes fall into the $16–$20 range.

Simply Crepes in Schoen Place, Pittsford, New York.
Photo by Larry Weill

Most popular menu item: The Nutella fruit crepe.

Entertainment: No.

Liquor license: Yes.

Description: The story of the family business and its founders is fascinating reading, as the Heroux family has traveled and lived all around the world. But family and food have always been central to their attitude and outlook on life, and this is reflected in every aspect of their restaurant in Schoen Place.

The Pittsford location is just one of four restaurants owned and operated by this family, and they all enjoy the same level of popularity. Their food is all homemade with fresh ingredients, including some unique ideas on adding flavor to their dishes. They use locally sourced maple syrup as a sweetener and also use apples from Schutts Apple Mill to take their dishes to new highs.

In addition to wonderful breakfasts, lunches, and dinners, patrons can also indulge in a variety of decadent dessert crepes, including "bananas and crème crepes" or "peanut butter brownie crepes" to end their meals. What a feast!

PITTSFORD FARMS DAIRY

Phone/Address: (585) 586-6610 / 44 N. Main Street, Pittsford, NY 14534.

Days/Hours: Open daily (Pittsford location) from 7:30 a.m. to 9 p.m.

Reservations accepted? No.

Restaurant size: A few tables, but most folks simply stand up while eating their ice cream.

Outdoor seating: A few more tables and benches.

Menu items: Ice cream and frozen yogurt, but the store sells a huge variety of dairy products including milk, cheeses, breads and cakes, jams and jellies, and lots more.

Price range: Their ice cream dishes and cones vary in price based on the size, but most are quite reasonable. Ice cream sundaes are listed at $8.50, and their banana splits are $9.50.

Most popular menu item: Any of their homemade ice creams, which are all great!

Entertainment: No.

Pittsford Farms Dairy, on the National Register of Historic Places, in Pittsford, New York.

Liquor license: No

Description: I have to admit, this is one of my favorite places in the Rochester area, as their ice cream is beyond good! I am also unsure whether their ice cream stand is within 445 feet and 10 inches of the Erie Canal, but I don't care. This place is worth it.

Pittsford Farms Dairy prepares a huge array of wonderfully flavored ice creams and frozen yogurts, and they serve them from behind a scoop counter inside their barn-style building. They also bake and sell many different kinds of breads and pastries, which are on display in their bakery corner. Many of the pastries would satisfy almost anyone as a dessert for any meal.

While visiting this store, one of the managers explained that they use a technique called "vat pasteurization" instead of "short-term pasteurization" to improve the quality of their milk products.

One quick warning: Pittsford Farms Dairy has such a great reputation that you can expect to find very long lines at the ice cream counter, especially in the evening. But the wait is well worth it.

CLEMENTINE COFFEE

Phone/Address: (585) 667-1801 / 6 N. Main Street, Suite 125, Fairport, NY 14450 (inside the Box Factory).

Days/Hours: Open Monday through Saturday, 8 a.m.–3 p.m.

Reservations accepted? Yes, but only for dinner.

Restaurant size: Approximately thirty-one tables between the main dining area and the bar, plus twenty-four tables on the outside patio (seasonal).

Outdoor seating: Yes (on patio).

Main dining room of Clementine Coffee in Fairport, New York. The same room is used by Lulu Taqueria at night.
Photo by Larry Weill

Menu items: Lots of great coffee and latte drinks, bagels, French toast, breakfast burritos, green chili, rice bowls, and so much more.

Price range: Most menu items are in the $8–$12 range, with breakfast dishes averaging slightly less than lunch plates.

Most popular menu item: Lattes, breakfast sandwiches, and burritos.

Entertainment: No.

Liquor license: Yes.

Description: This restaurant is built on a fascinating concept; it is actually two restaurants operating in the same space but at two different times of the day! From 8 a.m. through 3 p.m. it is Clementine Coffee, which serves up an appetizing selection of coffee drinks, breakfast dishes, and hearty lunches based mainly on Mexican cuisine. Then, after 4 p.m., it changes over to Lulu Taqueria + Mezcal, which stays open into the evening with even more great food and drink.

Clementine describes itself as a "contemporary coffee shop" with a warm, cozy atmosphere. It is located literally twenty to thirty feet from the edge of the canal, and boaters can step off their craft and into the shop within a matter of seconds. It is also a break from the big chain coffee shops, and the baristas behind the counter will be happy to brew you a custom-made java to get your taste buds off to a great start for the day.

For people who choose to drive, parking is available in the large lot behind the Box Factory.

LULU TAQUERIA + MEZCAL

Phone/Address: (585) 667-1801 / 6 N. Main Street, Suite 125, Fairport, NY 14450 (inside the Box Factory).

Days/Hours: Open Tuesday–Thursday, 4 p.m.–8:30 p.m., Friday and Saturday, 5 p.m.–9:30 p.m.

Reservations accepted? Yes.

Restaurant size: Approximately thirty-one tables between the main dining area and the bar, plus twenty-four tables on the outside patio (seasonal).

Outdoor seating: Yes (on patio).

The main dining room of Lulu Taqueria is the same room used by Clementine Coffee in the morning (see previous photo). Both restaurants share the same space.
PHOTO BY LARRY WEILL

Menu items: Starters include nachos, street corn, chips with salsa or guacamole, and loaded fries. Main course entrées include eleven (count 'em, eleven!) varieties of tacos, plus lots of burritos, pork belly torta, chiles rellenos, quesadilla grande, and more. There are even burgers and hot dogs on the kiddie menu.

Price range: The entire menu is extremely economical, with all items priced well below $20.

Most popular menu item: A fried chicken sandwich, served with jalapeño pickle slaw, a brioche bun, French fries and side remoulade sauce.

Entertainment: No.

Liquor license: Yes.

Description: Everything listed on the previous page, such as location and parking, applies to Lulu Taqueria. It literally springs to life an hour after Clementine Coffee shuts down for the day.

Lulu Taqueria describes itself as "contemporary food with heavy Mexican accents." From the look of the menu, it comes directly off the streets of the Mexican capital. (And the smells drifting out of the kitchen will make you think you are really there!)

Seating is available on the outdoor patio in the summer, where you can enjoy an amazing array of tequila and tequila drinks, including the following margaritas: original, strawberry, spicy, coconut, Paloma, and grandiose. The bar also serves a large selection of Mexican beers.

MULCONRY'S IRISH PUB & RESTAURANT

Phone/Address: (585) 678-4516 / 17 Liftbridge Lane E., Fairport, NY 14450.

Days/Hours: Closed on Mondays, Tuesday through Thursday 11:30 a.m.–12 a.m., Friday and Saturday 11:30 a.m.–1 a.m., Sunday 11:30 a.m.–12 a.m.

Reservations accepted? Yes.

Restaurant size: Fourteen tables downstairs with additional seating upstairs, including a large outdoor deck. Additionally, there is an upstairs party room that can accommodate forty to sixty people.

Outdoor seating: Yes (on deck).

Menu items: Traditional Irish fare including delicious starters (soft pretzels, pub wings, beer-battered chicken wings, and Irish poutine). A number of burgers (eight!) grace the entrée listing, along with the lengthy menu of traditional dishes, including fish and chips, bangers and mash, shepherd's pie, and boxtys. (If you don't know what these are, you've never dined "full Irish"!)

Price range: Most dishes here fall between $14 and $19, with a few items straying above $20.

Most popular menu item: Corned beef and cabbage, and Mulconry's boxtys. Also, don't miss their popular Irish curry sauce, which is served on French fries.

Entertainment: Yes, the stage in the barroom is often alive with the sounds of local musicians.

Mulconry's Irish Pub & Restaurant in Fairport, New York.
PHOTO BY LARRY WEILL

Liquor license: Yes. (Is there an Irish pub on the planet that does not have a liquor license?)

Description: Mulconry's is many things rolled into one. It is a great place to dine on authentic Irish cuisine. Your only difficulty will be selecting only one main course from the menu. (And their brown bread that comes with the food is also superb.)

If you are by yourself and want to be around other people, the bar area is a great place to plant yourself for a meal and drink. They have a superb lineup of Irish brews available on draft, including Guinness stout draught, Mulconry's Blueberry ale, Harp Irish lager, Smithwick's Irish red ale, Magner's Original Irish Cider, Young Lion IPA, and more.

The only thing that's difficult at Mulconry's is getting in the door on St. Patty's Day, so plan accordingly.

TK'S PIZZERIA

Phone/Address: (585) 388-1700 / 27 Liftbridge Ln. E., Fairport, NY 14450.

Days/Hours: Lunch hours are Monday through Friday 11 a.m.–1:30 p.m. Dinner hours are Sunday through Thursday 4 p.m.–9 p.m., Friday and Saturday 4 p.m.–10 p.m.

Reservations accepted? No.

Restaurant size: About ten tables plus some high chairs (seats around fifty people).

Outdoor seating: No.

Menu items: The focus of the menu at TK's is obviously the pizza, which is the main reason local residents and canal travelers alike flock to this location. Their pizzas are baked in three sizes: "mini" (which are eight inches and four slices, similar to a personal pizza). The other two sizes are small (which are fourteen

TK's Pizzeria, Fairport, New York.
PHOTO BY LARRY WEILL

inches and eight slices) and large (which are sixteen inches and twelve slices). They also offer pizzas that are gluten-free, as well as sheet pizzas (seventeen by twenty-six inches). The pizzas come with any of fifteen delicious toppings, which are listed on the menu. They also sell seven different submarine sandwiches in seven-inch or twelve-inch lengths, as well as chicken wings, salads, bread sticks, and more.

Price range: Pizzas are $7.50 for the minis, $14 for the smalls, and $18.50 for the large size. (Toppings are extra.) The subs range between $7 and $8 for the small size and $10 and $12 for the large. Salads are $5–$7, and the wings are $7.50 for a half dozen and $13 for a full dozen.

Most popular menu item: Just the old-school pizza they've made for the past fifty years.

Entertainment: No.

Liquor license: No (but people can bring in their own beer or wine).

Description: As several other restaurant owners in Fairport stated, "TK's has to be in this book! They are the oldest restaurant on the Fairport stretch of the Erie Canal! Indeed, TKs has been in business in this location for the past fifty years. Founded in 1975, they moved into what was originally an IGA grocery store. "Some of the old-timers still come in here and point out what used to be in which aisles of the original grocery store" said Max, son of the original business owner.

The business is entirely run by family and close friends, who proudly claim "We won't serve anything we wouldn't eat ourselves." Everything is homemade and fresh every day, and they wouldn't have it any other way. This is not a chain pizzeria restaurant. They run it as they'd bake in their own home kitchen. Stop in and sample one of their wonderful pizzas!

THE PORTERHOUSE

Phone/Address: (585) 364-0928 / 400 Packetts Landing, Fairport, NY 14450.

Days/Hours: Open Tuesday–Saturday, 4:30 p.m.–9 p.m. in the winter, Tuesday–Sunday in the summer months. They plan to expand to a Sunday brunch in the future.

Reservations accepted? Yes.

The Porterhouse, taken from across the Erie Canal in Fairport, New York.
PHOTO BY LARRY WEILL

Restaurant size: The restaurant can seat up to 120 people, which includes their outdoor deck overlooking the canal (seasonal). An additional fifteen seats are available in the bar area.

Outdoor seating: Yes (on deck).

Menu items: Wide variety of seafood dishes, steak, pasta, and more. Seafood includes entrées such as broiled Maine lobster tails, Aukra Norwegian salmon, pan-seared tuna, and mesquite grilled shrimp. Their steak offerings include porterhouse, grilled sirloin, New York strip, and twin petite filets.

Price range: $22.00–$36.00, although several of the top-choice seafood (lobster tails) and steaks are listed at "market price."

Most popular menu item: Diners here enjoy the entire variety of menu selections, and many specials are available throughout the week.

Entertainment: Yes (on the deck in summer months).

Liquor license: Yes.

Description: The Porterhouse describes itself as having "casual upscale, creative dining and entrées." This is another restaurant that I have personally visited on numerous occasions, and I've always experienced superior food and great service at every meal. In addition to preparing superb entrées, their side dishes that accompany the main courses are also uniquely flavorful. Their other customers share the same opinions, as seating is often limited, and reservations are highly recommended.

The outdoor deck offers a wonderful view in the summer months as it looks down directly onto the waters of the canal.

COLONIAL BELLE

Phone/Address: (585) 223-9470 / 400 Packetts Landing, Fairport, NY 14450.

Hours: The *Colonial Belle* cruises at different times on different days. Visit www .colonialbelle.com or call to make reservations for specific cruises.

Cost: Cost/person varies based on the type of tour and whether it includes a meal (see below).

Description: The *Colonial Belle* is the largest tour boat on the Erie Canal, and has been in business since 1989. (As of the writing of this book, it has been conducting canal cruises for thirty-six years.) Throughout that time, *Colonial Belle* has remained a family-owned and operated business. Tammee Poinan Grimes, the captain of the *Colonial Belle*, took over those duties from her father, Captain Lee Poinan.

The *Colonial Belle* is a wonderful boat with room for 149 passengers. It is certified by the US Coast Guard and has a well-trained and

Colonial Belle cruise boat, Fairport, New York.
PHOTO BY ANNE GOETZ, PROVIDED COURTESY OF COLONIAL BELLE ERIE CANAL CRUISES

friendly crew. Since the boat ties up very close to the company's office (in Packett's Landing, very close to the Fairport lift bridge), it is convenient for travelers on either the Erie Canal or the Canalway Trail.

There are many kinds of cruises offered by the *Colonial Belle*, many of which come with lunch or dinner. In addition to the lunch and dinner cruises, they also advertise many themed and event cruises, private chartered trips, and school trips. They also offer a special Fall Foliage cruise that starts from downtown Rochester. This voyage is held twice every year in October.

Some of their excursions last for two hours while others are three hours. Regardless of the type or length, they are all narrated by the captain. She is uniquely qualified to talk about any canal-related topic on any cruise, as she is very heavily involved in the administration of numerous canal groups and organizations. She can also tailor the narration to meet the interests of any specific group of guests, especially for charter groups with specialized interests.

Prices for various cruises: The "Family Special Cruise" is the least expensive venture on the *Colonial Belle*, and is only $19/person. It is just the cruise (narrated) but does not include a meal. The lunch cruise is $56 for a two-hour cruise and $65 for a three-hour trip. The dinner cruise ranges from $71 to $77 depending on the meal options that evening.

Reservations and departure point: All cruises (with the exception of the Fall Foliage cruise) depart from the pier below Packett's Landing in the Village of Fairport. Reservations for lunch, brunch, and dinner cruises must be secured forty-eight hours in advance. Some "cruise-only" reservations may be obtained on the day of the cruise, but advance purchase is always recommended.

ROYAL CAFE

Phone/Address: (585) 377-1430 / 15 N. Main Street, Fairport, NY.

Days/Hours: Most days 9 a.m.–9 p.m.

Reservations accepted? No.

Restaurant size: Inside the restaurant there are six tables, although most customers take their gelato dishes or cones outside to eat while strolling the canal.

Outdoor seating: Limited (one table).

Menu items: Lots of flavors of yummy gelato. In the winter months the number of flavors is limited. (There were sixteen flavors on the day I visited.) This number almost doubles in the summer months, so the selection is much larger.

Price range: Small portions of each gelato flavor were $4.95, mediums were $5.95, and large portions were $7.95.

Most popular menu item: Oreo cookie gelato, and pistachio and hazelnut.

Entertainment: No.

Liquor license: No.

Description: The Royal Cafe is a dessert mainstay in the village of Fairport, which is a small, picturesque community of about 5,500 people. It is located about one hundred yards north of the canal and is situated right on Main Street, so it receives a lot of walk-in traffic.

Royal Cafe in Fairport, New York.
Photo by Larry Weill

One of the main differences between the Royal Cafe and most ice cream scoop shops (or frozen yogurt parlors) is that it serves gelato, which is fundamentally different from other frozen desserts. Gelato is generally lower in fat than ice cream and also contains much less air. However, gelato has a higher sugar content than ice cream, and is recognized for delivering a more pronounced flavor than its sister dessert product.

The Royal Cafe serves premium gelato with flavors that burst out to the consumer. It has been in business in Fairport for eighteen years, so its product is loved and accepted by the local population.

The café also serves a variety of cakes, cookies, and baklava, all of which are baked in-house and available in the shop.

This is a great place to visit after you've finished dinner and are looking for the perfect dessert.

CHINA KING CHINESE RESTAURANT

Phone/Address: (585) 223-9440 / 120 Packetts Landing, Fairport, NY 14450.

Days/Hours: Tuesday through Thursday 11 a.m.–9:30 p.m., Friday and Saturday 11 a.m.–10:30 p.m., Sunday noon–9:30 p.m., closed on Monday.

Reservations accepted? No.

Restaurant size: Very limited (mostly takeout).

Outdoor seating: No.

Menu items: The menu lists fifteen different appetizers, from egg rolls and fried wonton to fantail shrimp and crab rangoon. (Some of the appetizers are portions for two to share.) They also offer nine varieties of soups, seven fried rice dishes, four chow meins, four lo meins, and many other traditional meals. The sweet-and-sour dishes come with chicken, shrimp, or pork. Their "Chef's Special" column of entrées lists twenty-eight different specials, which include the Happy Family (lobster, beef, chicken, shrimp, and pork with mushrooms, baby corns, and snow peas in a special sauce), Green Jade Scallops, and Orange Flavored Beef. They also list dishes featuring shrimp, chicken, beef, and pork, along with combination platters for each. They have a separate lunch special menu with twenty-six selections

China King Chinese Restaurant, Fairport, New York.
PHOTO BY LARRY WEILL

Price range: Most appetizers run from $3 to $7, although some of the larger platters are listed up to $16. The soups are $4–$7 per quart, chow mein dishes are $9–$11 per quart, the Chef's Specials are from $13 to $17, while the lunches range from $7 to $9.

Most popular menu item: General Tso's chicken and beef lo mein.

Entertainment: No.

Liquor license: No.

How to find it: To find this restaurant, walk south on South Main Street from the Fairport Village lift bridge until you get to Packett's Landing (on the left). Turn left and walk along Packett's Landing, which is on your left. China King is on the lower level, slightly below ground level, in the Packett's Landing concourse.

Description: China King is a standard Chinese restaurant with a very large menu of traditional Chinese dishes. This place is much more suited to purchasing "takeout" dinners, as their seating capacity is extremely limited. The local population has been coming to this spot for years for food that is prepared very quickly and is also very tasty. It is also a handy spot to tie up your boat and run in for a quick meal that can be consumed onboard your boat or on the pier-side dock.

SHORTS BAR & GRILL

Phone/Address: (585) 388-0136 / 35 N. Main Street, Fairport, NY 14450.

Days/Hours: Daily from 2 p.m. to 2 a.m.

Reservations accepted? No.

Restaurant size: Eight tables (including booths) plus bar seating.

Outdoor seating: No.

Menu items: Hearty bar food, starting with a great lineup of appetizers including pizza logs, fried ravioli, loaded tater tots, and poutine. They also serve outstanding jumbo wings, "super Spuds" (with all kinds of toppings), salads, seven different burgers, sandwiches, and quesadillas.

Price range: Appetizers are between $8 and $10, while most other dishes are $10–$14.

Most popular menu item: Wings, and their own "Barge Plate," which includes two burgers or hot dogs, homemade mac salad, home fries, onions, and a homemade meat hot sauce. (The full-size Barge Plate is $14, and a half-size version is available for $7.)

Entertainment: Yes (karaoke Friday and Saturday).

Liquor license: Yes.

Description: Shorts Bar & Grill is a comfortable neighborhood pub that consistently pulls in a regular crowd. (The bartender who spoke with me has been behind the bar for forty years!) It's simply one of those pubs where everyone knows everyone else, and the food and drink only adds to the comfortable and relaxed atmosphere of the place.

The menu is loaded with appetizers and dishes that are "pub fare." Plenty of good eating at a good price. It's also one spot in town where you can hang out

Shorts Bar & Grill, Fairport, New York.
PHOTO BY LARRY WEILL

with your friends until 2 a.m. every night, as long as you don't have to put in many miles on the canal the next morning.

Shorts also has a couple of special nights each week. Every Tuesday is "Taco Tuesday," with free pool and darts adding to the fun. They also have a "Wings Night" on Thursday, with fifty-cent wings.

This pub is just a few steps from the canal, so it's a quick in-and-out. Find out why it's been a success since 1976. Try it this summer!

MOONLIGHT CREAMERY

Phone/Address: (585) 223-0880 / 36 West Ave., Fairport, NY 14450.

Days/Hours: Monday through Thursday 2 p.m.–9:30 p.m., Friday 11:30 a.m.–10 p.m., Saturday 11 a.m.–10 p.m., Sunday 11:30 a.m.–9:30 p.m.

Reservations accepted? No.

Restaurant size: Six tables.

Outdoor seating: Yes.

Menu items: Lots of great ice cream flavors, plus other desserts to tempt your palate.

Price range: Small size ("itty bitty") ice cream $5, regular $5.95, large $6.85. You can also take home a hand-packed pint for $9.25, a two-pint deal for $16.50, or step up to a two-quart deal for $24.

Most popular menu item: The most popular flavor in the store is an oatmeal ice cream! (And since oatmeal is supposedly good for you, you should eat a lot of this.)

Entertainment: No.

Liquor license: No.

Moonlight Creamery in Fairport, New York.
<small>PHOTO BY LARRY WEILL</small>

Description: Moonlight Creamery is a modern and comfortable ice cream shop that has sat right next to the canal for many years. They proudly offer Giffords ice cream, which is a long-standing supplier of premium ice cream. They do also sell "soft serve" to those who enjoy that.

Moonlight's website displays an extensive list of flavors, although they can only carry a limited number (twenty-four) at any given time. You can call their store to inquire what flavors are in the shop at any given time.

Note: just to tempt your taste buds, flavors on their "extended list" include "Annie Wants S'More," "Bourbon with Sour Cherries," "Pineapple Upside Down Cake," and "New York Sugar Maple & Candied Bacon." (And that list goes on and on and on!)

If you decide you'd like to have a hot drink with your ice cream, they'll also pour you a cup of your favorite gourmet coffee, latte, or cappuccino. Also, inside the coolers are a selection of five signature cakes and three gourmet pies, along with lots of other gooey goodies.

So go ahead! With all the exercise you are getting on the canal path you can afford a few extra calories.

RIKI'S FAMILY RESTAURANT

Phone/Address: (585) 388-0139 / 25 N. Main Street, Fairport, NY 14450.

Days/Hours: Tuesday through Sunday, 7 a.m.–2 a.m., closed on Monday.

Reservations accepted? No.

Restaurant size: Thirty-three tables.

Outdoor seating: No.

Menu items: The breakfast menu includes a lot of egg dishes, including egg plates with corned beef hash, bacon, steak, and more. They also offer many different omelets, along with breakfast sandwiches, pancakes, waffles, and more. Their lunch menu offers salads, wraps, club and hot sandwiches, burgers, paninis, and several Greek specialties (see below).

Price range: Breakfasts can start as low as $7, but most range between $10 and $15. Most lunches also run around $10–$15.

Most popular menu item: Almost all of Riki's omelets are fan favorites in this local favorite restaurant.

Riki's Family Restaurant, Fairport, New York.
PHOTO BY LARRY WEILL

Entertainment: No.

Liquor license: No, but they do serve beer and wine.

Description: Riki's Family Restaurant is a very old establishment in the community. It dates back forty years (with the same ownership), and the customer base has become very attached to the cozy diner atmosphere of the eatery.

They serve a complete lineup of breakfast dishes, and their website proudly advertises that "if you can't find what you want on our menu, just ask for it." They genuinely enjoy providing their customers with whatever they desire, and their customers have become used to that level of service.

Their lunch menu lists the "Greek specialties" mentioned above, which include gyros, souvlaki, a "Greek burger," and "Greek fries" (which are topped with feta, tomatoes, onions, and spices).

If you're looking to hop off the canal trail for a quick breakfast or lunch, this would be a great option.

JUNCTION 361

Phone/Address: (585) 309-8651 / 24 N. Main Street, Fairport, NY 14450.

Days/Hours: Monday through Thursday 7 a.m.–8 p.m., Friday and Saturday 7 a.m.–9 p.m., Sunday 8 a.m.–3 p.m.

Reservations accepted? No.

Restaurant size: Thirteen tables.

Outdoor seating: No.

Menu items: This place offers not only standard coffee shop drinks and breakfast items, but also a wide variety of beers as well. Their hot drinks include coffees, lattes, espresso, cappuccino, and "cortado," which is half espresso and half milk. Their food menu items include flatbread pizzas, soups, chili, baked oatmeal, spinach and artichoke dip, hummus, bagels, and pastries. They also offer larger breakfast sandwiches, salads, and more.

Junction 361 in Fairport, New York.
PHOTO BY LARRY WEILL

Price range: Breakfasts sandwiches are $8–$13 while salads range between $9 and $13.

Most popular menu item: One of the most popular menu items is their cinnamon toast latte.

Entertainment: Yes (music on Friday nights, with new artists every month).

Liquor license: No.

Description: Junction 361 is a relatively new restaurant that has been open for a little over a year. It is a rather unique concept because it's the only establishment I've visited that will provide both a freshly brewed cup of gourmet coffee and offer you a choice of over fifty beers. It all depends on what time your boat crew went to sleep the previous evening!

The staff of this restaurant is also proud to point out that you can buy a beer or a coffee any time of day, all day long. (The beer must wait until 8 a.m., which is mandated by the law.)

Speaking of Junction 361's beer selection, it is positively *huge*, and most of them are locally produced. Almost all of these beers are in cans, but they always have four brews on tap, and those beers (which rotate frequently) are unusual brands that you've probably never seen before. During my visit, these were: Mortalis Thanatos, Grow Buried by the Future, Prison City Crispy Boys, and Noble Shepherd Happy Wizard. Ever heard of those? (Me neither.)

So, if you're not sure whether you want a coffee, a beer, or one of each, this is the place to visit.

DONNELLY'S PUBLIC HOUSE

Phone/Address: (585) 377-5450 / 1 Water Street, Fairport, NY 14450.

Days/Hours: Monday through Saturday 11 a.m.–11 p.m., Sunday noon–11 p.m.

Reservations accepted? Yes (for tables of six people or more).

Restaurant size: Nine tables with lots of bar seating.

Outdoor seating: Yes, about twelve tables on front patio in warmer months.

Menu items: Donnelly's offers an extensive menu of pub fare along with its lengthy selection of beers on tap. Lots of appetizers headline the menu, including wraps, mozzarella sticks, nachos, wings, curly fries, and more. Their smaller pub items include salads, beef on weck, and the "Ed Baronowski," which is warm corned beef on a toasted bomber roll with Brie, horseradish sauce, and jus. They also serve a few more substantial (and fancier) entrées, which include a Mahi Pineapple Glaze Salad or the Fried Shrimp Platter. These latter specials are written on a blackboard in the front of the pub.

Price range: Most dishes go for between $10 and $15, with some of the specials costing a few dollars more.

Most popular menu item: Customers at Donnelly's seem to prefer their wings above most other pub food items.

Entertainment: No.

Liquor license: Yes.

Donnelly's Public House, Fairport, New York.
PHOTO BY LARRY WEILL

Description: Donnelly's is one of those restaurants that people coming off the canal may not visit because it is out of sight, just down the road from the other dining spots on Liftbridge Lane. But it is another fan favorite for the locals in the area, as it's been there for many years and the Fairport residents are familiar with its friendly service and the quality of their food and drink.

They always carry a huge selection of beers, both imported and domestic. During my visit, the beers on tap included Ace Perry cider, Prison City Hitman stout, Paulaner Münchner Hell, Prison City Cream Ale, Rohrbach's Brewing Sunset Sorbet, Beer Tree Dunkel Hugh, and Twelve Percent Snappy Lager. And for those canal travelers who enjoy their brew, the list was a lot longer than that, so get ready to try one of each.

RUSTIC TACO

Phone/Address: (585) 364-0703 / 30 Fairport Village Landing, Fairport, NY 14450. (It's right on Main Street.)

Days/Hours: Tuesday and Wednesday 11:30 a.m.–8 p.m., Thursday through Saturday 11:30 a.m.–9 p.m., closed on Sunday and Monday.

Reservations accepted? Yes (parties of eight or more).

Restaurant size: Approximately twelve tables.

Outdoor seating: No.

Menu items: Craft cheeseburger taco, piña colada tilapia taco, sober spicy shrimp taco, rootstock pork taco, posh trash taco, rustic beer fry taco, whiskey barrel barbecue taco, mango margarita chicken taco, 3-B's taco (with buttermilk chicken, beer batter, and Buffalo sauce), and a veggie "wino" taco. (Notice a theme here?) They also diverge from the taco theme while presenting a nice listing of tasty appetizers, which include white chicken chili, lobster bisque, and drunken nachos, among others.

Price range: Single tacos go for $7.95, while two are $13.95.

Most popular menu item: The Craft Cheeseburger Taco, made with Angus beef, Rustic Kölsch cheese sauce, lettuce, tomatoes, red onions, chipotle aioli, and sour cream, double wrapped.

Entertainment: Yes (live music on Tuesdays and Saturdays).

Rustic Taco, Fairport, New York.
PHOTO BY LARRY WEILL

Liquor license: Yes.

Description: Rustic Taco's menu is a direct reflection of the restaurant's name. First and foremost, they are all about tacos, fresh ingredients, and providing a new taste experience to their customers. The owner is a self-taught chef who combines her unique culinary skills with an avid sense of imagination to create some truly innovative taco combinations.

The website for this trendy Fairport restaurant boldly points out that this is *not* Mexican cuisine. The owner stresses that Rustic Taco does not attempt to use "authentic Mexican ingredients." Instead, they stand out by using a bold array of American ingredients that are expertly blended and cooked with different spirits, including flavorful beers and wines for a truly unique taste. Regardless, the combinations of fresh ingredients, spices, and preparations have contributed to the success of this restaurant in the Fairport community.

ERIE CANAL BOAT COMPANY

Address: This outpost of the Erie Canal Boat Company is located just north of the canal, at the Fairport lift bridge. The address is 7 Liftbridge Lane, Fairport, NY 14450.

Background: This company is in business to provide rental boats (kayaks and other paddle boats), plus bicycles to the public for use on the canal or canal path. While the location described in this section refers to the Fairport area, this company also has facilities and resources in numerous locations along the canal, including Palmyra (at Aqueduct Park), Lyons (at Abbey Park), Lockport, and the Montezuma Anchorage.

Description of resources: The Erie Canal Boat Company offers a variety of boat type rentals, which include canoes and kayaks (both single and tandem), and stand-up paddleboards. Rentals are available for different time increments, including two-hour, half-day, and full-day rates. A variety of canoe models are available for general recreation, touring, and fishing. Guided tours are also available for groups.

Erie Canal Boat Company, Fairport, New York.
PHOTO BY LARRY WEILL

In addition to the canoes and kayaks, the Erie Canal Boat Company also offers a wide variety of rental bicycles, many of which are configured for people with different mobility issues. Even individuals who are limited to a single functional arm or leg can safely operate one of their recumbent trikes, which are designed with centralized controls that permit the rider to maintain control while steering, braking, and shifting. The Erie Canal Boat Company is the only Adaptive Paddling and Cycling Center in the United States, with adaptive kayaks and trikes available daily. Their ADA-accessible boat launch makes the entry and exit a breeze for people of all abilities.

Longer excursions: In addition to bike and boat rentals, this company also offers the opportunity to enjoy a weekend of paddling and camping inside the Montezuma Anchorage, located at the Erie Canal–Seneca River waterway. The Erie Canal Boat Company provides a cleared area for camp setup, potable drinking water, bathroom facilities, a communal firepit, and a recreation area.

Pets: Can't bear to spend the entire weekend away without Fido (the family poochie)? No worries! Not only are pets welcome on your excursion, but the Erie Canal Boat Company will even provide a dog life preserver.

Fees: Dependent on the type of equipment and duration of the rental period.

Contact points: Phone (585) 748-2628, or email at eriecanalboatcompany@gmail.com.

MAC'S PHILLY STEAKS

Phone/Address: (585) 377-0033 / 71 N. Main Street, Fairport, NY 14450.

Days/Hours: Every day of the week, 11 a.m.–8 p.m.

Reservations accepted? No.

Restaurant size: Seven tables, plus counter seating and outdoor tables.

Outdoor seating: Yes.

Menu items: Salads (seven different ones), hoagies, steaks, chicken dishes, Philly cheesesteak sandwiches, Philly's hots, pizza steaks, garlic Parmesan cheesesteaks, four different chicken sandwiches, and a choice of five different wraps.

Mac's Philly Steaks in Fairport, New York.
PHOTO BY LARRY WEILL

Price range: Most dishes range between $12 and $15. An eight-inch hoagie can be purchased for around $8 (depending on the total order and side dishes), while salads are available for about $16.00.

Most popular menu item: The garlic Parmesan cheesesteak, and also their plates dishes.

Entertainment: No.

Liquor license: No.

Description: Fairport has Italian food, Mexican food, Irish food, ice cream parlors, and American diners. So what's wrong with having a Philadelphia cheesesteak restaurant? Nothing!

Mac's Philly Steaks is a Fairport restaurant that is part of a four-store chain, with other locations in Rochester, Canandaigua, and Victor. The Fairport store is located just north of the train tracks on Main Street.

True to its name, this restaurant focuses its attention on the iconic chees-esteaks of Philadelphia. The restaurant has a continuous flow of customers lined up at the counter, a testament to the popularity of its cuisine.

The "plate" dishes are quite popular at this spot, including their three primary varieties, which are: the "Mac Plate" (mac salad with French fries, topped with a half-pound of your choice of meat, diced onions, ketchup, mustard, and meat hot sauce), the "Philly Plate" (with cheese served over a bed of mac salad, onion rings, and French fries, then smothered in hot sauce), and the "Fat Mac Plate" (a cheesesteak served in an Amoroso roll, topped with mac salad, French fries, ketchup, hot sauce, and mayo). If you can't drive to Philly tonight, you've got to come here!

WAYNE COUNTY

BUTTERFLY NATURE TRAIL

Location: The Butterfly Nature Trail is located the town of Macedon, inside the Erie Canal Park at Lock 30. To find the trail, turn into the park at Lock 30, which is located on Route 350 a short distance north of Route 31. From there, drive past the front of the South Macedon Fire Station (which will be on your left). Continue straight for another two hundred to three hundred yards, which ends in a small parking lot directly in front of the entrance to the Butterfly Nature Trail (see below).

Background: The trail was officially opened on August 25, 2014. It was a collaborative effort undertaken by a great many local corporations, volunteer

Archway marking the start of Butterfly Nature Trail in Macedon, New York.
PHOTO BY LARRY WEILL

organizations, and private citizens who not only raised the funds for development but also contributed many hundreds of hours to plan and shape the trail.

Description: The Butterfly Nature Trail is a short walkway that leads to a point on land about a quarter-mile due west. The route is not paved, although it is layered in compacted gravel and stone that provides secure, dry footing. Special shoes or hiking boots are not required.

Things to see and do: The entire length of the walkway is lined with displays, signboards, and other informational postings that describe the flora and fauna of the canal. Two of the main focal points are the butterflies and birds sighted in the immediate vicinity. There are also special bushes and flowers planted along the trail to attract as many species of butterflies as possible.

History is another focus of the Butterfly Nature Trail. Some of the signboards discuss the history of the canal dating back to 1825. They point out the locations of the three different canal segments: the original "Clinton's Ditch" (1825), the enlarged version (1862), and then the modern-day canal (completed in 1918) in its current location. The Butterfly Nature Trail is one of the few places along the entire length of the Erie Canal where all three eras of the canal's growth and expansion can be seen simultaneously.

Also displayed are some of the prominent citizens and contributors who helped fund and construct this worthwhile project.

Admission: There is no fee to enter the Butterfly Nature Trail.

Animals: Pets are welcome on this trail, but pet owners should take normal precautions and courtesies to control/leash their animals as well as clean up after them.

WEST WAYNE RESTAURANT

Phone/Address: (315) 986-7505 / 1900 State Route 31, Palmyra, NY 14502.

Days/Hours: Opens at 5 a.m. daily except closed on Monday. Closes at 3 p.m. on Tuesday–Thursday, 9 p.m. on Friday, 3 p.m. on Saturday and 2 p.m. on Sunday.

Reservations accepted? Yes, but seating is seldom a problem. (Call ahead for large groups.)

West Wayne Restaurant in the West Wayne Plaza in Macedon, New York.
PHOTO BY LARRY WEILL

Restaurant size: About twenty booths and numerous tables in their back room. Counter seating is available in the front of the restaurant.

Outdoor seating: No.

Menu items: West Wayne Restaurant has a very large menu for breakfast and lunch and can serve almost anything you can order. Their breakfast menu is loaded with all varieties of eggs, omelets, sausages, bacon, steak and eggs, waffles, pancakes, hash browns and home fries, and tons more. Their lunch is equally loaded with any kind of sandwiches, wraps, salads, and soups.

Price range: Most breakfast and lunch items on the menu are priced at $8 or less. Combination breakfast plates are also very reasonable.

Most popular menu item: Patrons enjoy all the items on the menu, but many are especially fond of the homemade soups. At least two choices are available every day.

Entertainment: No (unless one counts listening to all the "regulars" poking fun at one another).

Liquor license: No.

Description: This is one of my very favorite dining spots in the Rochester area, and I have breakfast here several times each week. The food is inexpensive and wonderfully prepared, and the waitstaff is always friendly and trying to make you feel at home. They will serve you anything from the breakfast, lunch, or dinner menu any time of day. This is also a restaurant where everyone knows everyone else, and many of the "regulars" occupy the same stools at the counter every day.

In the kitchen, Alex performs his magic on a daily basis, preparing large portions that cannot be outdone for flavor and price. This restaurant (diner) has my highest personal recommendation!

YELLOW MILLS DINER

Phone/Address: (315) 597-4613 / 2534 State Route 31, Palmyra, NY 14522.

Days/Hours: 7 a.m.–8 p.m. daily, but hours vary seasonally. Breakfast, lunch, and dinner served every day except Sunday.

Reservations accepted? No.

Restaurant size: About thirty tables.

Outdoor seating: No.

Menu items: The menu at this restaurant is loaded with comfort food that is all homemade and served in heaping portions. Perhaps the biggest crowds are for breakfast, which is also very economical. (Most items are under $9.) They include all the standards: eggs, pancakes, French toast, and a variety of waffles.

Price range: Most of the menu is set within the $9–$14 range. Some items do trend a bit higher (with the mixed grill set at $20.95), but the entire menu is quite reasonable.

Yellow Mills Diner, Palmyra, New York.
PHOTO BY LARRY WEILL

Most popular menu item: Chicken and biscuits.

Entertainment: No.

Liquor license: No.

Description: The Yellow Mills Diner has been in operation for twenty-five years, and many of their customers have been patronizing the place since its opening. Most of the customers are regulars, and include a lot of local residents in addition to many of the Latter-day Saints who frequent the area for the festivals.

The owner of the establishment emphasizes the fact that nothing on the menu is manufactured or brought in from off-site. Everything is homemade in the restaurant to ensure taste and freshness.

As a local customer myself, I highly recommend the eggplant Parmesan at this establishment. It is wonderful, and they have prepared it for me even when it was not on the menu. That's just the kind of people they are.

Although the restaurant does not accept reservations, it is large enough to accommodate fairly large parties. Counter seating is also available in the front area of the diner.

MUDDY WATERS CAFE & BISTRO

Phone/Address: (315) 502-4197 / 100 Division Street, Palmyra, NY 14522.

Days/Hours: 8 a.m.–2 p.m. most days. Schedules change between summer and winter.

Reservations accepted? No.

Restaurant size: About eight tables inside, seating approximately thirty people.

Outdoor seating: Yes (on deck).

Menu items: Muddy Waters serves primarily lunch dishes, although they also offer a "light breakfast" menu that includes bagels and breakfast sandwiches. Their lunch salads include the "Classic" and the "Barge." (All their menu selections are named after canal-related items.) They also offer a variety of sandwiches, wraps, and panini pressed sandwiches, all of which are hand-made at the deli-like serving counter.

Price range: Almost everything on the lunch menu is around $9–10.

Muddy Waters Cafe & Bistro in Palmyra, New York.
PHOTO BY LARRY WEILL

Most popular menu item: The "Hoodledasher," which is turkey with roasted red pepper, bacon, Provolone cheese, and red pepper sauce on a ciabatta roll. (Note: A hoodledasher is a hookup of two or more empty cargo barges to a full cargo barge. This allowed one team of mules to pull three barges at the same time.)

Entertainment: No.

Liquor license: No, but Muddy Waters does serve beer and wine.

Description: Muddy Waters Cafe & Bistro is a positively charming place tucked out of the way in the historic section of Palmyra, It sits directly behind the Port of Palmyra Marina, which enables boaters and bikers easy access to the facility.

Your host at this breakfast/lunch spot will be Donna, the affable owner who goes out of her way to make everyone feel at home. She is proud of mentioning that Hillary Clinton once held a conference in this very building.

Muddy Waters's food is not only all homemade, but the entire establishment feels as though you are eating in your own kitchen. The decor is entirely based on the canal, which adds even more to the experience. The patrons all gather and chat between the tables because they have all become friends over the years. This is a wonderful place to visit!

PORT OF PALMYRA MARINA

Location: The Port of Palmyra Marina is located off the canal at the intersection of Canal and Division Streets in Palmyra.

Note: This marina is neither restaurant, pub, nor "attraction." Instead, it is a service for the use and convenience of visitors who are hiking, biking, or boating on the canal.

Description of resources: The Port of Palmyra Marina is an incredibly useful and convenient contribution by the Village of Palmyra to the users of the Erie Canal and its associated walkway. The marina offers pier-side boat tie-up spaces where boats can stay overnight, free of charge. Both water (pump out) and electricity are available at no charge. There is also a launch area for kayaks and canoes. Camping is permitted at this marina as well, in case you are hiking or biking on the canal path.

Port of Palmyra Marina at Canal and Division Streets in Palmyra, New York.
PHOTO BY LARRY WEILL

Farther up the walkway from the marina is a beautiful comfort station, which offers restrooms and showers that are open to the public. The bathrooms and showers are open from 6 a.m. through 10 p.m., so plan accordingly.

In front of the comfort station is a large pavilion containing about eight picnic tables with benches. These are covered by a roof to enable large gatherings protected from inclement weather. This pavilion can be rented for group events. (Residents pay a deposit of $100, nonresidents pay $125.)

Problems: For issues at this marina, call the Palmyra Village Hall at (315) 597-4849.

Pets: Pets can be taken into the marina property, but they must be kept on a leash at all times. The Village of Palmyra also requests that you clean up after your pet to preserve the cleanliness of the grounds

Fees: There are no fees to use the Port of Palmyra Marina except to rent the pavilion at the comfort station.

AKROPOLIS FAMILY RESTAURANT

Phone/Address: (315) 597-5634 or (315) 502-0189 / 513 Canal Street, Palmyra, NY 14522.

Days/Hours: Every day of the week, 7 a.m.–9 p.m.

Reservations accepted? Yes (large parties only).

Restaurant size: About seventeen tables inside, plus bar seating.

Outdoor seating: Yes.

Menu items: This restaurant provides a full array of breakfast, lunch, and dinner selections. Breakfast includes a lot of egg dishes, with eleven different omelets, steak and eggs, pancakes, and French toast. Dinners include meat loaf, souvlaki, and roast beef, along with a nice selection of salads, sandwiches, wraps, and burgers. There is also a roast turkey dinner, a jumbo shrimp plate, chicken Parmesan, and five Italian dishes.

Akropolis Family Restaurant, Palmyra, New York.
PHOTO BY LARRY WEILL

Price range: Breakfasts list between $10 and $15 while lunches and many dinners are $10–$18. Some dinners (including steaks) are a little higher.

Most popular menu item: The two most popular dishes on the menu are the Greek salad and the fish fry.

Entertainment: No.

Liquor license: No.

Description: The Akropolis is another restaurant that offers breakfast, lunch, or dinner any time of day. They are open long hours, 7 a.m.–9 p.m., and will accommodate any order from morning to night.

The owners are proud of the fact that everything served in their restaurant is homemade, and the owner's mother is the primary chef in the kitchen. (You can't go wrong with mom doing the cooking!)

This restaurant has been open since 1999, and has developed a strong following of local diners who come in almost every day. There doesn't seem to be any favorite meal of the day; it is always crowded.

The Akropolis also caters to the Mormon visitors in the summer, which is why the crowds double in size during the season.

CHILL & GRILL

Phone/Address: (315) 597-8946 / 616 E. Main St, Palmyra, NY 14522.

Days/Hours: Monday through Saturday 11 a.m.–9 p.m., Sunday noon–9 p.m., but the grill closes at 8 p.m. every night.

Note: This is a seasonal restaurant, open each year from March 20 through September 1.

Reservations accepted? No.

Restaurant size: Five large tables outside, beneath the covered roof.

Outdoor seating: Yes.

Menu items: From the grill, they offer a nice selection of half-pound and full-pound burgers, including optional cheese, bacon, and all the toppings. They also have chicken fingers, sausages, and Zweigle's hot dogs (red and white), plus pizza logs, mozzarella sticks, and all the side orders. On the ice cream side, they proudly serve twenty-seven flavors of Perry's hard ice cream to go with their

Chill & Grill, Palmyra, New York.
PHOTO BY LARRY WEILL

Upstate soft ice cream. Their frozen menu also includes ice cream pies, ice cream sandwich cookies, sundaes, milkshakes, and an "ice cream nacho plate."

Price range: Most burgers are between $9 and $11, although the one-pound "Monster Burger" is $13.50. Jumbo white hots or red hots are $5.25, and most of the sides are $4–$8. Most of the ice cream cones (and sundaes) are from $6 to $8, with banana splits at $9.95.

Most popular menu item: Ice cream and their bacon cheeseburger.

Entertainment: No.

Liquor license: No.

Description: Jeff and Jennifer have owned this roadside ice cream and grill stand for twenty-eight years now. Jeff came to this job from a position as a plant manager and loves his new life without the "corporate stress." Every year they improve the place, making it better and more fun than before.

The motto of their ice cream business is: "That's a small?!!!" Their portions are huge, even the "small" cones. And their largest size is eight scoops, so you'd better arrive hungry!

When you visit, make sure to take your picture in the gigantic blue chair in front of the stand.

BLACK HART BBQ

Phone/Address: (315) 502-0297 / 623 E. Main Street, Palmyra, NY 14522.

Days/Hours: Only open on Saturday and Sunday from noon to 7 p.m.

Reservations accepted? No.

Restaurant size: Six tables, plus outdoor benches.

Outdoor seating: Yes.

Menu items: Award-winning barbecue smoked meats, including pork St. Louis cut spare ribs, beef brisket, and pulled chicken. All of these are also available as sandwiches, along with the "Breuben" (sliced brisket topped with Swiss cheese, coleslaw, and Black Hart special sauce on toasted marble rye bread). They also offer several specialty dishes, which are headlined by the "Hart Attack Plate." Think of it as the king of barbecue garbage plates. It has everything on it!

Price range: The sandwiches range between $8 and $12, while the ribs vary based on size. (Three ribs are $10, a half rack is $20, and the full rack lists at $36.) The Hart Attack Plate is also $36 for a whole lotta food.

Most popular menu item: Hart Attack Plate and the Four Meat Plate.

Entertainment: No.

Liquor license: No.

Description: Black Hart BBQ is as much an experience as it is a "restaurant." These people are seriously into barbecue, and have the trophies to prove it! They are only open on weekends for the time being, as the owners both hold down full-time jobs during the week. However they don't rule out adding additional weekdays to the schedule in the future.

While they do operate their Palmyra restaurant as a dine-in option on weekends, they are also busy bringing their brand of barbecued smoked meats and

Black Hart BBQ in Palmyra, New York.
PHOTO BY LARRY WEILL

other treats to other events. They cater to fundraisers, parties, grand openings, special events, corporate functions, and lots more.

Black Hart uses its food truck to serve any function in Wayne, Ontario, and Yates counties. They can handle large crowds, and provide details for catering on their website. And if you want to snag a peek at all their awards, log onto their website and click on "BBQ Competitions." The list is long and varied.

If you're looking to hop off your boat or the canal path for some quality barbecue, this is the place.

CRAFT 120

Phone/Address: (315) 573-7781 / 120 E. Union Street, Newark, NY 14513.

Days/Hours: Closed Monday and Tuesday, Wednesday and Thursday 4 p.m.–9 p.m., Friday and Saturday 4 p.m.–10 p.m., Sunday 4 p.m.–8 p.m.

Reservations accepted? Yes.

Craft 120 in Newark, New York.
PHOTO BY LARRY WEILL

Restaurant size: About sixteen tables inside, plus bar seating. There is also seating outside during the summer months.

Outdoor seating: Yes.

Menu items: Craft 120's menu starts with a tasty array of "small plates" which are made for sharing. They offer shrimp, mac and cheese, short rib poutine, charred Italian wings, a charcuterie board, plus salads and chicken Parmesan and four different varieties of flatbread pizzas, including margherita, meatball, NY State (with New York cheddar cheese and apples in a red wine reduction sauce), and garden.

Price range: Most dinner items range between $14 and $24, although a few items are a bit more.

Most popular menu item: The charred Italian wings are a favorite here, as is the fillet of sirloin.

Entertainment: No, although it appears they have had live music in the past.

Liquor license: Yes.

Description: Craft 120 is another scenic restaurant that sits right on the edge of the canal, with plenty of outdoor deck seating to take in the views.

This restaurant only serves dinner, as it opens at 4 p.m. most days. The interior dining room is very attractive, with large windows all around to provide the best views of the canal. A good way to describe this place is "trendy."

As they describe it themselves, "Craft 120 offers you an experience where sharing is encouraged." A complete bar and large selection of beers further complements the food.

In addition to the standard menu, Craft 120 also develops special menus to help celebrate special holidays. The 2024 Valentine's Day menu featured many unique items that do not appear on most of their regular dinner menus. The appetizers included seafood bisque; lobster, shrimp, and scallops; and crab cakes. That's a tough combination to beat.

MAIN STREET RESTAURANT

Phone/Address: (315) 332-8833 / 101 W. Union Street, Newark, NY 14513.

Days/Hours: Closed on Wednesday and Sunday, open all other days 11:30 a.m.–9 p.m.

Reservations accepted? Yes.

Restaurant size: Twenty-six tables inside plus counter/bar seating.

Outdoor seating: Yes.

Menu items: The menu here includes six great salad options, plus burgers, wraps, and some great-looking dinner entrées, which include herb-crusted salmon, chicken or veal marsala, lobster ravioli, and more. The desserts are all homemade and rotate frequently, so make sure to ask your waitress. (They are worth it!)

Price range: Most lunches are between $13 and $17, while dinners are mostly between $20 and $35.

Most popular menu item: Perhaps the most requested item on the menu is their chicken Parmesan. But the owner (Tom Tolleson) is extremely proud of the quality of their prime rib, which he claims is "the best around, hands down."

Main Street Restaurant, Newark, New York.
PHOTO BY LARRY WEILL

Entertainment: Yes. Main Street Restaurant has trivia contests on Tuesday.

Liquor license: Yes.

Description: Main Street Restaurant represents casual Italian American dining that welcomes the hikers, bikers, and boaters coming off the canal. It is one of those places with unusual "perks," many brought to you compliments of the owner. Tom is as inventive as he is creative. He created the bar (which is gorgeous) by hand from recycled wooden pallets he found along the roadside, which he then sanded, polished, and coated with polyurethane. Much of the wood behind the bar was similarly repurposed from discarded locations and artfully reused to form a beautiful front room.

Almost everything else inside this Newark restaurant is "different from the rest." The dinners come with salad and homemade focaccia bread, both of which are complimentary. Many area restaurants charge for one or both of these.

The owner is fond of saying the Main Street Restaurant is "the food and quality of the big city, but the hospitality of a small town."

CANAL VIEW FAMILY RESTAURANT

Phone/Address: (315) 331-4803 / 247 W. Union Street, Newark, NY 14513.

Days/Hours: Monday through Thursday, 7 a.m.–8 p.m., Friday and Saturday 7 a.m.–9 p.m., Sunday 7 a.m.–8 p.m.

Reservations accepted? No.

Restaurant size: About twenty-one tables. (No counter seating.)

Outdoor seating: No.

Menu items: This place has an extensive menu. (Many pages, similar to a large diner. It has everything!) Any breakfast, lunch, or dinner item is available all day long. Also features numerous soups, salads, sandwiches, wraps, seafood,

Canal View Family Restaurant in Newark, New York.
PHOTO BY LARRY WEILL

Italian entrées, and club sandwiches. Also of interest here is their "Texas Plate" (described below).

Price range: Almost everything on the breakfast menu is around $9–13, lunch and dinner ranges between $10 and $16, with a few seafood items priced a bit higher.

Most popular menu item: Lots of folks come in for the chicken wings, which were recognized as the "Best of the Finger Lakes." Patrons also enjoy the "Texas Plate," which is two hot dogs or Angus beef burgers or cheeseburgers, served with home fries, mac salad, topped with onions, cheese, and homemade meat hot sauce. Yeehaw!!!

Entertainment: No.

Liquor license: No.

Description: This restaurant resembles everyone's favorite hometown diner, but without the counter seating. It is a large, spacious restaurant that can handle anyone coming off the canal path for a hearty meal.

Another nice feature of the Canal View is the staff, who always have big smiles on their faces to welcome you inside. It's one more way they make you feel welcome to their establishment.

But the most distinctive factor about the Canal View is their menu, which appears to offer everything you could want. Whether you're looking for breakfast, lunch, or dinner (even if everyone in your group wants something different), this is the place to go. Eat in, or take it back to the boat!

MONTERREY MEXICAN RESTAURANT

Phone/Address: (315) 573-7493 / 833 W. Union Street, Newark, NY 14513.

Days/Hours: Closed on Monday, Tuesday through Friday 11 a.m.–9 p.m. (except for 2 p.m.–4 p.m.), Saturday 11 a.m.–10 p.m., Sunday 11 a.m.–8 p.m.

Reservations accepted? No.

Restaurant size: About twenty-nine tables inside, plus bar seating.

Outdoor seating: No.

Monterrey Mexican Restaurant in Newark, New York.
Photo by Larry Weill

Menu items: A full lineup of Mexican food, including tacos, fajitas, burritos, chicken plates, small plates, plus plenty of seafood entrées (including several dinners featuring shrimp). Vegetarian and gluten-free dishes are also available.

Price range: Lunches range from $9 to $11, while dinners are between $15 and $20.

Most popular menu item: This restaurant is best-known for its "La Bandera" plate, which features three corn enchiladas, one chicken with cheese sauce, one beef with green sauce, and one cheese with red sauce. These colors, of course, represent the Mexican flag. It is further graced with rice, beans, and guacamole salad. All that wonderful Mexican food for $15.99.

Entertainment: No.

Liquor license: Yes.

Description: In this day of fast-food franchises, it's nice to find a Mexican restaurant close to the canal that is different from the rest. All meals here are individually prepared and masterfully spiced. The sign out in front says "authentic," and they mean it.

Note: During weekdays, this restaurant closes down every day from 2 p.m. to 4 p.m. (This does not apply on Saturday or Sunday.) This won't affect lunch or dinner dining, but it will get in the way if you are looking for a midday snack, so be forewarned.

This restaurant is located in the first commercial plaza on the west side of town, so if you are hiking or biking from west to east be prepared to come off the canal path as soon as you hit town.

ERIE SHORE ICE CREAM SHOP

Phone/Address: (315) 830-0104 / 50 East Avenue, Newark, NY 14513.

Days/Hours: Monday through Friday 4 p.m.–9 p.m., Saturday and Sunday 2 p.m.–9 p.m. This location is seasonal: summer only.

Reservations accepted? No.

Restaurant size: Limited inside seating.

Outdoor seating: Yes.

Menu items: This canal-side shop offers both soft-serve and hard ("scoop") ice cream in three sizes, all of which are available in a cone or a dish. There are tons of flavors, all of which can rotate often throughout the season. Some of the more inventive flavors are: Fly Fishing Fudge, Scoop-a-Snack, Moose Tracks, and Lemon Lime Summertime. Also available are a huge variety of floats, sundaes, and specialty sundaes, which include homemade baked goods right in the ice cream.

Price range: Kiddie cones or bowls are $2.75, Small cones or bowls are $4.25, and large cones or bowls are $5.25. The floats, sundaes, and special sundaes range from $5.75 to $7.75.

Most popular menu item: Ice cream, ice cream, and more ice cream. (We're keeping this one simple!)

Entertainment: No.

Liquor license: No. (Alcohol on ice cream?)

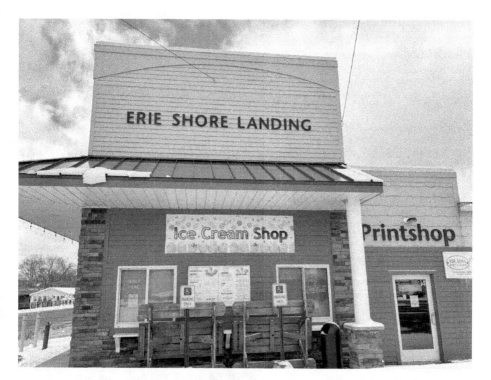

Erie Shore Ice Cream Shop, Newark, New York.
Photo by Larry Weill

Description: The Erie Shore Ice Cream Shop is a quaint little store on the end of the Erie Shore Landing building, situated right along the canal in Newark. The Erie Shore Landing is a retail business run by the Wayne County ARC. Every purchase made at Erie Shore Landing helps employ individuals with disabilities in the community.

Besides helping people with disabilities to gain employment in the local area, this shop also provides a great product of ice cream to those hikers, bikers, and boaters on the Erie Canal. The ice cream is all produced by Gifford's, a family-run operation that has been making the frozen stuff for over forty years.

Not only does this store provide great ice cream for you and your family, but they even sell a "Doggy Sundae," which includes soft-serve vanilla with mini Milk Bones for $1.50. Optional peanut butter sauce is also available if your poochie is into that. Woof!

THE POUR HOUSE

Phone/Address: (315) 665-0197 / 72 Geneva Street, Lyons, NY 14489.

Days/Hours: Monday through Thursday, 11 a.m.–10 p.m., Friday and Saturday 11 a.m.–12 a.m., Sunday 12 p.m.–9 p.m.

Reservations accepted? No.

Restaurant size: About fifteen tables inside plus a large bar, with some additional outdoor seating.

Outdoor seating: Yes (limited).

Menu items: Mainly pub food, with salads, wraps, burgers, sandwiches, pizza, and wings. They also feature a dish that is only available on every other Sunday called a "Beefy," which is a piled-high beef sandwich served with horseradish sauce. If you want one, come early because they often sell out within the first sixty to ninety minutes.

The Pour House, Lyons, New York.
PHOTO BY LARRY WEILL

Price range: Almost everything on the menu is between $9–$14.

Most popular menu item: The most popular item here is definitely the chicken wings, which have the reputation for being "big and delicious." You can customize your wings with any one of many great-tasting sauces. By the way, if you want a great plate of wings, stop by on Tuesday night, which is "Wing Night."

Entertainment: Yes. There are live bands on Friday nights, and karaoke on Wednesdays.

Liquor license: Yes.

Description: Make no mistake about it, this place is much more of a bar than it is a restaurant. Located right next to the waters of the canal, the bartender was very proud to declare that this is "the only bar in town."

This location also offers a lot to the folks who are hiking, biking, or boating on the canal. For boaters there are tie-up spots just below the Pour House building that provide electrical outlets for power. Additionally, the town fire hall is located next door to the bar, and canal travelers can get access to restroom facilities as well as to showers.

Finally, if you happen to be traveling the canal near Lyons in mid-July, check out the schedule of the annual Peppermint Days Festival. (Yes, the Hotchkiss Company began manufacturing peppermint oil in Lyons, New York, in 1839, and employed over one hundred people by 1844.) It's a fun time with food, crafts, and a huge fireworks display at night. Stop in for a great time.

PEPPERMINT MUSEUM (FORMERLY THE HOTCHKISS BUILDING)

Note: Another name for the museum is the H. G. Hotchkiss Essential Oil Museum

Address: 95 Water Street, Lyons, NY.

Hours: This museum only maintains regular hours in July and August, when it is open on Fridays and Saturdays from 10 a.m. to noon, and from 1 p.m. to 3 p.m. It is also open during those months by appointment. In June, September, and October the building will be by appointment only. To schedule an appointment, call Patty Alena at (315) 946-4596.

Description of resources: The Peppermint Museum is located in the old Hotchkiss Building, right next to the canal in Lyons. It is now owned by the Lyons

Peppermint Museum in Lyons, New York.
PHOTO BY LARRY WEILL

Heritage Society and is used to house and display artifacts from the booming peppermint industry, started in Lyons in the 1830s.

Hiram Hotchkiss started this business using peppermint that was found and harvested locally in the Lyons area. He began marketing his peppermint oil product in New York City in 1839, but did not achieve immediate success. Shortly thereafter, his oils were recognized in international competition overseas for purity and taste, which led to multiple prestigious awards. Commercial success quickly followed, and the business boomed.

The company remained in Lyons until it was acquired in 1982, and was later moved to Indiana in 1990. The building remains in place and is used as a museum dedicated to preserving literature and artifacts of the original peppermint industry started by Hiram Hotchkiss. Included in these documents are articles that outline the refining and production processes of the peppermint oil. The contents of the collection fill ten rooms inside this building.

Fees: There are no fees to enter the museum, but donations are greatly appreciated. The facility also offers a gift shop, and items sold inside also benefit the facility and the Lyons Heritage Foundation.

DIVERGENCE OF THE ERIE CANAL PATH (EMPIRE STATE TRAIL) AND THE ERIE CANAL WATERWAY

When the Canal Trail reaches a point about 1.5 miles southeast of the center of Clyde (about three hundred yards north of Lock 26), the Canal Trail diverges from the canal and the two head in different directions. The Erie Canal continues south, while the trail heads east for several miles, eventually passing through the town of Savannah in four or five miles. At this point, the Canal Trail turns south and then east, finally intersecting with the Erie Canal at the Montezuma Anchorage Paddle Camp.

The reunion of the trail and the canal is very brief. In fact, the Canal Trail simply crosses the canal at this point, continuing due east and then northeast through the towns of Port Byron, Weedsport, Jordan, Memphis, and Camillus before it crosses through the city of Syracuse. This entire length of trail is well south of the Erie Canal.

The distance between the canal and the trail is quite large at most points between Clyde and Stacy Basin (inside the town of Verona). While the canal is transiting across Oneida Lake, the trail is paralleling its course between eight and twelve miles to the south.

The divergence of these two routes is important to the users of this book because the restaurants, pubs, and attractions within "a stone's throw" of the boaters on the canal will be out of range for the hikers and bikers on the trail. Likewise, the hikers and bikers on the canal trail will not be inclined to travel all the extra miles to reach a canal-side location. (Even if they did, there is probably no direct route to cross that distance.)

For this reason, all restaurants, pubs, and attractions listed in these next sections will be noted as located on the Erie Canal or on the Canal Trail. I hope this helps to avoid any confusion along the way.

CAYUGA COUNTY

SENECA RIVERSIDE

Phone/Address: (315) 834-7002 / 9345 Stickle Road, Weedsport, NY 14522.

Days/Hours: Monday, Wednesday, and Thursday noon–9 p.m., Friday and Saturday noon–10 p.m., Sunday noon–6 p.m., closed on Tuesday.

Note: The pizza kitchen is closed on Monday and Tuesday, and has more restricted hours than the regular kitchen.

Reservations accepted? Yes.

Restaurant size: Twelve tables, plus a lot of bar seating. They also have tables outside.

Outdoor seating: Yes (in the summer).

Menu items: Lots of bar/comfort food fills this menu, with salads, sandwiches, wraps, wings, burgers, and chicken dishes. Appetizers on the menu include jalapeño poppers, fried pickle spears, pretzels, mozzarella sticks, onion rings, and egg rolls. To try an assortment you can order the "Riverside Sampler" for $11.99. There is also a separate pizza menu, which offers pizzas in six sizes (or just a slice). They have lots of toppings available to meet any taste.

Price range: Almost anything on the menu is between $10 and $15, and the appetizers run between $7 and $8. Pizzas are similarly inexpensive, with small pizzas at $9.75, medium $11.75, large $13.25, a half sheet costing $16, and the full sheet listed at $25. Some premium toppings (i.e., seasoned steak) are available for an additional charge.

Most popular menu item: Deveney tenders, and their mushroom Swiss burger.

Entertainment: Yes (live bands most weeks during the summer).

Liquor license: Yes.

Description: Seneca Riverside is a combination bar and restaurant that sits in a beautiful location next to the canal. (Many people there just call it "the river," as the waterway is really the Seneca River at this point.) The grounds extend right down to the banks, and patrons can sit outside on the deck and watch the canal traffic go by.

Seneca Riverside in Weedsport, New York.
PHOTO BY LARRY WEILL

The outside of the establishment is just as beautiful as the view, and owners take great pride in maintaining a gorgeous display of flowers while the season permits. This place has a great reputation for the great service and the low food prices. What a great combination!

MONTEZUMA HERITAGE PARK AND RICHMOND AQUEDUCT

Address: 8115 High Street, Montezuma, NY 13117.

Days/Hours: This park is open seven days a week and is generally accessible from dawn to dusk daily.

Admission Fees: There is no admission fee to enter or hike in this park.

Description and services: The Montezuma Heritage Park and Richmond Aqueduct is a large and diverse parcel of land that has been acquired and set aside by the Town of Montezuma for the purposes of preserving history, observing the historic background and structures of the Erie Canal, enjoyment of the nature, wildlife, and woodlands of the area, and providing trails for the enjoyment of the park's visitors.

Additional History: The park was acquired by the Town of Montezuma in the 1960s, and boasts 165 acres of beautiful greenery inside its borders. It also brings together four phases of the canal system, including the original "Clinton's Ditch" from the 1820s, the Cayuga-Seneca Canal (completed in 1828), the enlarged Erie Canal, and the Barge Canal System of 1918.

Much work has been invested developing this park into an ideal location for hikers, nature lovers, historians, and fishermen. Eleven different trails crisscross the grounds and provide users with a host of different views of the Erie Canal. Also located along the Aqueduct Trail (#2) are the remains of the historic Richmond Aqueduct, which used a series of thirty-one stone arches to elevate the Erie Canal up and over the Seneca River. It was completed in 1856 and was the second-largest aqueduct ever built on the enlarged Erie Canal. The remains of this majestic structure can be viewed by following the Aqueduct Trail for four-tenths of a mile, entering from Chapman Road on the enlarged Erie Canal towpath. It is well worth the walk.

The Montezuma Heritage Park is also noted for being "home" to the junction of the original Erie Canal and the Cayuga-Seneca Canals which joined here in 1828. This opened up navigable waters into the Finger Lakes in 1828. Also located along the canal's waters was the historic Exchange Hotel, which was used to stable extra teams of horse and mules for the boat companies.

Park Rules: Please sign in at the kiosk at the park entrance. Free maps are available at the sign-in location. Please carry out all garbage, as well as pet droppings. All pets must be kept on a leash. The park is smoke-free and alcohol-free. No motorized vehicles are permitted on the park's trails.

ONONDAGA COUNTY

TOWPATH PIZZA

Phone/Address: (315) 689-0043 / 2 S. Main Street, Jordan, NY 13080.

Note: This restaurant is only near the Empire Trail (canal path), not near the canal. This is not within walking distance for boaters.

Days/Hours: Sunday noon–8 p.m., Monday 11 a.m.–8 p.m., Tuesday through Saturday 11 a.m.–9 p.m..

Reservations accepted? No.

Restaurant size: Four tables.

Outdoor seating: Yes (picnic tables in front).

Towpath Pizza, Jordan, New York.
PHOTO BY LARRY WEILL

Menu items: They have thirteen special pizza varieties listed on their menu, with everything from Louisiana Chicken (with chicken, mozzarella, and their secret wing sauce), to their Deluxe Pizza (with pepperoni, sausage, onions, green peppers, garlic, and mushrooms). They also offer four different salads in small or large, a choice of fifteen different appetizers (how about some bacon cheese fries?), lots of specialty dinners, and a complete selection of Buffalo wings. And let's not forget the hot and cold subs. Listed among their dinners are various baked pastas, meatballs, and lasagna.

Price range: Pizzas vary in price based upon size and toppings. Medium pizzas are between $15 and $19, large from $17 to $21, and extra-large from $19 to $24. Sheet pizzas start at $24.99. Salads range from $5 to $11, and most dinners fall between $10 and $15, although the seafood platter is $21. Prices also vary as orders are customized with additional toppings.

Most popular menu item: Calzones, and their homemade lasagna, both served with their superb in-house sauces.

Entertainment: No.

Liquor license: No.

Description: Towpath Pizza is a small shop in this quiet little village that floods into their restaurant every day. The pizzeria is located directly across the street from the Empire Trail. The staff is extremely friendly, and will happily customize any pizza or dish to your liking. The staff is fond of saying "everyone in here is your best friend." They definitely make you feel that way. They also embrace the canal path and everyone on it. This place is worth a special stop.

CAMILLUS ERIE CANAL PARK

Phone/Address: (680) 800-5298 / 5750 Devoe Road, Camillus, NY 13031.

Days/Hours: This park is seasonal, but it is open year-round on Saturdays from noon to 4 p.m. The Sims Store Museum is open Wednesday, Thursday, Saturday, and Sunday from noon to 4 p.m.

Boat Tour Days/Hours: Boat tours are conducted on Wednesdays and Sundays, at 1 p.m., 2 p.m., and 3 p.m. Rides are 45 minutes in length.

Admission Fees: Entrance to the museum is free, Boat rides are $5 for an adult, $3 for a child, and $15 for a family. Tickets are purchased at the Sims Store.

Camillus Erie Canal Park, Camillus, New York.
PHOTO BY LARRY WEILL

Description and Services: This museum is modeled after the Sims' Canal Store, which was located approximately two miles east of its current location, also on the Erie Canal. The museum is designed to demonstrate what life was like in the early days of the canal, and also contains exhibits that display some of the early tools and devices used on and around the waterway.

The museum's website details the different sections contained inside the museum building, including a local history section, a display of an Erie Canal barge, an 1800s room, and an area that discusses the tools that were used in the 1800s to build the canal. There is also a gift shop where visitors can purchase period products that have been re-created for your enjoyment.

Visitors can also enjoy cruising down the canal waters on a beautiful canalboat that provides wonderful views of the shoreline en route to the 1842 Nine Mile Creek Aqueduct. This is the only navigable aqueduct that remains from the original first enlargement of the Erie Canal. These boat tours are all professionally narrated to enhance your knowledge of this piece of local history.

The boat tour can accommodate wheelchairs.

TASSONE'S WINE GARDEN

Phone/Address: (315) 635-5133 / 8133 Dexter Parkway, Baldwinsville, NY 13027.

Days/Hours: Closed Monday, Tuesday through Thursday 11:30 a.m.–8 p.m., Friday 11:30 a.m.–9 p.m., Saturday 4 p.m.–9 pm, Sunday 4 p.m.–8 p.m.

Reservations accepted? Yes.

Restaurant size: About forty-two tables inside, plus ample seating at the bar.

Outdoor seating: Yes (on front deck), three tables.

Menu items: Lots of Italian dishes fill the menu, but many of the dishes are American as well. The lunch menu includes grilled Reuben and Cajun prime rib sandwiches, triple-decker clubs, six kinds of burgers, pasta dishes, salads, and wraps. Dinner listings feature seafood (salmon, haddock, shrimp, scallops, and a fried seafood platter), lasagna, other pasta dishes, and chicken cacciatore.

Tassone's Wine Garden in Baldwinsville, New York.
PHOTO BY LARRY WEILL

Price range: Lunches are between $12 and $20 while dinners generally range between $20 and $27.

Most popular menu item: The Italian Platter, which contains a *heaping* serving of angel-hair pasta, lasagna, penne, sausage, meatballs, and chicken cutlets, all served with homemade sauce.

Entertainment: Yes (trivia and karaoke).

Liquor license: Yes.

Description: Tassone's Wine Garden is located about three-quarters of a mile west of the Oswego Street Bridge over the Seneca River (aka the Erie Canal). The restaurant is popular with the residents of Baldwinsville as well as with boaters who tie up at the marina across the street (Route 31).

Started in 1991, the place is well-known for its taste and authenticity. They prepare their own sauces, which are superbly seasoned and served on their own pasta creations. These delectable sauces include marinara, house Italian, Alfredo, and vodka sauce. (For an extra treat, try one of them on top of their Italian platter.)

The staff describes the restaurant as being a "comfortable place to come where the staff is helpful and friendly." Others say that the service is "spot-on every time," all while enjoying a dinner that was on top of its game.

The restaurant has its own parking lot, so it's a quick "in-and-out" even if you're not on a boat.

SAMMY MALONE'S

Phone/Address: (315) 635-5407 / 2 Oswego Street, Baldwinsville, NY 13027.

Days/Hours: Monday through Thursday, 4 p.m.–10 p.m., Friday and Saturday 12 p.m.–1 a.m., and Sundays from 12 p.m. to 8 p.m.

Reservations accepted? No.

Restaurant size: About fifteen tables inside, with another fifteen located outside on the deck. A few additional outdoor tables are available in front, with cold-weather heaters available.

Outdoor seating: Yes (on front deck), three tables.

Sammy Malone's in Baldwinsville, New York.
Photo by Larry Weill

Menu items: Food in this quaint Irish pub is not limited to that particular ethnic fare. Both barbecue chicken nachos and Bang Bang shrimp nachos are available as appetizers, as are eleven different varieties of wings. Included with the sandwich listings are lobster rolls, Philly cheesesteaks, and gyro wraps. (If that's not eclectic, nothing is!) Lots of burgers and salads round out the menu, along with cheese quesadillas and shrimp tacos.

Price range: Most dishes are between $12 and $15, although the lobster rolls weigh in at $19.

Most popular menu item: The roast beef sandwich is still the most popular dish in this Irish pub. It's topped with warm cheddar sauce on a locally made bun. You can't beat that!

Entertainment: No.

Liquor license: Yes.

Description: The inside of Sammy Malone's defines the word "cozy." It is a wood-lined space with lots of Irish-themed decorations gracing the walls from top to bottom. The deck has numerous tables to provide seating for boaters, hikers, and bikers coming in from the canal. The "inside" deck (on the right side of the restaurant) has the great feature of having fold-down partitions that convert the space to an outdoor deck in a matter of seconds. And that outdoor deck has a great view of the rushing canal waters directly below.

Sammy Malone's also offers a wide array of beers on tap: thirty-four drafts at any given time. These varieties are rotated through on a regular basis, so the beer menu varies on a regular basis. (Note: Some are Irish brews, although most are not.)

Their words to live by: "It's more fun to eat at a bar than it is to drink at a restaurant." How true!

THE SUDS FACTORY—RIVER GRILL

Phone/Address: (315) 579-2537 / 3 Syracuse Street, Baldwinsville, NY 13027.

Days/Hours: Weekdays 11:30 a.m.–8 p.m., weekends from 11:30 p.m. to 9 p.m.

Reservations accepted? No.

Restaurant size: About sixty tables, including upstairs and downstairs seating. There is also a beautiful deck that overlooks the canal.

Outdoor seating: Yes.

Menu items: While this restaurant used to offer fine dining options, it has scaled back to "pub food" since the pandemic. But their pub food includes a great many appetizing dishes that are served with mouthwatering sides for hungry visitors from the canal path. These include chili bowls with chips, cheese sticks, chicken quesadillas, and loaded chili skins. Want more? For even heartier fare, they advertise a listing of six salads, six pizzas, pulled pork, chicken sandwiches, and Big Bay Nachos (served with homemade chili, cheese, lettuce, olives . . . I'm getting hungry!)

Price range: Most dishes are between $10 and $15.

The Suds Factory—River Grill in Baldwinsville, New York.
PHOTO BY LARRY WEILL

Most popular menu item: The chicken sandwich, served with marinated chicken breast on flatbread with homemade mozzarella, roasted garlic aioli, roasted red peppers, and sweet balsamic onions, lettuce, and tomato.

Entertainment: Yes. Sundays is live music on the canal from 4 to 7 p.m.

Liquor license: Yes.

Description: "Fine dining? We don't need no fine dining!" The truth of the matter is that the throngs of customers who flock to this pub by the water's edge *love* the pub fare prepared by their kitchen. It's all wonderful and inexpensive comfort food that tastes great and doesn't break the bank.

The pub literally hangs over the banks of the Erie Canal (Seneca River) and draws on the energy of its waters.

The staff describes this place as a "secret gem, hidden from view of the casual passersby." Stop in when hiking or biking or boating by. It's well worth the stop, and you probably won't have to wait for a table. How great is that, especially in the crowded summer months?

ANGRY SMOKEHOUSE RESTAURANT

Phone/Address: (315) 800-6793 / 33 Water St., Baldwinsville, NY 13027.

Days/Hours: Tuesday through Thursday, 11:30 a.m.–11 p.m., Friday and Saturday 11:30 a.m.–midnight, Sunday 11:30 a.m.–10 p.m., closed on Monday.

Reservations accepted? Yes.

Restaurant size: Fourteen tables inside and another twenty tables outside, plus party room space.

Outdoor seating: Yes (for parties of eight or more).

Menu items: Their menu starts out with seven great appetizers (including "Candied Hot Links" and "Texas Twinkies), a selection of soups and salads, followed by a number of barbecue-inspired sandwiches (including a barbecue Shrimp Po-Boy sandwich and "The Coma," which is brisket, pulled pork, smoked bacon, slaw, smoked cheddar, candied jalapeños, and the special barbecue sauce), plus a couple specialty meals such as their pulled pork bowl and the smoked brisket mac and cheese. (Note: They offer a choice of five different barbecue sauces!)

Price range: Appetizers range from $11 to $15, sandwiches are $16–$19, half racks of ribs are $23 and full racks are $38 (both served with two sides). Side orders are $6.

Most popular menu item: Brisket, either on a sandwich or as part of one of their famous platters.

Entertainment: Yes (live music on Friday, Saturday, and Sunday).

Liquor license: Yes.

Description: "To gather, socialize, to smile, laugh, to meet new people, surround yourself with great people, to relax, appreciate those you're around, comfort food, messy, to reconnect with old friends, turn off the phones, to just be happy." This is the philosophy espoused by this beloved barbecue establishment in Baldwinsville, and the patrons would happily agree.

The Angry Smoke House is as much about the atmosphere as it is about the food. They are passionate about their Southern barbecue and making their

Angry Smokehouse Restaurant, Baldwinsville, New York.
PHOTO BY LARRY WEILL

patrons feel at home and at ease, They feature a wide selection of musical performers throughout the week to enhance the "vibes" of the place and make everyone happy. A large outdoor patio is available in case you want to stay close to your bike or boat. Get ready to have a good time!

THE WINDS OF COLD SPRING HARBOR MARINA

Phone/Address: (315) 622-2211 / 3642 Hayes Road, Baldwinsville, NY 13027.

Days/Hours: The marina and the restaurant/bar have different hours of operation. The bar is open from noon through midnight on Friday and Saturday, and noon through 8 p.m. from Monday through Thursday. Sunday is 9 a.m.–9 p.m.. The marina is generally open from 7 a.m. to 6 p.m., but it is always advisable to call ahead to confirm.

Description and Services: There is so much going on at this wonderful facility that it is almost impossible to describe. It is completely family-run, with several generations involved in all aspects of the operation. The father-daughter management team is augmented by the mother (who cooks) and the grandmother (who answers the phones).

The marina does a booming business and provides dock space, electrical power, water, gas, and pump-out services. There are no fees for boats to dock at the marina for short periods of time, although boat slips must be rented. The marina usually opens in May, assuming the weather (and ice) permits.

The grounds of the marina facility include a tiki bar, tables for outdoor dining, and a stage for musical performers. During summer months they sponsor live musical acts five nights/week, followed by karaoke on Monday evening and trivia night on Tuesday. They do not charge an entrance fee to customers who visit for these events.

Customers order and pick up food directly from the window outside the kitchen, and all dining is at their outside tables. They offer lunch and dinner on weekends and dinner during the week. The menu includes mainly bar food, with burgers, sandwiches, pizzas, and wings being the standard fare. They are especially well known for their quesadillas. Most food items range between $8 and $14.

The facility grounds can handle a crowd of about five hundred people, with room for fifty to sit and eat at their outside dining area. Space tends to fill up quickly because of the great food and festive atmosphere. At least 50 percent of their customers are "regulars" who have become accustomed to the good times and music. They remain quite active through the summer months, right up to their closing event which is a Halloween party on the third weekend in October.

This place is highly recommended for boaters and diners alike.

THE PRESERVE AT 405

Phone/Address: (315) 214-4399 / 405 Spencer St., Syracuse, NY 13204.

Days/Hours: Tuesday through Saturday, noon–9 p.m., closed Sunday and Monday.

Reservations accepted? Yes.

Restaurant size: About twenty tables plus bar seating.

Outdoor seating: Yes (lots of outdoor tables).

The Preserve at 405, Syracuse, New York.
PHOTO BY LARRY WEILL

Menu items: The menu lists a huge array of eleven appetizers, along with twenty pizzas, soups, salads (including a strawberry salmon salad), and lots of burgers and sandwiches. Their entrées include two chicken dishes, a salmon fillet, seafood scampi, chicken pepperoni Parmesan, and a selection of steaks.

Price range: Sandwiches are generally $15–$20, pizzas are $18–$26, basic salads are $8–$12, salads with add-ons are $15–$25, and the better cuts of steak range from $30 to $65.

Most popular menu item: Beef on weck and the "Cody" sandwich, made with grilled chicken, roasted red peppers, mozzarella, and pesto.

Entertainment: No.

Liquor license: Yes.

Description: The Preserve at 405 is a modern and attractive restaurant/pub with a sophisticated feel throughout the bar and dining room. It is adorned with an eclectic collection of artworks on the walls and attractive interior lighting.

This place is located right near the Canalway Trail and has plenty of outdoor seating, making it a great spot to pull up on your bike and enjoy a quick lunch or drink. Open since 2018, it has a large following of "regulars" who enjoy their great food and unique listing of cocktails. (I had the lobster roll here for lunch, which I thoroughly enjoyed.)

This restaurant not only cooks all the standard lunch/dinner dishes well, it also prepares a lot of dishes that are uncommon in the standard dining scene. For appetizers, how about a plate of perfectly browned coconut shrimp, or their Pump House Cheese Platter, which boasts cheddar, Monterey Jack, and pepper jack cheeses, with pepperoni, soppressata, sweet gherkin pickles, goat cheese, beets, crackers, spicy mustard, grapes, and fresh mozzarella?

DINOSAUR BBQ

Phone/Address: (315) 476-4937 / 246 W. Willow St., Syracuse, NY 13202.

Days/Hours: Sunday through Thursday 11 a.m.–9 p.m., Friday and Saturday 11 a.m.–10 p.m.

Reservations accepted? No.

Restaurant size: About thirty tables plus bar seating.

Outdoor seating: Yes (eight tables outside).

Menu items: The menu lists about five appetizers, several varieties of chicken wings, a "create-your-own-salad project," burgers, and lots and lots of smoked meats and ribs. The smoked categories include chicken, brisket, pork, catfish, and West Texas ribeye. Lots of these are available in combination platters, which include great sides and (of course) corn bread.

Price range: Appetizers are $10–$14, wings are six pieces for $10 or 13 pieces for $19, the smoked meat dishes run from $19 to $23, and the ribs are $22 for a half rack or $36 for a full rack (¼ and ¾ racks are also available).

Most popular menu item: The USDA Prime Brisket Plate and the mac and cheese side order.

Entertainment: Yes (live music plays several nights each week during the summer, outside in "the boneyard").

Liquor license: Yes.

Dinosaur BBQ, Syracuse, New York.
PHOTO BY LARRY WEILL

Description: "The Dinosaur" in Syracuse is another member of a restaurant chain that simply could not be left out of this book. For anyone who has never dined in one of these icons of the barbecue world, you have got to try it to fully appreciate the experience. The inside of the Dinosaur looks and feels like the quintessential barbecue joint, and everything (right down to the waiters/waitresses and bartenders) seems to play the role as well.

This restaurant is the first in the chain of six Dinosaur locations. It got its start in an old building that had been a bar since the 1920s. The Dinosaur opened its doors in 1988, and attracted a lot of bikers for its intensely flavorful barbecue. (The restaurant did not even operate a full bar until 1991.)

Located next to the Canalway Trail that transits through the city, Dinosaur BBQ offers hikers and bikers the chance to experience world-class barbecue without a lengthy break from their journey. By the way, this restaurant is also pet friendly, and welcomes well-behaved dogs (on leash) in the outdoor seating areas. They even provide water bowls for your animal.

ERIE CANAL MUSEUM

Phone/Address: (315) 471-0593 / 318 Erie Blvd. E., Syracuse, NY 13202.

Admission: Officially this museum is free, but the suggested donation is $10 per person. Any contributions are greatly appreciated.

Hours: Daily from 10 a.m. to 4 p.m. The museum is not seasonal, but open year-round.

Parking: Parking spaces can usually be found in the area immediately surrounding the museum building. Spaces are paid for on an hourly basis via the streetside parking kiosks.

Background: The Erie Canal Museum & Heritage Area Visitor Center is as close to the Canalway Trail as you can possibly get without getting run over by a cyclist. The trail literally runs along Water Street outside the building, and on the other side is Erie Blvd., the site of the old canal.

Erie Canal Museum & Heritage Area Visitor Center, Syracuse, New York.
PHOTO BY LARRY WEILL

The museum is built into one of the historic "weighlock buildings," (there used to be seven of these in Syracuse), of which this is the last one standing. These buildings were used at one time to weigh the boats on the canal. The structure was saved from the wrecking ball when it was purchased by Onondaga County in 1962 for the purpose of creating a museum to record the history of the Erie Canal.

This museum is different from other similar facilities because it is dedicated to an overview of the entire canal story. It is not a regional museum, focused on any one area or industry. Inside, you will find exhibits and stories on everything canal related, with lots of special activities and outdoor programs.

During my own tour, I had the opportunity to meet with the museum educator, Derrick Pratt, who described the many activities and events sponsored by the facility each year. In the winter months, they conduct gatherings such as the Gingerbread Gallery, with people baking gingerbread cakes and other fun activities related to that endeavor. In the summer time, they have their "Beers, Bikes, and Barges" tours through different cities and towns including Albany, Syracuse, and Lockport. There is a fee (often $25) for these guided events that provided a narrated ride through historic local sites followed by a brew at a local pub.

The museum features exhibits on all aspects of the communities and businesses surrounding the Erie Canal. It is also unique because it caters to the hikers and bikers of the Canalway Trail, and even offers a bicycle repair station for making minor bike repairs.

Pets are not permitted inside the facility, with the exception of service animals.

RED CHILI RESTAURANT

Phone/Address: (315) 446-2882 / 2760 Erie Blvd., Syracuse, NY 13224.

Days/Hours: Monday through Thursday 11 a.m.–9:30 p.m., Friday and Saturday 11 a.m.–10:15 p.m., Sunday 11:30 a.m.–9:30 p.m.

Reservations accepted? Yes.

Restaurant size: Twenty-six tables, all inside dining room.

Outdoor seating: No.

Menu items: The menu lists fourteen cold appetizers and eight hot appetizers, lots of soups, twenty-one dim sum dishes, a long list of entrées and traditional

Red Chili Restaurant, Syracuse, New York.
PHOTO BY LARRY WEILL

Chinese dishes, such as General Tso's chicken, kung pao beef, shrimp with mixed veggies, and twenty-one vegetarian entrées.

Price range: Appetizers are mostly $8–$12, entrées $19–$24, and classic Szechuan dishes from $22 to $28.

Most popular menu item: Chicken and beef entrées cooked with garlic sauce.

Entertainment: No.

Liquor license: Yes.

Description: There aren't many Asian restaurants close to the Canalway Trail, so this is a good one in case you are missing your hometown version of dim sum or Szechuan food. Red Chili sits on the south side of Erie Blvd., directly across from the Trail.

Red Chili offers a very extensive line of familiar and traditional Szechuan dishes that are served hot and delicious to your table, or can even be delivered for a small additional fee. (Exactly where are you right now on the bike trail?)

The interior of Red Chili is very nicely decorated in traditional Asian themes, and the tables have warming elements built in for cooking in front of the diners. The staff inside this place is also very warm and welcoming and will be happy to guide you through the menu if you are unfamiliar with Szechuan food.

If you are traveling on a budget and looking for an inexpensive place to purchase a large lunch without busting the bank, Red Chili has forty different lunch specials that come with soup or egg roll and white rice for only $9.99.

TEXAS ROADHOUSE

Phone/Address: (315) 445-4086 /3143 Erie Blvd E., Syracuse, NY 13214.

Days/Hours: Monday through Thursday, 4 p.m.–9:30 p.m., Friday 4 p.m.–10 p.m., Saturday noon–10 p.m., Sunday noon–9 p.m..

Reservations accepted? No, but there is a "call-ahead" list.

Restaurant size: Approximately fifty to sixty tables, all inside dining room.

Outdoor seating: No.

Menu items: A choice of eleven stick-to-the-rib appetizers, including grilled shrimp skewers and "rattlesnake bites" (which are diced jalapeños and jack cheese, lightly fried and served with Cajun sauce for dipping), various burgers and sandwiches, rib plates, ten different steaks, and seafood entrées (including salmon, grilled shrimp, and fish fry).

Price range: Appetizers are mostly $8–$14, burgers and sandwiches from $13 to $15, ribs (half rack for $20, full rack for $26), seafood from $17 to $21, and steaks (mostly from $20 to $30 depending on variety and size).

Most popular menu item: Hand-cut steaks and fall-off-the-bone ribs.

Entertainment: No.

Liquor license: Yes.

Description: Texas Roadhouse is the place to get your grilled steak or ribs fix while hiking or biking your way across the Canalway Trail. This book has avoided many of the chain restaurants along the trail, but Texas Roadhouse is a

Texas Roadhouse in Syracuse, New York.
PHOTO BY LARRY WEILL

great place to get a steak, which is important to many of our travelers along the route.

The restaurant is on the same side of Erie Boulevard as the Canalway Trail, so getting there should be easier than coming from the south side of the highway. (Erie Blvd. is a very busy road, so be careful if you need to ride on the shoulder.)

By the way, the food on the menu isn't the only thing here with a Texas influence. The cocktails have their own Lone Star flair and feature drinks such as the "Cactus Water," the "Southern Whiskey Long Island Ice Tea," and the "Peach Fuzz." Skoal!

BURIED ACORN RESTAURANT & BREWERY

Phone/Address: (315) 552-1499 / 881 Van Rensselaer St., Syracuse, NY 13204.

Days/Hours: Closed on Monday, Tuesday noon–9 p.m., Wednesday and Thursday noon–8 p.m., Friday and Saturday noon–10 p.m., Sunday noon–5 p.m.

Reservations accepted? No.

Restaurant size: Thirteen tables inside plus bar seating with an additional twenty tables outside.

Outdoor seating: Yes.

Menu items: A list of nine scrumptious appetizers (including spinach artichoke flatbread and pimento cheese dip), three Mediterranean-influenced salads, and a list of eleven sandwiches and wraps. They are even better known for their barrel-aged New York State beers and wines along with their lengthy list of other brews.

Buried Acorn Restaurant & Brewery, Syracuse, New York.
PHOTO BY LARRY WEILL

Price range: Most appetizers are $13–$16, sandwiches and wraps are $10–$15, salads are $9–$11.

Most popular menu item: Hand-cut steaks and fall-off-the-bone ribs.

Entertainment: Yes, including comedy, DJs, and live bands. They also sponsor a trivia night on Tuesdays.

Liquor license: Yes.

Description: The Buried Acorn is another one of those wonderful establishments that serves up a great meal in addition to maintaining its reputation as a brewpub and provider of first-rate local beers and wines. Their selections include not only barrel-aged beers, but also non-barrel-aged sours, lagers, Belgians, and New York State ciders.

The inside of the Buried Acorn is a beautiful place that is geared to the community and local brewing. The walls are decorated with a lot of artsy items that the owner described as "underground art." It all fits well with the feel of the business.

The Canalway Trail passes right by the patio tables outside this brewpub, so you will lose no time getting on and off the trail. The owners are delightful people who have operated this place for seven years, and thoroughly enjoy taking care of their customers, so you should have a wonderful time while enjoying your food and drink.

OSWEGO COUNTY

BARADO'S ON THE WATER

Phone/Address: (315) 668-5428 / 57 Bradbury Road, Central Square, NY 13036.

Days/Hours: Tuesday through Sunday, noon–9 p.m., closed on Monday. (Note: These are summer hours. These rest of the year it is only open from Wednesday through Saturday.)

Reservations accepted? Yes.

Restaurant size: This is a large restaurant with seventeen tables inside (plus bar seating), with additional tables under a covered front porch. There is also a large

Barado's on the Water in Central Square, New York.
Photo by Larry Weill

patio in back (next to the water) that can seat over 150 people. This is currently being expanded for even more seating.

Outdoor seating: Yes.

Menu items: This canal-side restaurant has a little bit of everything on the menu. Starting with a slew of appetizers, the menu extends to a list of four salads, some great-looking sandwiches, and an entire page full of specials. There are almost as many specials listed on the daily menu as there are regular items, and they include butter crumb haddock, pan-seared Akura salmon, and pan-seared scallops.

Price range: Appetizers are $13–$15, the salads range from $14 to $16, and the sandwiches go for $13–$16 (although the lobster roll is more). Dinner specials go for $19–$29.

Most popular menu item: They are well-known for their lobster bisque, which is available on Friday nights. The Bradbury Bay fish tacos are also quite popular.

Entertainment: No.

Liquor license: Yes.

Description: Barado's on the Water is a very popular restaurant and pub that is well known to both the local residents and the boaters on the canal. (Boat tie-ups are available on-site.) Although Barada's maintains a fun and festive atmosphere, people come for the food first and foremost.

The customers at this restaurant also benefit from the drink-making skills of Ericka, who has competed in the American Bartender Championship competition. She is best known for her Nespresso martinis, as well as her other amazing concoctions. (How about an Easter holiday martini topped with cotton candy!) You've got to try one!

BREWERTON REAR RANGE LIGHTHOUSE

Address: 792 County Rte. 37, Brewerton (Central Square), NY 13036.

Admission: There is no fee to visit the lighthouse. There is also no way to enter or ascend to the top of this structure.

Parking: There is a large parking lot in front of the lighthouse park that should accommodate all cars.

Brewerton Rear Range Lighthouse, Brewerton, New York.
PHOTO BY LARRY WEILL

Dock availability: There are docks on the river/canal in front of the lighthouse. However, these docks are very small (and may be unstable) and are unfit for medium-to-larger boats. There is docking suitable for larger platforms on the other (south) side of the river, accessible via the Route 11 bridge.

Background: This lighthouse, located on the west end of Oneida Lake, is one of three such structures built on the waters of the lake. They are also the only three lighthouses ever built along the entire length of the Erie Canal. For this reason, they were called the "three sisters," and all are still standing today. The Brewerton Rear Range Lighthouse marks the point at which the Oneida River enters Oneida Lake.

Construction of the Brewerton Rear Range Lighthouse was started in 1916, the same year that work began on the Verona Beach Lighthouse at the east end of the lake. Unlike the Verona Beach Lighthouse, the Brewerton structure is located inside a small park, with facilities for picnics and larger events. Picnic tables are available throughout the park grounds, and a sizeable pavilion is also available to rent for larger gatherings.

The towers were built to a fairly uniform height of eighty-five feet, although they appear to differ in size because their platforms vary a few feet in height from one to the next. They were built by barging in prefabricated eighteen-foot concrete sections which were then assembled on-site. This was a major engineering feat for the day.

Historically, the navigational lights on the three Oneida Lake lighthouses were originally lit by gas, although the Brewerton and Verona Beach lighthouses have long since been changed over to electricity. These two lighthouses are still illuminated today. The Brewerton lighthouse, when lined up with the beacon on the Route 11 bridge, is used as a navigational guide for boats heading west from Oneida Lake into the Oneida River channel.

The name given to the park that surrounds the Brewerton Rear Range lighthouse is the Oneida River Lighthouse Park, which was completed in 2009. It would make an ideal stopover point for a scenic lunch break.

OLIVER STEVENS BLOCKHOUSE MUSEUM IN OLD FORT BREWERTON

Phone/Address: (315) 668-8801 / 9 US-11, Brewerton (Central Square), NY 13036.

Hours/Days: The museum is open on Saturdays from June through September, but it is best to call ahead when planning a visit.

Admission: There is no required admission fee to enter the museum. However, donations are encouraged and always welcome.

Parking: Limited parking is available in front of the museum. However, visitors should expect to have to find their own parking nearby the site.

Dock availability: There are boat docks located on the other (South) side of the Route 11 bridge.

Background: The Oliver Stevens Blockhouse Museum is built into a re-creation of a log structure (or "blockhouse") that was part of the original Fort Brewerton. Fort Brewerton was built by the British during the French and Indian Wars (1754–1763) as a way to protect the passage from Albany to the Port of Oswego.

Fort Brewerton was a large structure for the day, built in the form of an eight-point star that was surrounded by a ten-foot moat. It was surrounded by a wooden wall (called a parapet) and a series of log blockhouses, which were used to store supplies and munitions.

Oliver Stevens Blockhouse Museum in Brewerton, New York.
PHOTO BY LARRY WEILL

The fort had fallen into disuse and disrepair by the time Stevens arrived in 1789. Oliver moved to the area from Connecticut with his wife, Nancy, and their children. Stevens immediately commenced modifying the military block-house, adding both a tavern and a trading post to the first level of the building. The store was added to supply goods to the people navigating on the Oneida River. The upper level of the building was converted into living quarters for Stevens and his wife along with their six children. This building served as the residence for Stevens until he died in 1813.

The reconstructed blockhouse building present on the site today was built using some of the original logs and bricks left over from the original fort and blockhouse. Additionally, the remains of the dirt formations of Fort Brewerton can still be seen on the grounds of the site nearby the Blockhouse.

The Oliver Stevens Blockhouse Museum is operated today by the Fort Brew-erton Historical Society. Its collections include thousands of years of artifacts and history documenting Native American life in the area, along with military artifacts excavated from the site surrounding the original Fort Brewerton.

WILD HORSE BAR AND GRILL

Phone/Address: (315) 403-8665 / 720 County Rte. 37, Central Square, NY 13036.

Days/Hours: Monday through Wednesday 11 a.m.–10 p.m., Thursday 11 a.m.–midnight, Friday and Saturday 11 a.m.–2 a.m., Sunday 10 a.m.–9 p.m.

Reservations accepted? Yes (for large parties).

Restaurant size: Twenty to twenty-five tables inside with considerable seating at the bar.

Outdoor seating: Yes.

Menu items: This casual country-and-western-theme pub has fifteen appetizers on its menu, including cheese and meat varieties of quesadillas. They also offer inexpensive pizzas, wings (regular and boneless), salads, sandwiches, wraps, and burgers.

Wild Horse Bar and Grill, Central Square, New York.
PHOTO BY LARRY WEILL

Price range: Most of their dishes range between $14 and $17.

Most popular menu item: Their most popular dishes are their pizzas and wings, but they have a special on steamed clams on Wednesday that also draws a crowd.

Entertainment: Yes. In summer they have music on Wednesday and Thursday, as well as groups playing on weekends. They also get quite active around Syracuse football and basketball games and NFL football on Sundays in season.

Liquor license: Yes.

Description: The Wild Horse Bar and Grill is an attractive pub built on a scenic stretch of the Oneida River (aka the Erie Canal). It has boat docks that permit up to twelve boats to tie up to visit the restaurant.

The kitchen is open early on Sundays to prepare a Sunday brunch. The rest of the week the Wild Horse is only open for lunch and dinner.

The rest of the Wild Horse is designed to be comfortable to the country-and-western crowd. It is decorated with Western art, bull horns, and other cowboy paraphernalia, while the main dining room also contains a pool table and dartboard.

Giddyap!

SANDBAR GRILL

Phone/Address: (315) 623-6022 / 1067 State Route 49, Bernhard's Bay, NY 13028.

Days/Hours: The restaurant opens at 2 p.m. on Tuesday and at noon on the rest of the week, except 9 a.m. on Sunday. The kitchen usually closes at 9 p.m., but the bar closing time varies based on how busy it is on any given night.

Reservations accepted? Yes (for large parties).

Restaurant size: The inside portion of the restaurant has 15–20 tables plus bar seating. However, there are many tables outside between the tiki bar, the back deck and the lawn.

Outdoor seating: Yes.

Menu items: The menu lists fourteen different appetizers (including beer-battered onion rings and "jalapeño cheese shrimp jammers"). It also offers

Sandbar Grill in Bernhard's Bay, New York.
PHOTO BY LARRY WEILL

seventeen varieties of wings at three heat levels, different-sized pizzas, specialty pizzas, tacos, fish fries, and more.

Price range: Appetizers are $7–$14, chicken dishes are $12–$15, burgers are $13–$15, pizzas are $12–$20 (although specialty pizzas are more), and seafood is $15–$23.

Most popular menu item: Taco Tuesday and Thursday wing nights. The fish and chips on Friday is also quite popular.

Entertainment: Yes (live music four days a week in the summer and two to three days a week in the winter).

Liquor license: Yes.

Description: The Sandbar is another restaurant/pub located right on the shoreline of Oneida Lake, with a boat dock to give boaters direct access to the facility. This place has a party atmosphere that people enjoy, especially during the summer months when the tiki bar is open and everyone can enjoy being outdoors.

If you need to stay out of the sun, they also provide shaded tables for your convenience.

You can bring your dog to the party, but please restrict them to the lawn only.

The Sandbar also welcomes children, as it maintains a family atmosphere during the early evening hours. (You will find lots of children here during the summer months.) Once the kitchen closes, the facility becomes more of a bar than a restaurant. Regardless, it is a fun and safe environment that everyone can enjoy.

NORTH SHORE COFFEE & TEA COMPANY

Phone/Address: (315) 929-1100 / 676 State Route 49, Bernhard's Bay, NY 13028.

Days/Hours: Tuesday through Friday 9 a.m.–2 p.m., Saturday and Sunday 8 a.m.–2 p.m., closed on Monday.

Reservations accepted? No.

Restaurant size: Seats about forty people inside the attached country store room.

Outdoor seating: Yes.

Menu items: This place is a coffee shop first and foremost. However, it still offers a wide selection of tasty baked goods to complement the various hot and cold beverages. These include lots of cookies, brownies, muffins, and pasties, which are on display in the coffee brewing room. They also prepare several superb breakfast sandwiches, fresh hot oatmeal, and yogurt parfaits.

Price range: Most coffee drinks are $3–$4, and teas are about the same price. The cookies, brownies, and pastries are between $3 and $5, yogurt parfaits cost between $6 and $7, and the breakfast sandwiches range from $8 to $12.

Most popular menu item: The biggest food items sold here are the breakfast sandwiches.

Entertainment: This coffee shop does not host bands, but it does sponsor an "Open Mike Night" twice each month. These are held twice each month (every other Friday) from 6 p.m. to 10 p.m.

Liquor license: No.

Description: North Shore Coffee & Tea Company is the quintessential coffee shop located on the roadside of a sleepy little town. It is located in a very old

North Shore Coffee & Tea Company, Bernhard's Bay, New York.
PHOTO PROVIDED COURTESY OF NORTH SHORE COFFEE & TEA COMPANY

building across from the shoreline of Oneida Lake with the storefront painted an array of eye-catching colors.

As at many coffeehouses, the aroma of freshly roasted coffee beans grabs you as soon as you set foot in the door. The owners of this business are firm believers in supporting the community and serving as many locally produced goods as possible. Likewise, the attached country store offers a great selection of products and works of art from nearby painters, craftsmen, and chefs.

Do your nose a favor and stop into this shop for coffee and a pastry.

THE CLEVELAND HOUSE

Phone/Address: (315) 675-6051 / 118 State Route 49, Cleveland, NY 13042

Days/Hours: Wednesday through Saturday 11:30 a.m.–11 p.m. Sunday 11:30 a.m.–9 p.m., closed on Monday and Tuesday.

Reservations accepted? No.

Restaurant size: 8–10 tables, plus bar seating.

Outdoor seating: Yes.

Menu items: Ten different appetizers (including a charcuterie board), plus a selection of eight salads, sandwiches, burgers, flatbread pizzas, pasta dishes, and several entrées including chicken Parmesan, shrimp scampi, fettuccine Alfredo, and Brianna chicken (which is chicken with roasted vegetables, and Asiago Caesar dressing served over pasta).

The Cleveland House in Cleveland, New York.
PHOTO BY LARRY WEILL

Price range: Most appetizers are $5–$10, salads and most burgers are $10–$15, sandwiches $12–$16, and most entrées range between $15 and $19.

Most popular menu item: The "steak bites" (which are pieces of beef tender-loin) are extremely popular. Patrons also enjoy the half-pound Black Angus beef burgers, which are served on handmade brioche rolls.

Entertainment: Yes. Small bands play here year-round (Friday and Saturday nights).

Liquor license: Yes.

Description: This very old and established restaurant/pub is a fan favorite along the north shore of Oneida Lake. It has a boat dock across the street, so you can simply pull in and tie up. And feel free to bring "Fido" inside, as dogs are welcome too.

The kitchen serves up a host of appealing bar foods, which include some imaginative dishes that bring people in from a wide area. While the Cleveland House looks like it's mainly a bar, it is really split 50–50 to include its great kitchen.

The customers in this establishment enjoy the small-town "Adirondacky" feel of the place and say it's a great place to make new friends. It has a lot of regular customers, but also many first-time visitors who immediately say they want to return on future trips.

MADISON COUNTY

FLO'S DINER

Phone/Address: (315) 697-7987 / 3223 NY-31, Canastota, NY 13032.

Days/Hours: Every day of the week, 8 a.m.–8 p.m.

Reservations accepted? No.

Restaurant size: Approximately twenty-one tables, plus counter seating.

Outdoor seating: Yes (covered front dining area).

Menu items: All the standard breakfast dishes including eggs/omelets, pancakes, French toast, bacon, sausage, and all the breakfast sides. Lunches include sandwiches, hoagies, soups, salads, burgers, and more. Their dinner menu continues with steaks, chops, different chicken dishes, and a fresh haddock dinner. They also offer twelve different side orders, in case you can't make up your mind!

Flo's Diner in Canastota, New York.
PHOTO BY LARRY WEILL

Price range: Most breakfasts run between $7 and $11, appetizers are $6–$12, sandwiches are $6–$8, and most entrées range between $12 and $15.

Most popular menu item: The "Big Breakfast" and the "Flo's Slop," which is ground ham, sausage, and pepperoni, combined with home fries, scrambled eggs, broccoli, mushrooms, onions, peppers, and tomatoes.

Entertainment: No.

Liquor license: No.

Description: There is one quick disclaimer to make about this diner. It is outside of the official distance limit for this book, being located six-tenths of a mile up Snell Road from the Lake Oneida shoreline. But I loved this place so much that I had to include it in this book. It reminded me so much of my favorite hometown diner, I simply could not exclude it.

The philosophy at Flo's is simple: "Serve a good, tasty, wholesome meal that people can afford."

You can order breakfast, lunch, or dinner any time of any day here. A cup of coffee costs ten cents (that is *not* a typo), and everyone inside seems like family. Both founders of Flo's have passed on, but the restaurant is still run by follow-on generations of the family.

Make sure to bring cash along, as credit and debit cards are not accepted.

BACK ROADS TAVERN

Phone/Address: (315) 363-9800 / 4299 Canal Road, Canastota, NY 13032.

Days/Hours: Monday through Friday 11 a.m.–2 a.m., Saturday and Sunday noon–2 a.m.

Reservations accepted? Yes (for large parties).

Restaurant size: Approximately 15–20 tables.

Outdoor seating: No.

Menu items: Mainly bar food, but with fifteen assorted appetizers (including chicken logs, and pulled pork nachos), fifteen varieties of chicken wings, sandwiches, salads, paninis, burgers, and pizzas (including personal-sized).

Price range: Most sandwiches are $10–$12, wings are $13 for an order of ten, salads range from $7 to $12, and burgers are around $10.

Back Roads Tavern, Canastota, New York.
PHOTO BY LARRY WEILL

Most popular menu item: The favorites here align with the nightly specials: tacos on Tuesday, wings on Thursday, and fish fry on Friday.

Entertainment: Yes (musical bands on the weekends).

Liquor license: Yes.

Description: This is a cozy restaurant/bar that is equally comfortable for a casual meal or a cold brew. The locals come here to hang out, be with friends, and make new friends. As one customer said, "No one is judging you when you come in here. Some folks who come here have no family, so we become their family. Even the workers here are like that."

Back Roads Tavern is very close to the Canalway Trail, but nowhere near the Erie Canal, so most of the visitors are hikers or bikers, who visit this place in droves during the summer months.

This establishment tries to provide entertainment during the warmer months, and their live music nights are quite popular. They also sponsor fun events such as beer pong tournaments to liven up the atmosphere.

CANASTOTA CANAL TOWN MUSEUM

Phone/Address: (315) 697-5002 / 122 Canal St., Canastota, NY 13032.

Museum is seasonal: This museum is seasonal, and is only open from May through October. However, group tours are available year-round by request by calling (315) 697-5002.

Museum Hours: From May to October: most days open by noon and closes at 3 p.m. The museum is closed on Sunday and Monday (even in season).

Admission: $5/person, children (twelve and under) and members are free. Individual memberships are $10 and family memberships are $20.

Mission: This museum, which is built into an actual historic building, focuses on the artifacts, memorabilia, and art of the Canastota area. As stated on the museum's website, "it contains exhibits illustrating Canastota's contributions to the canal, commerce, industry, and agriculture."

Description: This museum is located right next to the Canalway Trail, which followed the route of the original Erie Canal. The signs of that canal are all around the building, with numerous historic markers by the remaining waterway on the other side of Canal Street from the building.

The museum exhibits are arranged over the two floors of the building, and are divided into a series of ten galleries. Each of these galleries (A through J) focuses on a particular aspect of the canal's local history, art, industry, or culture. For example, Gallery A contains watercolor artwork of Canastota circa 1900, some original land surveys of the area, products from the Lee Chair Company, Victorian Era furniture (dresser and desk), and an exhibit on the birth of the local microscope industry. Each of the galleries has its own specific focus, and together they form a composite view of life along the Canastota section of the canal in the 1800s.

In addition to the in-house exhibits, the Canastota Canal Town Museum also participates in other outside events with the Canastota Public Library. This includes a series of "Canalside Talks," which are held on the second floor of the library, accessible by elevator. Recent topics included the "History of Abolition in Madison County" which was conducted in conjunction with Black History Month. Another program was "Madison County Women in World War II," which delved into the contributions women made to the victory in that conflict.

Canastota Canal Town Museum, Canastota, New York.
PHOTO BY LARRY WEILL

Of additional interest is that the museum building was built as a bakery around 1873, and is in the National Register of Historic Places.

ONEIDA LAKE BREW HAUS

Phone/Address: (315) 875-3462 / 6266 Lakeshore Rd. S., Canastota, NY 13032.

Days/Hours: Winter: Thursday and Friday 4 p.m.–10 p.m., Saturday noon–10 p.m., closed Sunday through Wednesday. (Note: In summer it is open from Wednesday through Sunday, so check their schedule online for current hours.)

Reservations accepted? No.

Restaurant size: Approximately eighteen tables.

Oneida Lake Brew Haus, Canastota, New York.
PHOTO BY LARRY WEILL

Outdoor seating: Yes—*lots* of outside seating (approximately thirty picnic tables).

Menu items: This place has a well-rounded menu for a brewpub, and includes a choice of seven appetizers, two salads, and five entrée specials on Friday and Saturday. The appetizers include a dish called the "Brew Haus Pig Pen," which is made with tortilla nachos covered with pulled pork, chicken brisket, plus salsa, and Haus beer cheese. How could you go wrong?

Price range: Appetizers are between $8 and $18, salads range from $10 to $13, and most entrées are around $12.

Most popular menu item: The Friday fish (which is broiled not fried), prime rib, and the selection of thirty-two beers on tap.

Entertainment: Yes (every day in summer).

Liquor license: Yes.

Description: The Oneida Lake Brew Haus is proud of saying that first and foremost, they are about their beer. Behind the bar are digital screens that display the current offerings. That list is both impressive and strikingly local. About 85 percent of the beers are "local craft beers," and that list changes every week. "Beer flights" are available to sample four brews at a time and find your favorite.

Opened in 2018, this place has something going on whenever it is open. Thursday night is Cornhole Night, although people are welcome to play anytime they feel the urge. Live music is offered almost every night in the summer, and the grounds are both kid-friendly and dog-friendly. The kids have their own playground, and the dogs have fun no matter what.

When visiting, make sure to check out the spectacular sunsets over the west end of the lake.

CHITTENANGO LANDING CANAL BOAT MUSEUM

Phone/Address: (315) 687-3801 / 717 Lakeport Rd, Chittenango, NY 13037.

Park Hours: Open Wednesday through Sunday, 10 a.m.–3 p.m., closed on Monday and Tuesday. Call ahead to confirm the museum is open. There is some inconsistency with these hours, and winter hours may differ. The facility also welcomes offseason tours (November 1–April 30) by appointment only.

Mission: The Mission of the Chittenango Landing Canal Boat Museum is to "educate and inspire the public with the stories of nineteenth-century canal boat builders, travelers, and businesses through the collection, preservation, exhibition, and interpretation of material related to the site, and its significance to Old Erie Canal State Historic Park." (This statement is from the museum's website.)

Donations and Event Fees: The museum operates as a nonprofit organization and always welcomes donations to further its work on construction and preservation. They also sponsor numerous events throughout the year that require a registration fee. Last season these events included: an Easter basket weaving class, a class in creating a winter table centerpiece, and various painting and sketching workshops. The prices on these events vary, so check their website for updated information.

Description: This museum is a wonderful facility in a parklike setting located right along the Canalway Trail. This was the site of the enlarged Erie Canal, and it contains a great many facilities that were used when this location was a bustling hub of canal activity. It contained a drydock facility for working on boats and

Chittenango Landing Canal Boat Museum, Chittenango, New York.
PHOTO BY LARRY WEILL

making repairs to the hulls on these platforms. The bays that held these facilities are still visible today.

Other structures inside the grounds include a rebuilt general store, a boat shop, a blacksmith shop, and a mule stable. Much of this site was developed from a series overgrown ruins using old photographs, archaeological surveys, and an old map from the 1895. The results have been simply amazing, reconstructing an entire canalboat-building community from the original parcel of ruins.

This facility also offers many programs that you will not utilize during your stroll/hike/bike along the Canalway Trail. However, you may decide to return sometime to revisit this idyllic historic location. There are also several connecting trails (e.g., the Chittenango Creekwalk Trail) that connect to the Canalway Trail. Free maps are available on the museum grounds.

ONEIDA COUNTY

VESCIO'S FRANKLIN HOTEL & RESTAURANT

Phone/Address: (315) 336-9974 / 301 South James Street, Rome, NY 13440.

Days/Hours: Tuesday through Saturday 11 a.m.–9 p.m., closed on Sunday and Monday.

Reservations accepted? Yes.

Restaurant size: Forty-two tables plus bar seating. The restaurant also has a party room that holds one hundred.

Outdoor seating: No.

Vescio's Franklin Hotel & Restaurant in Rome, New York.
PHOTO COURTESY OF MARY VESCIO

Menu items: The lunch menu lists a choice of about fourteen appetizers (including a grilled steak salad), soups, sandwiches, paninis, burgers, and pasta.

Price range: Lunch appetizers go for $9–$14, and almost everything else on the lunch menu runs between $11 and $14. The dinner sandwiches (i.e., chicken Parmesan and prime rib dip) range from $16 to $19, pasta dishes from $15 to $20, seafood dishes from $21 to $23, and other Italian specialties ranging from $21 to $25.

Most popular menu item: Lasagna, Cavatelli Milano, Broccoli Français, and "lobster tails" (which is a large and amazing dessert).

Entertainment: No.

Liquor license: Yes.

Description: Vescio's Franklin Hotel & Restaurant is currently enjoying its fifty-third year in business (family-operated since 1972), which is not an accident. They enjoy a loyal local patronage for their friendly service and outstanding food, which is prepared fresh "from scratch" every day.

The Franklin is located within the proverbial "stone's throw" from the Canalway Trail. They have officially earned the designation as a "cycle friendly" restaurant, and are visited by crowds of hikers and bikers every summer.

As long as you're stopping by for lunch or dinner, don't forget to visit Franklin's dessert case, where their chefs prepare a full lineup of delicious cakes, pies, and specialty desserts. Their listing of baked desserts is two full pages long, and features creations that include Black Forest cake, rum cake, peanut brittle torte, and lemon coconut cake. After all, with all that hiking and biking every day, you can afford the calories!

BELLAMY HARBOR PARK

Address: 139 E. Whitesboro St., Rome, NY 13440.

Park Hours: Most days 8:30 a.m.–4:30 p.m., but the hours vary based upon day of the week and time of year. (Some sources say open "dawn to dusk," but the park's buildings and facilities may be closed.) Check online for hours on the day of your visit.

Note: While this book does not normally discuss canal-side parks, this facility is rather extraordinary, and can be very useful to our canal users.

Bellamy Harbor Park in Rome, New York.
PHOTO BY LARRY WEILL

Background and Location: Bellamy Harbor Park is a spacious facility with plenty of open land for everyone. It is also loaded with history, as it marks some of the earliest excavation work in the construction of the original Erie Canal. It is located at the intersection of the Mohawk River and the current Erie Canal.

Facilities: The Bellamy Harbor Park contains many amenities that will be useful to boaters, hikers, and bikers. These include: benches and seating with beautiful views of the river, bike racks, small-boat launches, cell phone coverage throughout the park, boat dock and pier space, electrical outlets, cell phone charging, picnic tables, trash and recycling receptacles, as well as historic markers and information displays throughout the park. Several trailheads are present on the grounds to provide access to connected trail systems. Additionally, there is a visitor center located across the street with bathrooms and shower facilities.

Pet Policy: Pets are allowed on the park grounds.

Description: This park is friendly to just about every possible community, including boaters, bikers, hikers, and pet owners. The large boat dock provides a place to tie up even larger craft, and reports of the fishing in this area have been quite favorable, with bass, trout, and catfish all found in the waters of the river. So get ready to land yourself a whale!

If you are carrying youngsters on your boat, Bellamy Park also contains a full playground with an assortment of swings and slides, along with lots of open space to play and set up your picnic lunch. This is a great place to spend the day, or just take a long lunch break.

For those who do not mind the walk (approximately one mile), the Fort Stanwix National Monument is accessible via Mill Street and Dominick Street.

THE LAKE HOUSE AT SYLVAN BEACH

Phone/Address: (315) 356-1815 / 301 Park Ave, Sylvan Beach, NY 13157.

Days/Hours: Sunday through Thursday 11 a.m.–8 p.m., Friday and Saturday 11 a.m.–9 p.m.

Reservations accepted? Yes.

Restaurant size: Approximately fifteen tables (inside dining room), plus bar seating.

Outdoor seating: Yes.

Menu items: A choice of seven different appetizers (including "Spicy Bang Bang Bada Bing Shrimp"), burgers, tacos, sandwiches, and salads. Entrées listed on the winter menu include Korean barbecue chicken skewers, fish fry (not just on Friday!), twelve-ounce strip steak, and Cajun shrimp with chorizo pasta.

Price range: Most appetizers are $12–$16, burgers are $14–$16, sandwiches $14–$15, and tacos are $15–$16.

Most popular menu item: The "Churro Funnel Cake Ice Cream Sundae," which is an amazing dessert with a cinnamon sugar churro, vanilla and chocolate ice cream fudge, and caramel sauce, with candied walnuts, whipped cream, and a cherry.

Entertainment: Yes. The Lake House is constantly bringing in musical acts, live DJs, and other forms of entertainment.

Liquor license: Yes.

The Lake House at Sylvan Beach, New York.
PHOTO BY LARRY WEILL

Description: The Lake House is unique in this community because it is owned and operated by the Oneida Indian Nation of New York and offers slot machine gambling to the vacationing crowds. Most people recognize this as the same group who built Turning Stone Casino in Verona, New York, which means that they have refined entertainment, dining, and gaming like no one else in the state. Their gaming room is loaded with one hundred of the newest slot machines for your entertainment.

The Lake House was opened to the public in 2020 and offered new forms of entertainment to the tourists of Sylvan Beach. The restaurant at the Lake House offers indoor and outdoor dining, with menus that change from summer to winter. Guests must be eighteen or over to enter the restaurant.

In addition to the fabulous meal options, the bar also offers up a host of signature cocktails, including a "Raspberry Lemon Drop Martini" and their "Chocolate Martini." Yummy!

CANAL VIEW CAFE

Phone/Address: (315) 762-5623 / 9 Canal Street, Sylvan Beach, NY 13157.

Days/Hours: Closed on Monday and Tuesday, Sunday, Wednesday and Thursday 11:30 a.m.–8 p.m., Friday and Saturday 11:30 a.m.–9 p.m.

Reservations accepted? Yes (for parties of six or more).

Restaurant size: Approximately thirty tables, plus bar seating.

Outdoor seating: Yes.

Menu items: Their menu (serving lunch and dinner) includes sixteen appetizers and several salad dishes, including a "Bam Bam Shrimp Salad," handheld and covered sandwiches, chicken breast dishes, and burgers. They also have dinner entrées which include Delmonico steak, a steak and seafood plate with shrimp, lots of pasta dishes, and a choice of five Italian selections including lasagna, baked ziti, and ravioli.

Canal View Cafe, Sylvan Beach, New York.
PHOTO BY LARRY WEILL

Price range: Most appetizers are $15–$20, sandwiches range from $12 to $16, and the dinner entrées are mostly between $15 and $30 with some seafood dishes costing a bit more.

Most popular menu item: Customers here enjoy their "chicken riggies," as well as the fish fry (haddock), and their pasta and seafood dishes.

Entertainment: No.

Liquor license: No. Wine and beer only.

Description: The Canal View Cafe is a delightful combination of a restaurant, pub, and local gathering place for social interaction. I decided to have lunch in this place around midday and was mostly lost in my own thoughts for planning the day. However, I discovered that it is almost impossible to not get caught up in a conversation while reading the menu or waiting for your food. It is just that kind of a place. Fun!

The Canal View has been in business since 1977, so it has its share of long-time patrons. It really is a family affair, and everyone is interested in making you feel welcome. Another fascinating point about this place involves the decorations and artifacts found hanging on the walls, as well as on display behind the bar itself. As one patron (a local politician) stated, "This is history you see in front of you. We call it the 'Sylvan Beach Smithsonian.'" And it really is.

SYLVAN BEACH AMUSEMENT PARK

Address: 112 Bridge St., Sylvan Beach, NY 13157.

Park Hours: Noon until mid-evening in season. Hours may vary, please check the park website.

Seasonal: The park is open from mid-June until Labor Day. Please check the park website for specific details.

Note: This book will not be available until 2025, so readers will have to rely on the park's website for accurate dates, times, and admission prices (see below).

Admission Fees: Pay-One-Price Ride All Day wristbands are always available. Individual tickets and discount sheets of tickets may also be purchased. There is no admission charge. You are welcome to walk through the park at any time. Season passes are available along with special discount days.

Galaxi roller coaster at Sylvan Beach Amusement Park.
PHOTO COURTESY OF PAT GOODENOW

Description: What could be better in the middle of a weeklong cruise down the Erie Canal than a detour through an old-fashioned amusement park? That is exactly what you will get if you take a few hours of your journey to visit the Sylvan Beach Amusement Park.

Located on the eastern end of Oneida Lake, this park offers you the opportunity to venture back in time and frolic around the entertaining rides and games of the 1800s. (The park's origins date back to the 1870s.) Whereas some newer amusement parks have migrated to the shiny, electronically dominated feel of the future, Sylvan Beach has retained its old-fashioned goodness that will remind you of your family vacations with Mom and Dad (and maybe the grandparents).

The rides inside "the midway" include a host of favorite rides including the Galaxi roller coaster, which will send your cart rising and falling as you swirl around tight curves and bends in the track. (Don't forget to scream!) Other classic rides include the Tilt-A-Whirl, the Scrambler, the Super Slide, and let's not forget the bumper cars (and bumper boats too!). This park also has its own "Kiddieland" section with ten rides just for small children. (Must be under forty-eight inches to ride.)

In addition to all the rides, Sylvan Beach Amusement Park also provides multiple locations to purchase fun food like hot dogs and hamburgers, pizza, ice cream, and picnic fare. Do you miss the candy apples, popcorn, and cotton candy of your youth? No worries, you can get all that as well. Then, after you finish eating, try your hand in the arcade playing all your favorite games.

Note: There are height restrictions on many of the rides, so check those out online.

VERONA BEACH STATE PARK

Address: 6541 Lakeshore Road S., Verona Beach, NY 13162.

Park Hours: Area and trails are open year-round, dawn to dusk. Dates and hours for swimming, camping, and use of shelters can be found on their website.

Seasonal: Many of the park's resources and services are seasonal. These can be found on the park's website, but it is usually from mid-May through mid-October.

Admission Fees: The entrance fee for a vehicle (non-bus) is $7. Campsite rentals range between $18 and $43/night, with additional fees for electrical power and other add-ons. Rentals of the various shelters or community room vary between $50 and $300 depending on the size of the shelter and the day of the week. (Weekend rentals cost more.)

Description: Verona Beach State Park is a large and gorgeous facility located on the east end of Oneida Lake, near the Verona Beach Lighthouse. It is a perfect spot to camp overnight in the middle of an extended boat trip down the Erie Canal.

This park has so many amenities to offer that you may decide to stay an extra day or two, although most camping reservations need to be confirmed well in advance. The park offers biking, camping (including campsites, cabins, and lodging), horse trails, fishing, food stands, ice fishing, a swimming beach, playgrounds, pavilions and shelters, and bathroom/shower facilities. It also provides trails for snowmobiles and snowshoeing/cross-country skiing in winter.

Entrance to Verona Beach State Park, Verona Beach, New York.
Photo by Larry Weill

The hiking alone in this park is worth at least one day, given that it advertises thirteen miles of hiking trails that are open year-round. The "Woods and Wetland" nature trail has a great reputation for providing hikers with wonderful views of both forest and aquatic environments.

Pet Policies: Pets are welcome inside the park, but there are a number of restrictions to observe. Campers may have a maximum of two pets in a campsite, but they must be kept on a leash (six foot maximum) or inside a crate. Pets must be vaccinated for rabies, and are not permitted in playgrounds, buildings, or guarded beaches. (This policy does not apply to service animals.)

Reservations: Campsite reservations may be made up to nine months in advance. Pavilion reservations must be made at least fourteen days in advance and up to eleven months in advance. For reservations call (315) 762-4463.

EDDIE'S

Phone/Address: (315) 762-5430 / 901 Main St., Sylvan Beach, NY 13157.

Days/Hours: Open daily from 11 a.m. to 8 p.m. (Hours may differ in the offseason.)

Reservations accepted? Yes.

Restaurant size: Approximately eighty tables, plus counter seating.

Outdoor seating: Yes.

Menu items: They have a full slate of breakfast dishes including eggs, bacon, sausage, pancakes, and waffles. Their lunches include sandwiches, salads, soups, chicken wings, and tenders. Their dinners feature Italian dishes such as lasagna, chicken Parmesan, manicotti, and "Fifi's Special," which contains pieces of pork and beef braised in Eddie's famous sauce.

Eddie's in Sylvan Beach, New York.
Photo by Larry Weill

Price range: Breakfasts range from $10 to $14, lunch sandwiches are $10–$15, burgers are $14–$17, and the Italian specials range between $15 and $22.

Most popular menu item: Fresh haddock and their Eddie's "hot ham" dinner.

Entertainment: No.

Liquor license: No.

Description: Eddie's is truly an institution in this lakefront community. It has been a fan favorite of the local population and the vacation crowd for ninety years. It was started as a hot dog stand by a husband-and-wife team in 1934 and has grown into the popular restaurant it is today.

This is also the kind of restaurant that people revisit every year, no matter how many "pilgrimages" they make to the Sylvan Beach area. According to the staff, roughly 98 percent of their customers are "regulars," and they know many of them by first name.

The restaurant is known for their amazing Italian classics, and their sauce is a secret combination of ingredients that enhances each dish.

"Seriously, this place is like community," said one staff member. "You'd be surprised how many couples had their first date in this restaurant." It's just that kind of place.

HARPOON EDDIE'S

Phone/Address: (315) 762-5238 / 611 Park Ave., Sylvan Beach, NY 13157.

Days/Hours: (Summer hours) Monday through Thursday, 4 p.m.–11 p.m., Friday through Sunday noon–10 p.m.

Reservations accepted? Yes.

Restaurant size: Approximately ninety tables, many of which are outdoors.

Outdoor seating: Yes.

Menu items: Harpoon Eddie's has a gigantic menu of great-tasting appetizers, including their sausage and clams, or their lager onion rings. They also list five salads, lots of varieties of pizza (including a pulled pork pizza), lots of pasta dishes, sandwiches, and paninis.

Harpoon Eddie's in Sylvan Beach, New York.

Price range: Appetizers range from $8 to $14, burgers are $13–$14, sandwiches run from $13 to $17, and the surf and turf (with steak, shrimp, and scallops) is $28.

Most popular menu item: Fresh fish tacos and fresh steamed clams.

Entertainment: Yes (live music seven nights a week in the summer).

Liquor license: Yes.

Description: This restaurant/pub is so popular with both the locals as well as the vacation crowd because of its incredible beach party atmosphere. With so many of their tables located outside, right on the lakeside beach, it's a real crowd pleaser.

Every Thursday night they sponsor beach volleyball. It's a great place to play, or simply enjoy watching with your favorite summer cocktail. Harpoon Eddie's has a whole menu of unique cocktails, mixed up by their superb bar staff. How about sampling the "Harpoon Fish Bowl," or maybe a "Poon's Punch?"

If you happen to have your kids along with you on your watercraft, bring them along! Harpoon Eddie's is both kid and dog friendly. (Dogs are welcome on their outdoor patios.)

Are you feeling particularly strong? How about stopping by in August to watch the "Battle at the Beach" Arm Wrestling Championships? This event draws a crowd every year, so why not stop by the beach patio to watch them battle it out? Even if you can't win the arm wrestling championship, you can still have fun doing some left-handed curls with your favorite drink.

CAPTAIN JOHN'S

Phone/Address: (315) 762-9949 / 1424 Main St., Sylvan Beach, NY 13157.

Note: This is a seasonal restaurant open from May through mid-September. Check online for dates.

Days/Hours: Closed on Monday and Wednesday. Open on Tuesday and Thursday 4 p.m.–9 p.m., Saturday 3 p.m.–9 p.m., Sunday 1 p.m.–8 p.m., opens at noon on holidays.

Reservations accepted? Yes (parties of ten and more).

Restaurant size: About sixty-five tables inside and fourteen more tables outside.

Outdoor seating: Yes.

Menu items: This is a very large menu that starts with eleven appetizers (including coconut-crusted fried shrimp), five soups, prime rib, three steaks, five chicken dishes, six pasta entrées (including lobster and seafood fra diavolo), three lobster and crab plates, and eight seafood plates. The menu also includes lots of tropical drinks from the bar as well.

Price range: The appetizers are $12–$15, prime rib runs from $37 to $48, the steaks are $40-–$50, chicken entrées range between $25 and $30. Their signature ten-ounce lobster tail is $45, and the pasta plates are $19–$49.

Most popular menu item: Prime rib and lobster tails. Also their two-for-one margaritas from the bar.

Entertainment: No.

Captain John's, Sylvan Beach, New York.
PHOTO BY LARRY WEILL

Liquor license: Yes

Description: Captain John's is a very good and very cool restaurant! It's been in business for fifty-two years, and the original owner (who is now over one hundred years old) greets diners at the door on weekends! The entire inside is adorned in Island vibes and nautical decor, with each booth named after an old ship.

Margaritas are always two-for-one, and they feature an amazing (and *huge*) bar drink called "The Shipwreck." Each one is made with a half-gallon of rum, brandies, and tropical fruit juices. You even get to keep the glass after you're done with it.

I ate dinner here during my visit, and the seafood was amazing. Their prime rib is known for being just as good. The owner said boaters could even call for a ride to their restaurant!

WHAT'S THE SCOOP

Phone/Address: (315) 761-4022 / 604 Main St., Sylvan Beach, NY 13157.

Note: This is a seasonal restaurant that is only open from May through September.

Days/Hours: Thursday and Friday 5 p.m.–9 p.m., Saturday and Sunday noon–9 p.m. (After the end of June they are open every day of the week.)

Reservations accepted? Yes.

Restaurant size: Eight tables, all outside.

Outdoor seating: Yes.

Menu items: Ice cream, ice cream, and more ice cream! They have both hard-scoop and soft-serve ice cream available in lots of flavors. Also on the menu are sundaes, smoothies, hand-spun shakes, slushes, flurries, floats, and banana splits.

What's the Scoop in Sylvan Beach, New York.
PHOTO BY LARRY WEILL

You can also purchase ice cream flights (any four hard ice cream flavors), ice cream nachos, "brownie delights," and the famous Sylvan Sundae.

Price range: Soft-serve portions are from $3.75 to $6.75 depending on size, sundaes run from $6.50 to $8, smoothies are $7, hand-spun shakes are $6.50, slushes are $2.75–$3.75, flurries are $6.50, and banana splits are $8. Finally, ice cream flights are $8, ice cream nachos are $8.50, and both the Sylvan Sundae and the Brownie Delight are $8.

Most popular menu item: The Sylvan Sundae, which is twist ice cream with hot fudge, peanut butter, whipped cream, and a cherry on top.

Entertainment: No.

Liquor license: No.

Description: What's the Scoop is a quaint little ice cream stand on Main Street in Sylvan Beach that has been serving premium ice cream to the community for thirty years. It was founded by Joseph Rizzo, who, upon his retirement, converted an old garage into this dessert mecca that has become so loved by the town. His entire family became involved in the business and still run it to this day.

What's the Scoop offers Perry's hard scoop ice cream, which is preferred by ice cream lovers everywhere. They offer thirty flavors during their first few months every year before adding many more in the summer months.

The Sylvan Sundae is a new creation invented by the people at this popular spot. Try one!

PANCAKE HOUSE

Phone/Address: (315) 761-4303 / 516 Main St., Sylvan Beach, NY 13157.

Days/Hours: Open 7:30 a.m.–2 p.m. every day of the week (in summer months).

Reservations accepted? No.

Restaurant size: Fourteen tables inside plus counter seating, and eight tables outside.

Outdoor seating: Yes (large covered patio).

Menu items: The Pancake House has an extensive breakfast and lunch menu, but it is hardly limited to pancakes. In addition to the pancakes and French toast,

The Pancake House, Sylvan Beach, New York.
PHOTO BY LARRY WEILL

they also list several egg dishes and five omelets, English muffins and bagels, three breakfast sandwiches, "breakfast combinations," eggs Benedict, breakfast quesadillas, and more. Their lunch menu includes six sandwiches (including a turkey club and a honey barbecue melt), California Vegi-wrap, and numerous other enticing dishes. They also offer a complete selection of alcoholic and non-alcoholic drinks.

Price range: Pancake and French Toast breakfasts range from $9 to $10, the omelets are $11–$16, breakfast sandwiches are listed from $12 to $14, the "breakfast combination" plates are $11.49–$14.49, and lunch sandwiches are $13–$16.

Most popular menu item: The Crabcake Benedict and the Cinnamon Swirl pancakes are the most popular breakfast items, while the panini sandwiches are most requested for lunch. Their drink menu also features the ever-popular mimosas and handcrafted Bloody Marys.

Entertainment: Yes (occasionally they have live music in the summer months).

Liquor license: Yes.

Description: This is the only restaurant in the area that focuses primarily on breakfast, although they also prepare outstanding lunches as well. Staying true to its name, customers flock to this place for their signature dishes while enjoying exceptional service and the nostalgic atmosphere.

The Pancake House has been a mainstay of the Sylvan Beach community since it opened its doors in 1957. Many famous people have dined here, including Rodney Dangerfield, Foster Brooks, Tony Bennett, Tom Jones, and Liza Minnelli. (The Pancake House was one of Rodney Dangerfield's favorite restaurants.) This is a great place to visit for a fantastic breakfast or lunch while enjoying the history of the town. But if Rodney shows up, give him some respect!

THE BEACH AT SYLVAN BEACH

Location: Eastern shoreline of Oneida Lake.

Days/Hours: The lake and beach are accessible 24 hours/day, 7 days a week.

Admission: Free.

Access points: Please avoid cutting through the private property of houses and businesses to access the beach. There are two public access points to reach the sandy beaches. These are from Akehurst Avenue (between Eleventh and Twelfth Avenues) and through Sunset Park (near the new bathhouse).

General Notes: What could be better on a sunny summer day than pulling up to a white sand beach and burying your toes in the sand? The eastern shoreline of Oneida Lake offers just that opportunity! The beach is between one and two miles long (depending on who you ask), and has great views down the entire length of the lake.

The lake itself is very shallow near the shoreline, and bathers can walk out some distance without going beyond "waist-deep" in the water. Children should be supervised at all times since lifeguards are not on duty on the beach.

The beach is surrounded by lots of great places to dine, play, and relax. There are public restrooms located at Sunset Park and at the Carello's Corner parking lot (at the corner of Main Street and Akehurst Avenue.) There are also playgrounds, pavilions, picnic areas, benches, and green space available for public use. Parking, however, is not free. Parking kiosks are conveniently spaced along

Sylvan Beach on the eastern shoreline of Oneida Lake.
Photo by Larry Weill

the nearby roads, and tickets are written to cars that do not display a current parking receipt tag. The parking kiosks do accept credit cards.

If you have arrived by boat (assuming you are boating the Erie Canal), you are permitted to anchor your vessel off the beach and wade ashore. Pulling your boat up onto the beach is not permitted.

Rules:

- No open containers of alcoholic beverages are permitted on the beach.
- No glass or glass containers are allowed on the beach.
- No dogs are permitted on the beach. They may be kept on a leash on any of the grassy areas behind the beach.
- Motorized vehicles, including motorcycles and ATVs, are not allowed on the beach.
- Smoking is not permitted on the beach due to excessive litter from "butts" in past years.
- Grills are not permitted on the beach, although barbecue grills are provided in the grassy areas behind the beach.

VIENNA FARMERS MARKET

Phone/Address: (561) 246-0148 / 6839 Lakeshore Drive N., Verona Beach, NY. (Look for the tents in front of the Farmhouse restaurant.)

Days/Hours: Only on Thursday afternoons, from 3 p.m. to 6:30 p.m. This event runs from early May through late October.

Admission: Free.

General Notes: The Vienna Farmers Market is a fun collection of vendors who enjoy getting together once a week to display and sell their wares. They come from all over the state, although many are locals. You truly never know what you are going to find as you meander between the tent displays. When asked why they like to participate in these markets, several of the vendors replied that they "just want to be around other people" in addition to selling their crafts. It's simply a very friendly place to shop for handmade goods.

Vienna Farmers Market in Verona Beach, New York.
PHOTO BY LARRY WEILL

The market has been running since 2016, although it has been held at numerous locations other than the Farmhouse. Its previous home was at the Transportation Department at the intersection of Routes 13 and 49. However, the vendors and the organizers both enjoy the current location, which is right next to the main road going from Verona Beach into Sylvan Beach. Boaters traveling the Erie Canal can tie up within a couple hundred feet of the market.

The Vienna Farmers Market attracts a regular group of eighteen to twenty vendors who make or prepare a plethora of goods, crafts, and edibles. A short list of these items would include cookies, cakes, pies, fudge, breads, fresh fruit and vegetables, herbs, woodcraft, birdhouses and feeders, soaps, honey, and more. One vendor even makes and sells customized cornhole bags!

A major focus of the Vienna Farmers Market is to educate people to shop for and cook healthy meals. They work in conjunction with Cornell Cooperative Extension of Oneida County and SNAP-Ed New York for those who qualify or receive SNAP benefits. Patrons who possess EBT/SNAP cards can double their benefits when purchasing goods at the Vienna Farmers Market. For every $2 in EBT benefits redeemed for tokens, patrons will receive a $2 Fresh Connect coupon.

For more information about the Vienna Farmers Market, visit https://www.Facebook.com/ViennaFarmersMarketNY.

CINCO DE MAYO

Phone/Address: (315) 761-4058 / 412 Main St., Sylvan Beach, NY 13157.

Days/Hours: 11 a.m.–9 p.m., every day of the week.

Reservations accepted? Yes.

Restaurant size: Twenty tables inside, but a large door opens in summer to provide outside exposure.

Outdoor seating: Yes.

Menu items: This restaurant is pure Mexican, with a large menu full of standard south-of-the-border fare. There are thirty-seven items on the lunch menu including fajitas, enchiladas, nachos, and taco salads. They list over twenty "special dinners," which include a burrito Mexicano, mole ranchero, and hot tamales. They also offer thirteen fajita plates, ten steak plates, fifteen chicken dishes, three

Cinco de Mayo, Sylvan Beach, New York.
Photo by Larry Weill

pork entrées, and eight seafood plates. All come with their own authentic blends of Mexican sauces and seasonings.

Price range: Lunches range from $11 to $14, the special dinners list from $13 to $18, the fajita plates are $14–$20, steak dishes are $18–$23, chicken plates are $15–$20, and the seafood dinners are $19–$23.

Most popular menu item: The Tex Mex Nachos.

Entertainment: Yes (live Mexican music on Saturday nights).

Liquor license: Yes.

Description: Cinco de Mayo is a relative newcomer to the Sylvan Beach food scene, but it has been very well received by both the local population as well as boaters coming off the canal (through Oneida Lake). The kitchen produces authentic flavors and dishes that achieve the same tastes as one would experience dining "south of the border."

"Many of our chefs were born and raised in Mexico and learned how to cook from their family members," related one of the bartenders at Cinco de Mayo. He said that background made them wonderfully adept in the kitchen at creating culinary masterpieces that were "true Mexican." Additionally, the owner makes his own margarita mix from scratch, so the bar drinks are authentic Mexican as well.

The interior of Cinco de Mayo is attractively decorated in a Southern style, with old license plates, signs, and antique gas pumps on the walls. It's a great stop after a long day on the boat.

THE SPAGHETTI FACTORY

Phone/Address: (315) 762-9948 / 6800 NY-13, Verona Beach, NY 13162.

Note: This restaurant is slightly outside of the "stone's throw" range from the canal but not by much. (Perhaps two stones' throws!)

Days/Hours: Monday and Thursday noon–9 p.m., Friday and Saturday noon–9:30 p.m., Sunday 1 p.m.–8 p.m. Closed on Tuesday and Wednesday.

Reservations accepted? Yes.

Restaurant size: Forty-five tables inside, twelve tables outside on their side deck.

Outdoor seating: Yes.

Menu items: The menu lists ten appetizer options featuring dishes like eggplant bruschetta and shrimp Parmesan. They also offer seven soups and salads, eleven pasta dishes (including homemade lasagna and stuffed rigatoni), eight chicken dishes, seven varieties of steaks and chops, nine seafood dishes (including scallops alla Rossi and crab cakes Pasquale), and lots of spaghetti dishes. They also offer thick-crust pizzas of various sizes and with lots of great toppings. On Fridays, they have fresh haddock on the menu served seven different ways.

Price range: Appetizers are $10–$16, the pasta dishes range from $11 to $23, the steaks and chops entrées run from $22 to $39, seafood dishes are $17–$28, pizzas are $9–$22 depending on size and toppings, and the fresh haddock Friday dinners are $19–$21.

The Spaghetti Factory, Verona Beach, New York.
PHOTO BY LARRY WEILL

Most popular menu item: The fresh haddock dishes on Fridays, along with the veal dinners.

Entertainment: No.

Liquor license: Yes.

Description: The Spaghetti Factory is another restaurant in this resort area that dates back many years, in this case to 1978. Back in those days, it was called Gallagher's Bar, and it was a small place perhaps half the size of the current restaurant.

The current owners were invited to take over the restaurant after the previous owners retired in 2019. They maintained the same staff and paid meticulous attention to preserving the same recipes and quality of service to their dedicated customers. This focus on quality has kept patrons coming back year after year. It's the best pasta in town.

VERONA BEACH LIGHTHOUSE

Address: 6765 Forest Avenue, Verona, NY 13157.

Admission: There is no fee to visit the lighthouse. There is also no way to enter or ascend to the top of this structure.

Parking: There is a small parking lot for cars, but space is very limited (five or six spaces). Please respect the privacy of the property owners who live directly behind the lighthouse plot.

Dock availability: There currently is no dock available for larger boats, although small canoes, paddleboats, and other very small craft can be pulled up to the sand beach. Plans to construct a boat dock are in the works for future development.

Verona Beach Lighthouse, Sylvan Beach, New York.
Photo by Larry Weill

Background: This lighthouse, located on the east end of Oneida Lake, is one of three such structures built on the waters of the lake. For this reason, they were called the "three sisters," and all are still standing today.

Construction on the Verona Beach lighthouse was started in 1916, the same year that work began on the Brewerton lighthouse at the west end of the lake. The third lighthouse in this series is not located on the shoreline, but rather on French Island, which is much closer to the west end of the lake than the east. This lighthouse (on French Island) no longer stands out like its two sisters, as it has become obscured by trees and other vegetation on the island.

It's important to note that the lighthouses were not built until almost ninety years after the initial completion of the Erie Canal because the original canal did not transit across Oneida Lake. That only happened once the canal was expanded and rerouted to accommodate much larger vessels, thus the name "barge canal."

The towers were built to a fairly uniform height of eighty-five feet, although they appear to differ in size because their platforms vary in height a few feet. They were built by barging in prefabricated eighteen-foot sections which were then assembled on-site. This was a major engineering feat for the day.

In 2002, a group of local citizens funded the Verona Beach Lighthouse Association for the purpose of preserving the lighthouse and performing any repair and restoration work that was needed. They have also replaced a door and several windows to the lighthouse as well as performed landscaping work on the grounds around the base.

If you are on the lake around sunset, look to the west for superb photographic scenery.

UTICA MARSH WILDLIFE MANAGEMENT AREA

Location: Utica, New York—best access route is off N. Genesee in between the Mohawk River and the Erie Canal. There you will find a large parking lot that is seldom crowded.

Hours: Officially the hours for this park are 6:30 a.m.–11 p.m., seven days a week. However, like most parks, the practical hours are from dawn to dusk.

Admission: Free.

Note to boaters: While there are no rules restricting boats from this area, there is no way to access it from the Erie Canal, and no boat docks are located nearby.

Sign kiosk at the entrance to the Utica Marsh Wildlife Management Area, Utica, New York.

Photo by Larry Weill

Description: This large and underused area is a marshy wetland environment set aside for the preservation of wetland flora and fauna. It provides visitors with the opportunity to observe these species in a natural setting while also affording visitors with walking, running, and biking routes across the landscape. The wildlife management area contains several hundred acres of land, and looks even larger from the inside. There are no motorized vehicles permitted inside the tract, so visitors must either hike or bike on the Canalway Trail to enter the grounds. The hike from the parking lot to the entrance of the wildlife management area is over one mile, so wear comfortable shoes. (The trail can get muddy in places.)

Once inside, visitors can either follow the Canalway Trail all the way through or follow the loop trail that passes between the East Pool and West Pool bodies of water. On the northwest corner of this location (where the two pools come together) is an excellent wooden observation tower that overlooks both the East Pool and the West Pool. It was built in 2017 and is about twenty feet tall.

Animals present in the Utica Marsh area: Species of birds can include wood ducks, mallards, American black ducks, Canada geese, snow geese, ring-necked ducks, northern pintails, American wigeon, green-winged teal, great blue herons, common egret, both hooded and common mergansers, and more. Osprey and bald eagles have also been spotted within the area or flying overhead. Many people see painted and snapping turtles on the trail and in the aquatic vegetation. Also present in this area are beaver, muskrat, mink, raccoon, weasel, skunk, opossum, red and gray fox, and coyote.

Rules: There is no camping permitted in the Utica Marsh Wildlife Management Area. There is also no hunting or target shooting, horseback riding, snowmobiling, ATV use, camping, swimming, or fires allowed inside the area. Accumulation of trash has been a problem in the past, so please be respectful and carry out anything you carry in.

ROSIE'S ORISKANY DINER

Phone/Address: (315) 790-5395 / 8404 NY Route 69, Oriskany, NY 13424.

Days/Hours: Wednesday through Saturday 7 a.m.–2 p.m., Sunday 7 a.m.–noon, closed on Monday and Tuesday.

Reservations accepted? No.

Restaurant size: Fourteen tables.

Outdoor seating: No.

Menu items: Their breakfast menu includes lots of egg and omelet dishes, pancakes, French toast, Belgian waffles, and giambrotte (scrambled eggs with mushrooms, onions, peppers, sausage, Utica greens, topped with mozzarella and home fries). Their lunch dishes feature burgers, sandwiches, lots of wraps (including the BLT wrap and the taco salad), along with lots of tempting side orders.

Price range: Most egg dishes are $6–$11, omelets are $9–$12, eggs Benedict are $12.45, and most sandwiches and wraps are between $8.45 and $11.45. Side orders run from $3 to $7.

Most popular menu item: Garbage plate and their hidden (secret) menu items.

Entertainment: No.

Liquor license: No.

Rosie's Oriskany Diner in Oriskany, New York.
PHOTO BY LARRY WEILL

Description: Rosie's Oriskany Diner is another one of those places where everyone knows everyone, and you become an instant friend the moment you walk in the door. Rosie is fond of coming out of the kitchen and chatting with her customers whenever time permits.

Although only in business a few short years, the diner has built a large and devoted following in the community. As proof of this, make sure you look to the left when entering the restaurant. There, on the wall in the area to the left, is "the Breakfast Club" board where customers pin their photographs below the club sign. There are an astonishing number of photos pinned up, all smiling and enjoying their meals.

Rosie adds her own ideas to the menu dishes, many of which are local to the area. Her "Rosie Greens" are different from the standard Utica greens and are frequently ordered by her patrons.

Rosie is proud of the food served in the diner, all prepared fresh and locally sourced. Her brother owns the nearby Ramon's Bakery, who delivers all of their breads fresh daily.

ORISKANY FLATS WILDLIFE MANAGEMENT AREA

Location: City of Rome, New York, although it is in the towns of Marcy, Rome, and Whitestown. The easiest entrance is off River Street (Route 32), and the Canalway Trail runs right past it. There are two parking lots providing access to the northern and southern grounds.

Hours: Dawn to dusk, seven days a week.

Admission: Free.

Hazard: Ticks are common in this area. Use a tick repellant, and always check yourself for ticks after using this wildlife management area.

Description: The Oriskany Flats Wildlife Management Area is a large (806 acres) tract of land that was predominantly used as farmland over the past century, but has now been left to naturally revert to a wetland wildlife habitat and recreation area. Those areas that were used for agriculture (which comprise over 50 percent of the wildlife management area) are in various stages of ecological succession. Some of these fields are home to milkweed and grasses, while other areas representing later phases are sprouting wild raspberry and blackberry bushes and other transitional species. About 15 percent of the total tract is considered a true wetland habitat.

Visitors to this wildlife management area (WMA) have access to a wide variety of recreational activities, including hiking, biking, hunting, trapping, fishing, and observing wildlife. Persons engaged in hunting must follow all established state hunting regulations. Fishermen who venture into the Mohawk River in this area will find largemouth and smallmouth bass, yellow perch, and brown bullhead. Fishing can be done from either the Mohawk River or the shore. There is a canoe launch at the parking facility on the north side of the river.

Animals present in the Oriskany Flats Wildlife Management Area: Species of birds can include American crow, black-capped chickadee, American robin, goldfinch, blue jay, wild turkey, wood duck, mallard, Canada geese, snow geese, and great blue heron. Also present in this area are white-tailed deer, beaver, muskrat, mink, and river otter. Reptiles and amphibians in the area include the

Sign kiosk at the entrance to the Oriskany Flats Wildlife Management Area, Oriskany, New York.
Photo by Larry Weill

northern water snake, garter snake, bullfrog, northern leopard frog, green frog, eastern American toad, snapping turtles, and Jefferson's blue-spotted salamander.

Rules: There is a "Leave No Trace" policy in force in this WMA, so please carry out everything you carry in. No motorized boats shall be used inside this area. Mooring, anchoring, or storing a boat in this area is forbidden. No other motorized off-road vehicles are authorized here unless formally authorized by the Regional Manager. Camping in this area is not permitted. Please read the remainder of the rules posted on the signboards at the WMA entrance kiosk.

HERKIMER COUNTY

GEMS ALONG THE MOHAWK

Phone/Address: (315) 717-0077 / 800 Mohawk St., Herkimer, NY 13350.

Hours: 9 a.m.–5 p.m., every day of the week. This center is open year-round.

Admission fee: This center does not charge an admission fee to enter. Boat tours must be paid for in advance at the kiosk inside the building.

Location: The location of this visitors' center is ideal because it is centered at the crossroads of several major cities. Albany is located to the east, Utica to the west, Cooperstown to the south, and Old Forge to the north. The New York State Thruway is also nearby and provides easy access to Herkimer. It is also located right on the river/canal, providing boaters with easy boat access.

Gems Along the Mohawk, Herkimer, New York.
PHOTO BY LARRY WEILL

Description: Trying to describe Gems Along the Mohawk in a single paragraph is very difficult. It is similar to attempting to describe a really good buffet restaurant with a single adjective. It really can't be done.

The official term to describe Gems Along the Mohawk is a "visitor center," although there are lots of components to the place. The only thing they all have in common is to provide tourists and other visitors with a great time and the opportunity to engage in fun activities.

The first thing you'll see upon entering the front door is a large floor space filled with great merchandise of all kinds. The store area contains items brought together from about fifty local artisans, and it covers the gamut of treasures from jewelry to clothing to books to locally produced food items. They are also affiliated with the Herkimer Diamond Mines and carry a large selection of their beautiful jewelry. It just goes on and on and on, so if you are looking for gifts or souvenirs to bring home from your trip, this is the best place in the region to shop.

Boat Trips: Inside the building, you will find a kiosk where tickets can be purchased for a local boat ride and a narrated tour. These tour boats go out twice/day with most of the standard excursions lasting for ninety minutes. These tours take you to many of the local historic sites up and down the canal and through the local communities. Special charter tours for groups are also available.

Services: This center does have boat docks that are available for tying up. No additional services are available at these docks, although local marinas in the area can supply services as needed.

Food: Finally, if you are looking for a great meal instead of just a snack, check out the Waterfront Grill (see below), which is located at the far end of the plaza.

WATERFRONT GRILL

Phone/Address: (315) 717-0700 / 800 Mohawk St., Herkimer, NY 13350.

Days/Hours: Wednesday through Saturday 11:30 a.m.–3:30 p.m. and then from 5 p.m. to 9 p.m., closed on Sunday, Monday, and Tuesday.

Reservations accepted? Yes.

Restaurant size: About twenty tables seating about eighty people.

Waterfront Grill, Herkimer, New York.
PHOTO BY LARRY WEILL

Outdoor seating: Yes.

Menu items: Appetizers abound at this waterfront restaurant, with sixteen choices listed on the lunch menu and eighteen appearing on the dinner version. These include a plate of greens tossed with prosciutto, hot peppers, and a squeeze of lemon served with garlic bread. The lunches also feature five salads, lots of sandwiches and grilled dishes, and several pizzas. The dinner menu offers several salads, Italian specialties, "Rocky's Pasta," ravioli, stuffed rigatoni, chicken Français, and more. They also include a choice of three steaks and five seafood dishes.

Price range: Appetizers run from $12 to $17, salads range from $8 to $18, most burgers and sandwiches are $14–$15, and lunch pizzas are $13–$15. For dinners, veal and chicken dishes are $21–$25, and the seafood entrées range from $23 to $27 (although the fish fry is $10–$16).

Most popular menu item: Steaks, veal, scallops, and pasta with homemade marinara sauce or vodka sauce.

Entertainment: No.

Liquor license: Yes.

Description: The Waterfront Grill has been in business since 2002, and has built up a large and faithful local following. Their dining room is beautifully decorated in a nautical theme to go with the waterfront setting. It is located in the visitors' center plaza with Gems Along the Mohawk.

In case you were wondering, "Rocky's Pasta" is named after the owner. Rocky and Barbie Fiato have run this restaurant since its inception, and have contributed to the Italian American influence on the menu and the food. They are fond of describing their establishment as having "comfort food served in an atmosphere of water and the canal." They also have a private party space for up to forty people on Sunday, Monday, and Tuesday.

Another great feature of this place is the incredible view from the dining room. In most waterfront restaurants the diners clamor for a table at the window to get the best view. In this location, every table has a great view of the river. It is a superb place to dine and "feel the canal."

FORT HERKIMER CHURCH

Phone/Address: (315) 866-1523 / 575 Route 5S., East Herkimer, NY 13350.

Hours: Monday through Thursday 10 a.m.–2 p.m., closed Friday through Sunday.

Note: If the name "Fort Herkimer Church" sounds odd, don't worry. The name itself is an oxymoron, but it is correct; this church was used in both capacities as a house of worship and also as a place of protection. It was also known as the Reformed Protestant Dutch Church of German Flatts.

History: While this is a beautiful and historic church and landmark in Herkimer County, details of its background are a bit sketchy and hard to find. It is known that the church was constructed between 1753 and 1767, prior to the United States becoming an independent country. It was later expanded in 1812 to increase the height of the building by eight feet. Also during that year, a second row of windows and a new entrance were added to the west end of the building. The raised pulpit, which is flanked with twin sets of stairs on either side, was moved to the east end of the church at the same time.

Fort Herkimer Church in East Herkimer, New York.
PHOTO BY LARRY WEILL

Of additional interest is that the Fort Herkimer Church is one of the oldest remaining churches in New York State. It is also the oldest building in Herkimer County. It is unique in that the church walls include gun ports used to defend those inside the building. This was a necessary feature in the years that included the French and Indian War as well as the American Revolution.

Access to the church: As many visitors have noted, the church is seldom open for inside tours. There are hours listed, although most people have found the doors locked on most days. It is still possible, however, to walk around the outside grounds, which also serves as a cemetery. The stones in this burial ground are quite old, with most dating from the 1750s and on.

There are individuals on social media accounts who claim that the church is open in the month of September for the Living History Weekend, and also for Thanksgiving Day mass. There is also a video posted online of an Easter morning service that shows the stark but beautiful interior of the church. Arrangements can be made if someone desires a church wedding at this location. However, for the purposes of this book (hikers, bikers, and boaters), most people will have to be satisfied with the "walk by" tour, which is still worth the time and effort.

Credit: Many of these details are taken from an old publication, *The History of Fort Herkimer Church*. This eleven-page pamphlet is not dated, and no author's name appears on the front or inside its covers. Rev. Forest L. Decker of the Reformed Church in Herkimer wrote the Foreword to this publication on November 21, 1966. It can be found on the fortherkimerchurch.com website.

ANN STREET RESTAURANT AND DELI

Phone/Address: (315) 823-3290 / 381 Canal Place, Little Falls, NY 13365.

Days/Hours: Every day from 7 a.m. to 3 p.m.

Reservations accepted? Yes.

Restaurant size: About twenty tables.

Outdoor seating: Yes.

Menu items: Ann Street Restaurant has a full breakfast menu, with lots of combinations and ten different omelets, breakfast sandwiches, and side orders of meats, muffins, potatoes, and more. Breakfast also includes their fresh waffles, pancakes, French toast, and fruit salad. Their lunch menu features a long list of seventeen grilled sandwiches, five cold sandwiches, main course salads, and "something different" selections (including one with red pepper hummus and fresh vegetables rolled in a garlic wrap).

Price range: Most breakfasts range from $4.50 to $8. At lunch, the sandwiches are mostly between $6 and $9, while the main entrée salads are from $10 to $12.

Most popular menu item: The Mediterranean turkey sandwiches are very popular, although several customers voted with "Reubens" while I was asking this question!

Entertainment: No.

Liquor license: No.

Ann Street Restaurant and Deli, Little Falls, New York.
PHOTO BY LARRY WEILL

Description: The Ann Street Restaurant and Deli is a bright, wide-open spot that is fully embraced by the local community. Situated in the historic Canal Place neighborhood, it is filled with local residents, antique hunters, and employees from the nearby hospital. Many workers from the surrounding factories also stop in, often for take-out orders.

If you enjoy dining outside, the Ann Steet Restaurant and Deli has a lovely outside porch that is completely screened in, open from May through October. If you'd rather dine inside, the large windows across the front give you a bird's-eye view of the street while the open kitchen affords you a view of your meal as it is being prepared.

The restaurant serves breakfast until 11 a.m. on weekdays and until 1 p.m. on weekends. Lunches are available from 11 a.m. to 3 p.m. daily. They also post a whiteboard every day with a listing of specials, so don't forget to look for that before you order.

CANAL PLACE

Location: This attraction does not have a single street address or phone number. Instead, it is the name of a small district adjacent to the Mohawk River/Erie Canal in downtown Little Falls, New York.

Hours: This area is open to the public twenty-four hours/day, year-round. Business hours vary based on the business. Check independent websites for hours of operation for your destination.

History: The area surrounding this part of Little Falls was filled with factories and other manufacturing buildings from the 1800s. It was a thriving community that revolved around the Mohawk River and the Erie Canal. Thousands of people lived and worked in this area, thus forming the core of the Little Falls' industrial base.

Following the heyday of the Erie Canal and the gradual shutdown of the major factories in Little Falls, the entire Canal Place district fell into disuse. Buildings were abandoned and shut down, gradually falling into disrepair and

Canal Place, Little Falls, New York.
PHOTO BY LARRY WEILL

decay. Major industry was no longer able to support this infrastructure, and the massive stone buildings became forlorn symbols of the past.

The transition: It wasn't until the 1980s, when some of the old factory buildings were being torn down, that the town started to realize the potential of the area including some of the abandoned structures. In 1988, a group of local business owners, residents, and town officials formed the Canal Place Development Association and started planning. They began development on a couple of parks as well as planning how to reuse some of the incredible abandoned factories to reinvent this "Canal Place" neighborhood as an asset to the community.

What you will find today: The Canal Place district, while still under development, has become a thriving community and visitor destination. It is filled with artsy businesses and boutiques, beautiful hotels, residential apartments, antique stores, breweries, and lots more.

Perhaps the most abundant businesses found in this area are the antique shops. There are a number of them, and they are literally loaded to the gills (windowsills?) with all kinds of items from the past, from tools and books to jewelry and glassware. It's all there, assuming you have time to browse all these quaint little shops.

Many of the other stores have an extremely artistic emphasis, with paintings and sculptures on display, sometimes created by the gallery owner. These shops are nestled between stores that offer health products and other holistic products.

For those looking to come off the Canalway Trail and grab a quick lunch, there are plenty of places to purchase a great meal and drink. These can be seen from Canal Place (the street) itself, and are a quick "off-and-on" from the trail. Plan to spend at least an hour roaming this area.

HERKIMER HOME STATE HISTORIC SITE

Phone/Address: (315) 823-0398 / 200 State Route 169, Little Falls, NY 13365.

Hours: Wednesday through Sunday 10 a.m.–5 p.m., closed on Monday and Tuesday. (Open some Mondays on holidays.) The grounds around the buildings are open every day from dawn until dusk. Tours of the mansion start every hour on the hour. (Call ahead to reserve a spot.)

Seasonal: This museum is only open from Labor Day through Columbus Day.

Herkimer Home State Historic Site, Little Falls, New York.
Photo by Larry Weill

Admission: Adults are $4, seniors and students are $3, children under twelve are free.

History: This mansion was the home of General Nicholas Herkimer (also known as Nikolaus Herchheimer). It was completed in 1764 and was situated on the south side of the Mohawk River on a spot described as the edge of the American frontier.

Herkimer had been involved with the Tryon County Militia since 1758 and was commissioned as a captain in January 1758. His promotion path was rapid, and he was appointed colonel of the district militia in 1775 and then further promoted to brigadier general in September 1776. In July 1777, he marched his Tryon County Militia to Fort Stanwix (in current day Utica) to repel a force of British soldiers, Tory militia, and Mohawk warriors. His column was ambushed in what became known as the Battle of Oriskany, and he was badly injured in his leg. Although his leg was amputated in an attempt to save his life, the operation went poorly, and he died of his wounds ten days later. He was forty-nine at the time of his death.

The Herkimer Home mansion today: The site today is easily accessed from either the Erie Canal (Mohawk River) or the Canalway Trail. Both are located a very short distance down the hill from the mansion. The original Erie Canal ran directly past the mansion, as did the first train railway in the area. It is possible today to see residual signs of each situated near the mansion.

Many parts of the mansion built by Nicholas Herkimer are still standing today. The exterior brickwork is all original, as is the framing of the building. The interior, however, has been remodeled over the years. The well and the root cellar are all original, and the family cemetery (where Nicholas Herkimer is buried) looks much as it did two hundred years ago.

Plans are in the works to construct a signpost and info station on the bike trail pointing up the hill to the historic site. (The mansion is easily viewed through a wide clearing in the trees.)

This attraction is also a bike-friendly site and offers restrooms, water, and picnic sites on the grounds. Dogs are welcome on the grounds but not inside the mansion.

EL TREN DE VILLA

Phone/Address: 315-210-4040 / 95 East Main Street, Mohawk, NY 13407.

Days/Hours: Monday through Saturday 11:30 a.m.–8 p.m., Sunday 11:30 a.m.–7 p.m.

Reservations accepted? Yes.

Restaurant size: Twenty-two tables plus bar seating.

Outdoor seating: No.

Menu items: Ten different appetizers, a choice of three salads, four enchilada dishes, combination dinner (make your own choices), six taco dishes, burritos, chimichangas, quesadillas, and lots of house specialties. The specialties include carnitas with fried shredded pork, and a carne campirana, which includes sliced steak cooked with sliced nopales (cactus), potatoes, onion, and tomato sauce. They also offer a full lunch "combo box" with one of six entrées, including a guacamole salad along with rice and beans.

Price range: Most appetizers are $6–$9, salads are $11–$15, combo dinners are $12.50, taco dishes range from $6 to $13, burritos are $12–$17, and chimichangas are $13–$16.

El Tren de Villa, Mohawk, New York.
PHOTO BY LARRY WEILL

Most popular menu item: Super burritos. These are your choice of barbacoa beef, steak, grilled chicken, carnitas, al pastor (marinated pork), or Buffalo chicken. It is served with green sauce, cheese sauce, lettuce, sour cream, guacamole, and pico de gallo.

Entertainment: No.

Liquor license: Yes.

Description: This is a new Mexican restaurant that has attracted a lot of attention since its opening. Most of the customers have given it a hearty approval with comments about the authenticity of the food and the freshness of the ingredients. As in many Mexican restaurants, diners are given a large dish of freshly baked chips and homemade salsa as soon as they sit down for their meal. Everything is made fresh on the premises.

The jumbo burritos are not only among their most popular dishes, but they are also *huge*. Patrons who have reviewed this dish claim that these are big enough to feed two to three people.

El Tren de Villa also has a full bar that specializes in Mexican drinks, with margaritas available in regular, jumbo, and by the pitcher. They offer a wide variety of beers (both Mexican and domestic), along with a full menu of mixed drinks and cocktails. For those not drinking, their bar also lists several "mocktails," that are alcohol-free.

INDIAN CASTLE CHURCH

Phone/Address: (315) 823-2099 / 141 Dillenbeck Rd, Little Falls, NY 13365.

Note: Some sources online list the address as 109 Dillenbeck Road. However, since the church stands alone on the hillside it is easy to locate.

Days/Hours: Memorial Day to Labor Day, Monday through Sunday 10 a.m.–6 p.m.

Admission: Free.

History: Indian Castle Church is a historic Indian mission church that was built by Sir William Johnson in 1769. Johnson served as the British Superintendent of Indian Affairs and was a highly influential figure in many facets of pre–Revolutionary War life. The church was built primarily for the Mohawk inhabitants of the area. Mohawks were part of the larger Iroquois nation.

The land for the church was donated by Joseph Brant and his sister Mollie. Joseph was a prominent military leader among the Mohawks and was allied with the British. He was also the one who originally planted the seed to have a church built in the area that was then called "Mohawk Castle." The

Indian Castle Church, Little Falls, New York.
PHOTO BY LARRY WEILL

church was started in 1769 and completed in 1770. Sir William Johnson provided all of the funding to construct the building.

The church was originally aligned with the Anglican denomination, although many of the Mohawk parishioners left the area for Canada at the beginning of the Revolutionary War. After a period of vacancy, several other denominations used the church, including the Reformed Dutch, Presbyterians, Lutherans, and Universalists.

The church saw continued use throughout the rest of the 1800s and into the 1900s when the Union Church Society adopted the building and made major repairs and structural changes to the interior and exterior appearance. The church ceased conducting services in 1925.

Church activities today: The Indian Castle Church is managed today by the Indian Castle Church Restoration and Preservation Society. It is open to the public during the summer months and also sponsors a series of events for educational and community purposes. These events have included a 250th anniversary celebration, Mohawk cultural demonstrations, and an eighteenth-century living history demonstration day. Events for future years are not yet known but should be available online at https://indiancastle.church.

MONTGOMERY COUNTY

KEEP RIGHT CAFE

Phone/Address: (518) 673-0003 / 80 Erie Blvd., Canajoharie, NY 13317.

Days/Hours: Open 8 a.m.–3 p.m. daily. Closed on Wednesday.

Note: This cafe is open all year. Hours may change slightly seasonally.

Reservations accepted? On occasion.

Restaurant size: Six tables plus counter seating for twenty-four persons. Occupancy under fifty.

Outdoor seating: Yes.

Menu items: Organic coffee and teas, Puremade Italian sodas (try the "Dummy"), daily salads, smoothies, and bowls, oat and yogurt parfaits, breakfast

Keep Right Cafe in Canajoharie, New York.

cookies, "waffle balls" (which are seven waffles on a shish-kabob), breakfast panini, and grain bowls.

Price range: There are many selections to choose from that are low to moderately priced ranging from $3 to $15.

Most popular menu item: The "Gravy Master Special" is turkey, mild cheddar cheese, cranberry sauce, "Gravy Master" mayonnaise, walnuts, and potato sticks. It's like a beautifully crafted Thanksgiving meal on a grilled panini.

Entertainment: Yes. Special event nights such as open mic and game nights are posted on their Instagram and Facebook pages.

Liquor license: No.

Description: Keep Right Cafe is a delightful café inspired by Canajoharie's historical Dummy Light (which is a traffic light on a pedestal in the middle of an intersection). It is a wonderful and cozy little spot with a fun and engaging staff that revels in creating a great atmosphere for its customers. They love being part of the Canajoharie community and embrace the local town and its history. Bonnie, the café owner, created the tasty and health-conscious menu they offer to the public.

Their coffee is organic and locally roasted. Their original house blend is called "Can-Jo," and is available for purchase in the store. The meats used in their sandwiches are roasted and sliced on the premises. They believe in bringing their customer a menu of selections that are good, whole, fresh, nourishing, and delicious. They are also very serious about reducing their footprint. The to-go packaging is biodegradable, compostable, and/or postconsumer recycled. They also love to promote unique small-footprint retail products and local artists. (Their breakfast cookies are delicious!)

ARKELL MUSEUM

Phone/Address: (518) 673-2314 / 2 Erie Blvd, Canajoharie, NY 13317.

Hours: Tuesday through Friday 10 a.m.–5 p.m., Saturday and Sunday noon–5 p.m., closed on Monday.

Note: The Arkell Museum is attached to the Canajoharie Public Library.

Seasonal: The Arkell Museum is closed in January and February, although the Canajoharie Library remains open year-round.

Arkell Museum, Canajoharie, New York.
PHOTO BY LARRY WEILL

Admission: Adults are $9, senior citizens and students are $6.50, children under age eleven and military are free.

Facilities: This is a bike-friendly facility. Bikers coming in from the Canalway Trail have access to the bathrooms, plus free water bottle fill-up stations, free Wi-Fi, and a bicycle repair kit.

Background: Both the library and the museum at this location owe their origins to Bartlett Arkell (1862–1946), an entrepreneur and industrialist with a passion for the arts. He was responsible for taking a small smoked meat company and turning it into the Beech-Nut Packing Company, which became known worldwide for producing baby food and chewing gum. From the rear windows of the museum, one can see the now-empty grounds of the massive Beech-Nut factory complex.

The library portion of the building was built in 1924, and the museum was added in 1927. Many of the stones used in the construction of the building were taken from an original Erie Canal storehouse.

The museum has grown significantly over the years and was finally expanded in 2006–2007. That massive expansion added two to three times the floor space to the facility, which now has the capacity to display much more of its impressive collection to the public.

The museum houses a great many pieces of artwork collected by Arkell, including some purchased in Europe as well as across the Mohawk Valley in New York State. There are twenty-one artworks by Winslow Homer, the famous American artist, in their collection. Other notable painters and artists represented in their exhibit halls are John Singer Sargent, George Inness, Thomas Eakins, and William Merritt Chase.

The Arkell Museum is very close to the Canalway Trail, thus offering bikers and hikers a quick off-and-on to tour the facility. Visitors should figure on spending one to two hours to enjoy all six galleries inside museum. All tours are self-guided, although guided tours can be arranged.

MOHAWK VALLEY WELCOME CENTER

Location: Accessed from westbound lanes at mile post 187 on the New York State Thruway, between the Fultonville and Canajoharie exits. For boaters, it is located next to Lock 13 on the canal.

Note: This resource is aimed more toward the boaters than the bikers or hikers, because the canal path is not next to the waterway at this point. Instead, it is located on the other side of the Thruway from the canal. There is no pathway (road) crossing under the Thruway, and it is unsafe and illegal to cross the Thruway on foot.

Description of resources: The Mohawk Valley Welcome Center could easily be confused with the many service centers that appear along the Thruway at twenty- to thirty-mile intervals. However, this location is very different in almost every regard. The center, which was built about eight years ago, is jointly managed and operated by Taste of New York (through the New York Department of Agriculture and Markets), and the Liberty ARC.

Boaters are welcome to tie up to the section of canal wall near Lock 13. Unfortunately, there is no water or electrical service available at the site, but it still represents a safe spot to tie up and spend the night.

The Mohawk Valley Welcome Center provides a host of services and educational opportunities through interactive displays. There are several display boards set up inside the building. There is also a trail outside the building that is lined

Mohawk Valley Welcome Center, on the New York State Thruway.
PHOTO BY LARRY WEILL

with signboards explaining the history of the Erie Canal, along with other displays that describe the contributions of local civilians who were influential in the development of the waterway.

Inside the building, visitors can find clean bathrooms, cell phone charging stations, and stands offering free information brochures and maps. All the agriculture products on display are available for purchase. This serves to showcase the numerous varieties of maple syrup, apple butter, honey, jams, baked goods, granolas, barbecue sauces, spices, beef jerky, and more that are raised or produced in New York State

Other resources located outside the Welcome Center are targeted solely at the drivers coming off the Thruway. There are three charging stations for "refilling" electrical vehicles, and at least one is usually available at any given time. Finally, there is also a beautiful ADA-compliant playground available for the kiddies.

Summary: This is a wonderful, convenient stop for boaters or Thruway travelers. Check it out!

THE DAIRY BAR

Phone/Address: (518) 853-4727 / 22 S. Bridge Street, Fonda, NY 12068.

Seasonal: This restaurant is only open from April through September, depending on the weather.

Days/Hours: 11:30 a.m.–9 p.m. every day except Saturday, which is 11:30 a.m.–10 p.m.

Reservations accepted? No.

Restaurant size: Three tables inside and a few more outside.

Outdoor seating: Yes.

Menu items: Despite the appearance and name of this dessert palace, it is also known for serving items that are not dairy and do not melt. The menu also listed numerous appetizing edibles such as hamburgers, cheeseburgers, potato and mac salads, pretzels, and pulled pork sandwiches. Even Philly cheese sandwiches are

Dairy Bar (offseason) in Fonda, New York.
Photo by Larry Weill

on the window menu board. (In case you are interested, it is 272 miles between Fonda, New York, and Philadelphia, Pennsylvania.)

Price range: Almost everything on the lunch menu is around $4–9. Most ice cream dishes and desserts are in the $4–$6 range.

Most popular menu item: Hot dogs with meat sauce, Philly cheesesteaks, and ice cream.

Entertainment: No.

Liquor license: No.

Description: The Dairy Bar is primarily an ice cream stand located directly across the roadway from the Fonda Fairgrounds. This doesn't mean that most of the Dairy Bar's business comes from the Fair (which only operates six days/year), but the location doesn't hurt.

The owner, Jim, has run this ice cream stand for the past forty-six years and has built a large local following. The Dairy Bar is one of those places that offers not only a huge array of ice cream flavors, but also a variety of ways to process it into award-winning desserts. They produce a lengthy list of milkshakes, "slushes," sundaes, and ice cream sodas. Among the "shakes," they advertise the "Boston," the "Hand Made," and the "Malt."

There is also a small arcade attached to the stand to keep the little ones occupied while you eat.

FONDA FAIR

Note: This is a limited-time event. It only runs for six days each year.

Phone/Address: (518) 853-3133 (fair office) / 21 S. Bridge Street, Fonda, NY 12068.

Days/Hours: The 2025 Fair will be held between August 27 and September 1. The hours are 8 a.m.–11 p.m. every day (although the midway has shorter hours).

Admission Fees: $12 general admission, $5 for seniors on Wednesday and Friday, $2 for children ages six to eleven, and free for children under six.

Reservations accepted? No (but tickets are purchased that do the same thing).

View of the end of the grandstand at the Fonda Fair, Fonda, New York.
PHOTO BY LARRY WEILL

Description of resources: The Fonda Fair has been held every year since its inaugural event in 1841. The location has changed several times since its original version, but many of the events remain the same, rooted in tradition.

The Fonda Fair grounds are located in close proximity to the waters of the canal. This is actually one of those spots where the Erie Canal borrows a section of the Mohawk River and claims it as its own, but that happens at times along the route.

Smoking: The entire premises has been designated "nonsmoking," which includes cigarettes, vaping, and that "other stuff." There are a few designated smoking locations for cigarettes inside the fairgrounds. Please be considerate to your fellow visitors and comply with the rules.

Summary: The Fonda Fair is an annual event that is similar in nature to a volcano. The site sits dormant for much of the year, quietly awaiting its period of activity. Then, for one week in late summer, it erupts into a fun-filled, action-packed spectacle that brings in visitors from miles around.

No matter what you enjoy, the Fonda Fair has something for everyone. A list of events would be too long to fit on one page but includes 4-H animal displays and competitions, cut flower demonstrations, tractor pulls, demolition derbies, goat milking, musical group performances, talent shows, bingo and other senior events, antiques, craft vendors, Miss Fonda Pageant, midway rides and other activities, horse and pony rides, "barnyard Olympics," fireworks, sand sculptures, racing pigs, auto engine displays, and so much more.

For more information, visit: www.thefondafair.com

OUR LADY OF MARTYRS SHRINE

Phone/Address: (518) 853-3939 / 136 Shrine Rd #2, Fultonville, NY 12072.

Days/Hours: 10 a.m.–3 p.m. daily, Sunday mass celebrated at 3 p.m. (beginning in May).

General Notes: This shrine is one of the few religious "attractions" in this guidebook. It is located across Route 5S from the Canalway Trail, and is a bit more than the prescribed 445'10" from the from that trail. However, its incredible beauty and the architectural grandeur of the building and grounds is worthy of a viewing.

Directions: If heading east on the Canalway Trail, look for the point where Noeltner Road intersects with Route 5 in Fultonville. Looking up the grassy hill, you will see the impressive statue overlooking the trail and the canal. If boating down the Mohawk River, look for the site to the south about a mile west of where the Mohawk merges with Schoharie Creek.

Statue on the northern slope of the property of Our Lady of Martyrs Shrine in Fultonville, New York.
Photo by Larry Weill

History: Our Lady of Martyrs Shrine is a historic site originally built in 1884 to commemorate the three Jesuit missionaries who were martyred in Ossernenon (a Mohawk Indian village) in 1642 and 1646. Missionaries Rene Goupil, Isaac Jogues, and John LaLande were captured and killed in separate events in 1642 and 1646 while attempting to reach a settlement of Huron Indians in New York. Both met their deaths at the hands of the Mohawks, a tribe of the Iroquois Confederacy who were enemies of the Huron tribe.

The site for the shrine was purchased in 1884 by Father Joseph Loyance, who believed it was the location of the village of Ossernenon. On that site he built the original shrine, which was called Our Lady of Martyrs, and led followers from Albany and Troy to visit and worship. A large round "coliseum" shrine followed, built in 1930, that could hold six thousand worshippers.

The grounds of this shrine encompass approximately six hundred acres, with stunning buildings spread across the site. The grounds are open to visitors from mid-April through mid-November, and all are welcome to conduct self-guided "pilgrimages."

Fees/Admission: There is no mandatory charge for visiting the shrine, although donations are gratefully accepted. There is also a gift shop on the grounds with merchandise and books (and lots more) available for purchase. Proceeds from the sale of the merchandise benefit the upkeep and growth of the shrine.

NELLIS TAVERN

Phone/Address: (315) 866-2619 / 7355 NY-5, St. Johnsville, NY 13452.

Hours: Open every Sunday from 1 p.m. to 4 p.m. from June through September.

Seasonal: As stated above, this museum is only open from June through September.

Admission: Recommended donation is $5.

History: The "Nellis Tavern" was originally built as a farming homestead in 1747. Several reliable sources state that Christian Nellis built the home in 1747. There were several differences between the original construction and the structure that is standing today. The most visible of these differences was the size of the home, which was originally only one and a half stories tall. Also, the "front door" was on the back of the building, as Route 5 did not yet exist. The old front

Nellis Tavern, St. Johnsville, New York.
PHOTO BY LARRY WEILL

door faced the Mohawk River (away from Route 5), and the Erie Canal was still over eighty years in the future.

In 1767 Nellis's son purchased the property and the farmhouse. In 1790, he performed some major renovations, including switching the front door to the other side of the building and adding the completed second floor to the top of the house. Further renovations and construction followed, including a major expansion in 1820. Five rooms were added to the side of the building which enabled it to serve as both a tavern and a hotel.

The Nellis Tavern proceeded to survive through some extremely difficult times. The fact that it withstood the violent battles of the French and Indian War and the Revolutionary War is nothing short of remarkable. (Some people in that day referred to it as a "fort.") Perhaps just as surprising is the resilience of the Nellis Tavern to the brutal weather in the Mohawk Valley region, especially considering that the structure was left to decay after the state condemned it in the 1960s. It is a testament to the superb craftsmanship of the original building, which has finally been restored and preserved for the benefit of the visitors of the current day.

Nellis Tavern today: The Palatine Settlement Society was formed in 1982 to restore a group of properties and structures in the area around St. Johnsville into a living museum. The Nellis Tavern was one of the first buildings that attracted their attention. The project was quite large in scope, as the old wooden building was completely surrounded and engulfed in large trees and vegetation to the point where it was hidden from the road. A great amount of work was performed simply to clear away all the growth so the building could be viewed and evaluated.

The restoration already completed is astounding, and the Nellis Tavern (while not completely finished) is an incredible piece of work. If passing along the Canalway Trail on a Sunday, this museum is definitely with the stop, We are very lucky to still have it in existence today.

FORT KLOCK HISTORIC RESTORATION

Phone/Address: (518) 568-7779 / 7214 NY-5, St. Johnsville, NY 13452.

Seasonal: This museum is open from Columbus Day through Labor Day.

Summer Hours: Open Thursday through Monday 10 a.m.–4 p.m., closed on Tuesday and Wednesday.

Fall hours: Friday through Sunday, 10 a.m.–4 p.m.

Admission: General admission is $10, under age sixteen is free.

History: The site of the Fort Klock Historic Restoration traces its roots back to 1750, when Johannes Klock erected the fortified home for his family. The term *fortified home* is quite justified, as its stone walls are over two feet thick, and gun ports are poked through the walls to provide protected positions from which to shoot. All the windows and gun ports have thick, heavy wooden covers for protection when needed. Some of the original covers are still present inside the home. For additional protection, there is a freshwater spring present in the cellar of the house, thus ensuring the inhabitants would not have to risk venturing outdoors to fetch water in times of crisis.

The house was expanded in the 1760s, during which time a larger kitchen was added and other interior doors, walls, and fireplaces were moved and rebuilt. The fortified house survived both the French and Indian War and the Revolutionary

Fort Klock Historic Restoration, St. Johnsville, New York.
PHOTO BY LARRY WEILL

War, and probably served as a temporary refuge for other local inhabitants through the many local skirmishes. It is thought that the Battle of Klock's Field, which took place in 1780, was fought on land just west of the house.

Although the home stayed in the Klock family until the 1950s, it was vacant for most of the years following the 1930s, during which time the building fell into severe disrepair. In 1953, Willis "Skip" Barshied Jr. and his group, the "Tryon County Muzzleloaders" decided to lease the property and use it for their historical militia-related organization. Their hard work and perseverance led to the fort being opened for tours in 1961, and the rest has been wonderful. In 1973 they were designated as a National Historic Landmark.

Fort Klock today: The Fort Klock Historic Restoration is open to the public five days a week during the summer, and provides tours through the historic buildings on a regular basis. They also conduct many special events throughout the year, including a geneaology day, a basket-weaving class, the Young Pioneers Days, an annual craft fair, and battle reenactments. Many of these events fill up quickly, so call early if interested. The staff really means what they say with their slogan, "Let's Make History Come Alive Together!

FORT PLAIN MUSEUM & HISTORICAL PARK

Phone/Address: (518) 993-2527 / 389 Canal St., Fort Plain, NY 13339.

Days/Hours: Thursday through Monday 10 a.m.–4 p.m., closed on Tuesday and Wednesday.

Admission: Adults $10, children under sixteen and military free.

History: If the building that houses the Fort Plain Museum looks old, it is. The structure was built in 1848 by David Lipe and family and functioned as a residence for many years. It became a museum in 1961 as the Fort Plain Restoration, with a focus on rebuilding the history of the Revolutionary War in the Fort Plain area.

Fort Plain Museum & Historical Park, Fort Plain, New York.
PHOTO BY LARRY WEILL

The grounds on which the museum was built were of great importance to the early security of the Mohawk Valley. The hillside behind the museum was the site of the original Fort Plain, which was also called Fort Rensselaer. It was originally used as an outpost and protective fortification to protect the local families from the British and loyalist Indians. Numerous skirmishes and battles were fought in the region from 1777 to 1783, including the Battle of Oriskany, the Battle of Stone Arabia, and the Battle of Klock's Field. In July 1783, George Washington visited the site and used it as a base camp for touring military installations as far north as Rome.

Modern-day archaeological excavations and discoveries: Excavations began on the site of the hillside fort in 1963 and continued through the 1960s. Numerous artifacts were excavated around the fort and the various outbuildings. Many of these shed light onto the life and times of those days. Further excavations in 1975 uncovered the fort's original stockade, barracks building, a dining hall, officers' quarters, and a small blockhouse.

Exhibits and events: The museum operates today as an educational facility with a focus on Upstate New York and the Mohawk Valley, especially through the years leading up to and following the Revolutionary War. The museum receives about three thousand visitors each year, and also encourages student tours from the local schools.

Plans are in the works to add a ten-thousand-square-foot expansion onto the museum, which will enable them to display a lot of Native American artifacts that are part of their collections.

The museum also hosts a number of special events throughout the summer months, including the Revolutionary War Conference (which is held at the Fulton-Montgomery Community College Theater), and "Rebels, Recoats, & Zombies." For a complete schedule of special events, refer to their website at https://fortplainmuseum.org/viewevent.

FORT PLAIN FREE PUBLIC LIBRARY

Phone/Address: (518) 993-4646 / 19 Willett St., Fort Plain, NY 13339.

Hours: Open on Monday, Tuesday, Wednesday, and Friday from 10 a.m. to 5 p.m., Thursday from 10 a.m. to 7 p.m., Saturday from 10 a.m. to 1 p.m., closed on Sunday.

Fort Plain Free Public Library, Fort Plain, New York.
PHOTO BY LARRY WEILL

Seasonal: No. The library is open to users all year long.

Admission: Free.

History: The concept for establishing a library in the town of Fort Plain was the idea of the Women's Library Association, which was a literary society organized in 1885 by Martha A. Bortel. Bortel had been an educator, lecturer, and Universalist minister who taught at the Bortle Seminary in Rochester, New York from 1871 to 1879. From there, she moved to Fort Plain and served as an instructor at the Clinton Liberal Institute. It was there, in 1885, that she founded the Fort Plain Free Public Library.

The library's collection of books was started in a Fort Plain home, where many of the town's citizens contributed to a large book donation. Even though the library lacked a permanent home, they were able to find a librarian in the person of Mrs. Maria Langdon, who used her own residence to house the initial collections.

The Fort Plain Free Public Library was housed in several temporary buildings until 1909, when James and Harvey Williams donated a house to the library association. The Greek Revival building was located at the corner of Willett and River Streets. It was built in 1836 and still serves as the Fort Plain Free Library.

The site today (including services): The current library houses over ten thousand volumes, and is part of the greater Mohawk Valley Library System. This means that library users can search and access books and research materials from thirteen other area libraries, including those in Amsterdam, Canajoharie (and Arkell Museum), Cobleskill, Fort Hunter, Fonda, Gloversville, Johnstown, St. Johnsville, Middleburgh, Northville, Schoharie, Sharon Springs, and Schenectady.

Many hikers and bikers coming off the Canalway Trail make use of this library, which opens its doors and facilities to the trail users. The library offers free library cards to everyone and also permits visitors to use their computers. (Users must be thirteen years old and have a valid email address to apply for a library card.) Even if you only stop in to rest, or to use the park across the street, you are more than welcome. Service animals are also welcome.

Donations: Even though the library is free, donations are welcome and always appreciated. They are used to expand the book collection and to refurbish and expand the library building.

YANKEE HILL LOCK 28 AND PUTMAN STORE

Location: The Yankee Hill Lock is at the eastern entrance to the Schoharie Crossing State Historic Site (on the western end). The GPS address to enter for this site is 550 Queen Ann Road, Amsterdam.

Hours: This portion of the site is open daily from dawn to dusk.

Admission: Free.

History: The Putman Store was built in 1856 and operated by Garret Putman. He had purchased the land almost a decade earlier when he learned that the Erie Canal would be enlarged, with a new lock to be constructed at that spot. His store was conveniently located on the canal towpath, making it the perfect place to sell provisions to the men who shepherded the boats and barges through the waterway. Additionally, workers and passengers on the boats could purchase

Putman Store, at the site of Lock 28, Amsterdam, New York.

whatever supplies they needed, and feed for the horses and mules could also be purchased at the store.

At that site is Yankee Hill Lock 28, which was a double lock built to accommodate boats going in either direction on the canal. It opened in the 1850s and remained in service until the early 1900s. The Putman Store did a booming business through the last half of the nineteenth century until the decline of shipping on the canal. Once the Barge Canal opened in the Mohawk River, the store closed down, circa 1917.

After the Putman family shuttered the store, there is some record of other interests renting the building, which kept it open in other capacities. There are also stories about this building having connections to Prohibition-era activity, although this cannot be confirmed. Later efforts by community groups and then departments within the New York State government stepped in to provide restoration works that kept this piece of history intact.

The site today (including services): The original Lock 28 still sits on the enlarged canal and is slated to undergo restoration. Meanwhile, the reconstructed Putman Store rests on land about two hundred feet from the Canalway Trail. Cyclists use the covered front porch as a resting place, especially during inclement weather. The site has an ADA-configured porta-potty present in the summer for cyclists and others traveling on the trail. There are also picnic tables and hibachis there for public use, along with bike racks and a kayak rack.

RUSSO'S GRILL

Phone/Address: (518) 842-2630 / 365 W. Main St., Amsterdam, NY 12010.

Days/Hours: Monday through Wednesday 11 a.m.–8 p.m., Thursday through Saturday 11 a.m.–9 p.m., Sunday noon–8 p.m.

Reservations accepted? Yes.

Restaurant size: About twenty-five tables.

Outdoor seating: No.

Menu items: The menu lists nine different appetizers, including their "Brick Oven Meatballs," and their famous Greens & Beans. They also feature seven different salads, including a large and elaborate Sicilian antipasto dish, along with hot and cold sandwiches, burgers, pasta dishes, pizzas, and a number of Italian classics. These include chicken/veal/eggplant Parmesan, stuffed eggplant, and stuffed shells melanzane, which is giant pasta shells filled with creamy ricotta cheese and homemade marinara sauce.

Price range: Appetizers run from $11 to $18, salads range from $12 to $27, most sandwiches are around $12, pasta dishes range from $15 to $20, and pizzas list from $10 to $18, although their signature pizzas can be up to $27.

Most popular menu item: "The Special" pizza, which is sausage, mushroom, and anchovies.

Entertainment: No.

Liquor license: Yes.

Description: Russo's Grill is a very friendly, "homey" restaurant that just makes people feel like they belong there. It's been in business since 1920, and all in the same family, so they know how to do it right! When asked about their longevity, the bartender is quick to point out that there was a short break in their continuous service. During the flood of 2011, when a good part of Amsterdam was underwater, they had to close for four months to make repairs due to the high water that infiltrated their bar and dining room.

Russo's Grill, Amsterdam, New York.
Photo by Larry Weill

Russo's has a very interesting and unique history. Through its earlier years in the 1920s, it functioned as a speakeasy, serving alcohol during Prohibition. Women were supposedly not permitted in the bar, although the nurses from St. Mary's did somehow find their way into the back of the pub where they were served.

Russo's is very proud that all their food is fresh every day and their breads are all homemade.

MOHAWK VALLEY GATEWAY OVERLOOK PEDESTRIAN BRIDGE

Address: 1 Bridge Street, Amsterdam, NY 12010.

Hours: All day every day.

Seasonal: The bridge is open from spring until the first snowfall of the winter.

Access: The bridge is located a couple hundred feet from the Canalway Trail on the south side of the river.

Mohawk Valley Gateway Overlook Pedestrian Bridge, Amsterdam, New York.
PHOTO BY LARRY WEILL

Background: This artistic and historic marvel is not only a landmark of the Amsterdam community, but also a proud tribute to the entire Mohawk Valley. The idea for a bridge connecting the north part of the town to the south began in 2003 with a waterfront revitalization plan. Completed in the summer of 2016, it is the culmination of a full decade of collaboration, planning, designing, and construction.

The concept for this project was immediately embraced by the residents of the city and its leadership. The main concern of the populace was to design a large, open area that would serve as an outdoor gathering place that would bring together the neighborhoods on opposite sides of the river. More than simply a bridge, the designers attempted to create a living, breathing "park over the water." They also wanted to include major pieces of art (sculptures and interpretive displays) that represented the cultures of all inhabitants of the area, both past and current.

The bridge is over five hundred feet long and thirty feet wide and spans from the north to the south sides of the Mohawk River. Two of the first things to notice about the bridge is that it is not straight, but curved. Secondly, it is adorned with sculptures and other artistic works across its entire length. The curved form is to represent the shape of the river itself as it snakes through the landscape of the region. The works of art represent different facets of the community and its people across not only decades but many millennia.

Approaching the bridge from the south, the first things you will notice are the tall, wavelike gates on either side of the entrance walkway. A large metallic sculpture of a mother and child in a swirling, aquatic setting graces the circular viewing area immediately to the right. Continuing across the bridge you will encounter a series of twelve different stations, each with its own artwork representing another facet of the history of Amsterdam and its inhabitants, reaching back over five thousand years to its Native American ancestors.

This attraction is unique to the city of Amsterdam and is right next to the overlook, so it's worth your while to take a detour of a few minutes and check it out.

GUGE'S DOGS

Phone/Address: (518) 212-2679 / 43 Bridge St., Amsterdam, NY 12010.

Days/Hours: Monday through Saturday, 7 a.m.–2 p.m., closed on Sunday.

Reservations accepted? No.

Restaurant size: Eight tables.

Outdoor seating: No.

Menu items: Breakfast sandwiches, breakfast wraps, Monte Cristo sandwiches, home fries, hash brown patties, hot dogs served six or seven different ways, hamburgers, and chicken sandwiches.

Price range: Most of Guge's breakfasts are $6–$7. For lunch, the hot dogs are $3–$4.50 and the burgers are $6–$7.50.

Most popular menu item: Hot dogs with their homemade meat sauce.

Entertainment: Yes (they do sometimes have a band playing in the summer months).

Liquor license: No.

Guge's Dogs in Amsterdam, New York.
PHOTO BY LARRY WEILL

Description: Guge's is a popular Amsterdam restaurant and stopping place for bicyclists along the Canalway Trail. First and foremost, it is a hot dog stand, one of which the owner (Joe) is justifiably proud.

"We're only three years old here," said Joe. "We got started as an actual hot dog stand and then moved up to a full concession trailer. But we've always done well because people around here really love our food."

Working out of a mobile stand had its challenges, but Joe always found ways to overcome them. "In the beginning, people wanted our dogs for lunch but didn't know where to find our stand on any given day because we moved around. So I started posting our location on Facebook so our customers could find us."

The name "Guge's" comes from Joe's last name, which is Gugliemelli, and he really has a large local following. Everyone who comes into his store seems to know his name and has a personal connection to him. It's not only personal loyalty; people just love his hot dogs and meat sauce.

Guge's is mainly a breakfast and lunch spot, but they also stay open for festivals and special events. It's located right near the river and the Canalway Trail, so stop in and grab a dog!

VALENTINO'S RESTAURANT

Phone/Address: (518) 843-0592 / 110 Riverside Drive, Amsterdam, NY 12010.

Days/Hours: Monday through Saturday 4 p.m.–9 p.m., Sunday noon–8 p.m.

Reservations accepted? Yes.

Restaurant size: About thirty-five tables (including some large-capacity tables, plus bar seating.

Outdoor seating: Yes.

Menu items: A choice of ten appetizers (including frog legs), several seafood and grill dishes (including broiled or fried sea scallops, fresh salmon, and jumbo fried shrimp. The menu also features an assortment of French cuisine dishes as well. These include coquilles St. Jacques, frog legs, and steak au poive, which is steak covered with crushed peppers and flamed with cognac and cream. They also offer eleven different Italian pasta specialties.

Price range: Appetizers range from $10 to $13, the Italian pasta specialties are $18–$22, the French specialties are $25–$29, and the osso buco is $34.95.

Most popular menu item: Osso buco, which is a two-inch-thick veal shank slowly braised with fresh vegetables, wine, tomatoes, broth, and fine herbs. Another favorite at this restaurant is the cavatelli with homemade braciole.

Entertainment: No.

Liquor license: Yes.

Description: The restaurant currently called Valentino's has been in operation as a restaurant for a very long time. Once called "The Tower Inn," it traces its roots back to 1936. The building still looks much as it did almost ninety years ago, although both the owner and the menu have changed.

Vittorio, the new owner of Valentino's, has used his culinary training to bring high-end Italian and French cuisine to the area. Vittorio served overseas when he was a young man working for an American delegation in France. Following that

Valentino's Restaurant, Amsterdam, New York.
PHOTO BY LARRY WEILL

duty, he studied cooking at the famous Cordon Bleu, where he earned his basic diploma in the culinary arts.

Valentino's is a wonderful representation of Vittorio's vision of French and Italian cuisine. It is a large restaurant where seating is usually available. They also offer a great lineup of decadent desserts (how about a piece of chocolate mousse layer cake?), just in case you can still fit it in!

LORENZO'S SOUTHSIDE

Phone/Address: (518) 212-2256 / 1 Port Jackson Square, Amsterdam, NY 12010.

Days/Hours: Wednesday through Saturday 4 p.m.–9 p.m., Sunday 4 p.m.–8 p.m., closed on Monday and Tuesday.

Reservations accepted? Yes.

Lorenzo's Southside, Amsterdam, New York.
PHOTO BY LARRY WEILL

Restaurant size: This is a large restaurant that seats 190 diners inside and another 100 outside.

Outdoor seating: Yes.

Menu items: Seven different appetizers (all Italian), three salads, four panuozzo (Italian sandwiches), seven pasta dishes, and lots of pizzas. There were also nine specials listed including appetizers, salads, soups, and entrées.

Price range: The appetizers were listed from $10 to $20, salads from $15 to $20, pizzas from $15 to $19, and the pasta dishes from $24 to $30.

Most popular menu item: Their hand-made meatballs, which are "the best ever."

Entertainment: Yes (on city festival days).

Liquor license: Yes.

Description: This popular Italian restaurant has been a fixture in Amsterdam for over one hundred years. It was all started by the owner's grandfather as "Lanzi's" on Bridge Street. The current owner of Lorenzo's Southside is Joe Lanzi, who loves everything about the business, his staff, and his customers. Lanzi explained how four generations of his family have contributed to the growth of the restaurant dynasty in their family. He is an absolute fanatic about offering high-quality authentic Italian food in his place. They make their own pasta and pizzas from scratch with ingredients imported directly from Italy. Nothing is taken for granted; it's all genuine Italian.

Joe enjoys telling the story of his grandfather's restaurant that operated through the Prohibition era. "He was arrested fourteen times," said Joe with a smile. "But he always paid someone else to do his jail time!"

The Lanzis operate five restaurants in the area, and they are all a little different. For example, they run a restaurant on Sacandaga Lake that specializes in "beach food." However, Lorenzo's Southside is the place you want to be if you are on the Erie Canal or the Canalway Trail, which goes right by their front door. You can't help but love their food!

MICHAEL'S DINER

Phone/Address: (518) 853-3549 / 26 S. Main St., Fultonville, NY 12072.

Days/Hours: Monday through Friday 7 a.m.–1 p.m., Saturday 7 a.m.–11 a.m., closed on Sunday.

Reservations accepted? No.

Restaurant size: Six tables plus a lot of counter seats.

Outdoor seating: No.

Menu items: Standard diner fare for breakfast and lunch. The breakfast includes seven egg dishes, six breakfast sandwiches, six options of pancakes or French Toast, and the full array of extras and side orders, including bacon, sausages, home fries, and lots more. The lunch menu includes five different varieties of burgers, fifteen sandwiches, eight grilled sandwiches, and five salads.

Price range: The breakfast sandwiches are $4–$6, egg dishes are $4–$7, and pancakes or French Toast ranges between $5 and $8. On the lunch menu, burgers are $5–$7, and all sandwiches (regular and grilled) are $3–$6.

Michael's Diner, Fultonville, New York.
PHOTO BY LARRY WEILL

Most popular menu item: Biscuits and gravy.

Entertainment: No.

Liquor license: No.

Description: Michael's Diner is a great little place (and the only diner) in the small town of Fultonville. It is filled every day with a loyal band of patrons who come for Michael's food as well as his personality. This is only natural, as one of the biggest attractions of Michael's Diner is Michael himself. When asked what their most popular item was, Michael proudly stated "my sarcasm and my personality." Michael is a marvelous one-man-show who has created this local establishment and run it for the past seventeen years. Working with the assistance of just a cook, he seems to keep everyone happy and well fed on a daily basis.

You have to read this: In addition to serving up daily portions of great breakfast and lunch food at great prices, Michael is also a host of the warmshowers.org organization. This wonderful group of benefactors welcomes cyclists into their homes to use their personal bathrooms and showers, as well as allowing them to pitch a tent in their yard. Go to their website (above) to read more.

KAREN'S ICE CREAM AND PRODUCE

Phone/Address: (518) 829-7397 / 2311 NY-5S, Tribes Hill, NY 12010.

Days/Hours: Monday 3 p.m.–9 p.m., Tuesday through Sunday 11 a.m.–9 p.m.

Reservations accepted? No.

Restaurant size: Twelve large picnic tables inside (between two rooms) and eight tables outside.

Outdoor seating: Yes, in summer.

Menu items: Lots of ice cream choices, including hard and soft-serve ice cream cones, flurries, sundaes, banana splits, milkshakes, and floats. On the day of my

Karen's Ice Cream and Produce, Tribes Hill, New York.
Photo by Larry Weill

visit, the chalkboard listed thirty-eight flavors of Hershey's ice cream! From the grill they offer hot dogs, burgers and cheeseburgers, regular fries, waffle fries, and more. They also have additional food items on display inside their covered dining area (to the right of the ice cream window), where they sell a large array of jams, jellies, pies, and produce (when in season).

Price range: Ice cream cones are $2.60–$3.10 for baby size, $3.10–$3.60 for regular, and $3.85–$4.35 for large. Pints go for $4.85–$5.55, sundaes range from $3.60 to $5.60, a banana split is $6.10, and milkshakes are $3.60–$4.60. Items off the grill include hot dogs at $2.30–$2.55, hamburgers and cheeseburgers are $5.90–$6.70, and extra add-ons are slightly higher. You can also order grilled cheese sandwiches for $4.85–$6.25, different varieties of fries from $3.50 to $4.00, and chicken tenders for $6.50.

Most popular menu item: Burgers, and also sweet corn and peas from their produce section (when in season).

Entertainment: Yes (music outside in the summer months).

Liquor license: No.

Description: This roadside store has been in the owner's family for twenty-two years now, and its popularity just keeps increasing every season. It is located directly across NY Route 5S from the Canalway Trail and attracts a crowd of bikers to sample their ice cream and meals off the grill.

This truly is a family gathering spot, with large picnic tables available both inside and out. In addition to the jars of jams and jellies for sale inside the covered area, they also offer a large selection of Smith's Orchard Pies, including mouthwatering flavors like Apple Crumb, Apple Blackberry, Raspberry Peach, and Blueberry Crumb. You've got to try one, they're irresistible.

SCHENECTADY COUNTY

HUNGRY CHICKEN COUNTRY STORE

Phone/Address: (518) 879-9442 / 661 River Rd., Schenectady, NY 12306.

Hours: Monday through Friday 7 a.m.–4 p.m., Saturday and Sunday 8 a.m.–5 p.m.

Location: This unique store is located on the northwest side of Schenectady, on the south side of Route 5S, It is located directly across the road from the Rotterdam Kiwanis Park.

Description: This is another place that you just have to visit to truly understand and appreciate. Sitting beside the road and the bike trail, it has become a standard stopping place for bikers as they pedal by on their excursions. The Hungry Chicken is still more of a store than it is a restaurant, although it is filled with good things to eat and drink as well.

Hungry Kitchen Country Store, Schenectady, New York.
Photo by Larry Weill

The merchandise inside the story covers the gamut of food, art, decorations, and everything in between. Whether you want coffee, baked goods, salad dressing, or a birdhouse, you'll find it all inside. Almost everything for sale comes from local artists, most of which come from their own personal workshops. The owner (Louise) personally creates jams, candles, and knitted goods. Her son makes the birdhouses that are displayed in the store. There truly is something for everyone.

The rest of the story: Louise and her husband, Jeff, purchased the property in 2016. It had been a store in prior years, but the previous owners had moved on and left the building vacant. It sat for many years before the industrious couple decided to buy it and become shopkeepers. This was not an easy task, as the building had been empty for so long and required significant work to recondition the inside and outside.

Another project the new owners tackled after moving in was to rehab and expand the existing apple orchard, which is located on the hillside behind the store. This has been immensely successful and has supplied them with enough apples to produce about 350 gallons of cider every year. Bikers coming off the trail have come to enjoy this drink and stop in specifically for this liquid refreshment. Plans are in store to produce hard cider sometime in the near future.

Food is also available inside the store. Their six different breakfast sandwiches (including a gluten-free variety) are favorites, and they now also offer chicken sandwiches and hot dogs.

Boaters can also access the Hungry Chicken Country Store if they are staying across the river in the campground. If they have bicycles, they can cross the river on the Route 890 bridge (about one mile east). Anyone with a lunch can use the picnic tables which are set out on the grass in front of the store. Well-behaved dogs are welcome too, and dog treats are sold inside the store.

MABEE FARM HISTORIC SITE

Phone/Address: (518) 374-0263 / 1100 Main St., Rotterdam Junction, NY 12150.

Seasonal: This attraction is open for its season from July through September.

Hours: Winter (from September 1 through June 30) Friday and Saturday, 11 a.m.–4 p.m. Summer hours (from July 1 through August 31) Wednesday through Saturday, 11 a.m.–4 p.m.

Mabee Farm Historic Site, Rotterdam Junction, New York.
PHOTO BY LARRY WEILL

Admission: $10 for adults, children and students (with ID) free.

History: The Mabee Farm Historic Site is a genuine working museum and is the oldest farm in the entire Mohawk Valley. It was established in 1705 by Jan Mabee and Anna Boorsboom, who moved into the area when it was true wilderness frontier. They lived in this location along with eight children and fourteen African slaves, who helped raise the early buildings and plant the crops.

The Mabee Farm would expand and thrive over the next three centuries under the control of the Mabees and generations of their offspring. It has been noted that, while the names and histories of their children are well documented, much less is known about their slaves, who toiled on the farm and helped to build this cherished landmark. Current efforts are underway to research this part of the farm's history so it can be added to the story of the farm.

About the surviving farm: The grounds are home to three eighteenth-century houses along with a Dutch barn, numerous animal buildings and pens, a family cemetery, and the impressive Franchere Education Center. There is also a dock on the river (which runs directly along the property border) with an eighteenth-century bateau (which is a reproduction).

Activities and tours: The Mabee Farm Historic Site conducts regular tours throughout the day and also provides numerous activities across its grounds. In the winter hours tours are conducted on Friday and Saturday at 11 a.m., 1:30 p.m., and 3 p.m. Summer tours are conducted from Wednesday through Saturday, also at 11 a.m., 1:30 p.m., and 3 p.m.

Visitors should also plan on spending some time inside the Franchere Education Center, which hosts a number of display galleries and educational exhibits for public viewing. The center also houses a community room, meeting rooms, and a classroom, in addition to a climate-controlled storage facility for historical artifacts.

Special events: The Mabee Farm Historic Site also sponsors other special events throughout the year. Past events have included a "Cider & Moonshine at the Mabee Inn" day, an "Earth Night at Mabee Farm," and more. Tickets may be required in advance for any of these events.

Access: All buildings except for the Brick House are wheelchair accessible.

JUMPIN' JACK'S DRIVE-IN

Phone/Address: (518) 393-6101 / 5 Schonowee Ave., Scotia, NY 12302.

Days/Hours: 11 a.m.–9 p.m., every day.

Note: This restaurant is seasonal. It opens every year on the last Thursday in March and closes the day before Labor Day.

Reservations accepted? No.

Restaurant size: Forty-three tables (picnic size).

Outdoor seating: Yes (there is no indoor seating).

Menu items: The menu includes lots of varieties of burgers, fish fry and clam fry, sandwiches, chicken and beef dinners, and fish and shrimp dishes. The building located right next to the main restaurant is the dessert building, where they serve ice cream, cone dips, "freezes" (with your choice of chopped cookies, M&M's, Reese's Pieces, Snickers, or Butterfingers), milkshakes, floats, and slush puppies. Oh, and let's not forget the banana splits!

Jumpin' Jack's Drive-in, Scotia, New York.
PHOTO BY LARRY WEILL

Price range: Basic hamburgers are $3.75, most other burgers (with extras) are $4–$7, fish fry and clam fry sandwiches are $5.75, and the larger dinner plates (beef, chicken, shrimp, or fish) range from $12 to $15. Jackburgers (see below) are $8.25.

Most popular menu item: The "Jackburger," which is a hamburger and a cheeseburger (the cheese is in the middle) served on a three-decker sesame roll with coleslaw on top.

Entertainment: Yes (music at least three days a week, plus waterskiing shows on the river).

Liquor license: No.

Description: Jumpin' Jack's Drive-in is such a cool place. It wasn't originally going to be included in this guidebook until I visited for the first time. In addition to the great food and ice cream, the place is simply loaded with nostalgia from "the old days," although people of all ages love coming here. It's been operating at this location since 1952. The current owner is Mark Lansing, who has worked there for thirty-four years. "Making customers happy is number one," he says proudly. It's a strategy that has obviously worked well, as they have over thirty thousand Facebook followers.

There are plenty of picnic tables outside, which are beautifully stained and laminated. Diners enjoy coming to Jumpin' Jack's and just hanging out. "Lots of first dates happened here" says Lansing. "We've even had a bunch of them end up getting married!"

There is a lot to see here; it's as much about the experience as it is about the eating.

KNOTTY PINE HOUSE

Phone/Address: (518) 887-2281 / 1216 Main St., Rotterdam Junction, NY 12150.

Days/Hours: The hours can vary from day to day, but they are generally open on Wednesday through Saturday from 10 a.m. to midnight, and on Monday and Tuesday from noon to 9 p.m. Call ahead on the day of your visit to confirm.

Note: If you search for this pub online, you may see a note saying that the Knotty Pine is closed. This is not true. Both the pub and the kitchen are still open.

Reservations accepted? No.

Restaurant size: Six tables inside plus additional tables outside (in back and on the side).

Outdoor seating: Yes.

Menu items and prices: Chicken wings $14, chicken tenders $9, fish fry $8, poppers $7, deep-fried pickles $7, breaded mushrooms $8, mozzarella sticks $7, French fries $4, onion rings $6, tater tots $4, and salted pretzel with cheese sauce $5.

Most popular menu item: Chicken wings.

Entertainment: Yes (live music, plus horseshoes on Wednesday or cornhole if it is raining).

Knotty Pine House, Rotterdam Junction, New York.
PHOTO BY LARRY WEILL

Liquor license: Yes

Description: The Knotty Pine House is the local pub that residents of the area visit for a laid-back lunch of wings and a cold brew. Kelly (and her husband) have run the place as owners for the past twenty-five years, although it's been in the family for fifty-five years. It was started by their parents, who owned a tavern on the opposite side of the river. They had the first live music of any bar in the area.

Today, this is still a place you can visit if you want to take time off the canal and come in for a quick meal and a drink. It is almost entirely patronized by locals, but everyone is welcome. The menu is small, but inexpensive and filled with all the "pub food" favorites.

One last note: This pub has hours that sometimes fluctuate based on how many people are still inside. Call ahead to confirm they are still open before visiting.

BLATNICK PARK

Phone/Address: (518) 386-4504 / 2545 River Rd., Niskayuna, NY 12309.

Days/Hours: Monday through Friday, 9 a.m.–4 p.m. Look online for updates.

Admission: Free, except the bark park requires a paid dog park permit card. To obtain a permit, call the Town Clerk's Office, at (518) 386-4510. (Local residents pay $30 for their first dog and $15 for additional animals. Nonresident fee is $100.)

Pavilion rental fees: Residents can rent a pavilion for groups of twenty or more for $180.

Background: Blatnick Park is a spacious tract of land that offers a great many activities to many kinds of users. It was originally a stone quarry that was made into a public park in the 1960s. It still holds a beautiful waterfall that flows down a rocky gorge that is often photographed by nature viewers.

Blatnick Park, Niskayuna, New York.
PHOTO BY LARRY WEILL

For those who are hiking or biking along the Canalway Trail, the trail literally crosses over the main entrance to this park. One of the public restrooms is located along the road immediately next to the park entrance.

Facilities: Blatnick Park contains an almost endless array of facilities for grownups, children, and pets. Most of these are available for use without an admission fee, which makes its proximity to the Canalway Trail all that much better. These facilities and services include:

- Splash park for the kids
- Playgrounds
- Softball fields
- Tennis courts
- Driving range (just south of the park, enter at the Recycling Center)
- Hockey rink
- Bark park
- Basketball courts
- Disc golf course
- Ponds
- Picnic pavilions
- Open restrooms for use by all travelers

Remember: If you carry it in, carry it out!

BROUWER HOUSE CREATIVE

Note: This house, which is now owned by the Schenectady Historical Society, is operated as a store for a small group of local artists and craftspersons. It does not provide historical tours of the building. To check for hours of operation, go to https://www.sweetsprig.com.

Phone/Address: (518) 374-0263 / 14 N. Church Street, Schenectady, NY 12305.

Days/Hours: Wednesday through Friday noon–5 p.m., Saturday and Sunday 11 a.m.–4 p.m., closed on Monday and Tuesday.

Admission: Free.

Front entrance to the Brouwer House, Schenectady, New York.
PHOTO BY LARRY WEILL

Historical background: Many people claim that the Brouwer House is the oldest residence in Schenectady. There is a historical marker in front of the Yates House on Union Street that makes the same claim, and there is often debate regarding the order in which they were completed. Evidence points back to the period of time between the 1720s and 1730s, with various bits of archaeological and architectural evidence, combined with historical documentation. Regardless, they are both fascinating remnants of the earliest residential buildings inside the Stockade District of Schenectady.

Stepping inside the Brouwer House you are immediately impressed by the wide wooden floor planks that cover the front room. They are extremely wide and are reported to be part of the original structure. Other parts of the front room, including the beams and the framing of the fireplace, have reportedly been replaced over the years, but some of the wood is still original.

At one time, the lower level was divided into three small apartments. Those were torn out in later years when the newer owners tried to restore some of the original structure to the house. However, it was determined that a full restoration to the 1700s configuration would have been cost-prohibitive, and the idea was abandoned.

The house was last owned by Fred and Catherine Kindl, who passed away in 2009 and 2016, respectively. It was their wish, aided by the efforts of their four daughters, that the house should be donated to the Schenectady Historical Society to be managed as a historical site in perpetuity.

The Brouwer House today: This historical residence today serves as a craft store for local artists to display and sell their creations. It is called "Brouwer House Creative," and the main store on the lower level is Sweet Sprig. The shop makes and sells scented candles, soap bars, sachets, and skin care products. The attendant also has access to historical information, in case you are interested during your visit.

JOHNNY'S

Phone/Address: (518) 982-5657 / 433 State St., Schenectady, NY 12305.

Days/Hours: Tuesday through Saturday, 5 p.m.–9 p.m., closed on Sunday and Monday.

Happy hour: Although the restaurant is not open until 5 p.m., the bar opens at 4 p.m. for happy hour.

Reservations accepted? Yes (and highly recommended).

Restaurant size: About forty tables inside (plus twenty-six bar seats). They also have a private party room (seats up to fifty people). Their front patio has another ten tables.

Outdoor seating: Yes, in summer.

Menu items: Choice of nine appetizers, including fried calamari and "Frankie's wings." They offer a soup

Johnny's, Schenectady, New York.
PHOTO BY LARRY WEILL

de jour and several substantial salads. Their main entrée list starts off with thirteen classic Italian dishes including chicken cacciatore and lobster alla Elena. Their carne (steak) offerings include five meals that range from a "Sicilian Cowboy Burger" to "Filet Madagascar." Finally, they offer a full lineup of authentic Italian pasta dishes that are all fully homemade along with their sauces.

Price range: Appetizers are $12–$18, the salads are $10–$14, the main course Italian entrées range from $24 to $39, the carne dishes list from $8 to $14, and the pasta dishes are $6–$19.

Most popular menu item: The most popular appetizer is their Italian nachos, and the most popular dinner entrée is the chicken Parmesan.

Entertainment: Yes (music on Thursday night once per month).

Liquor license: Yes.

Description: Johnny's is a long-standing landmark for Italian food in Schenectady. Joe Mallozzi (current manager) is the son of Johnny, who founded the restaurant back in 1965. It has remained a proud family business that describes itself as a "casual Italian American family restaurant with a very upscale dining experience."

Joe Mallozzi's grandfather, who was also named Joe, started the nearby Villa Italia Bakery, which still bakes all the breads and desserts served in the restaurant. This is a genuine first-class dining experience that is well worth the stop.

MING'S FLAVOR CHINESE RESTAURANT

Phone/Address: (518) 347-1288 / 9 Mohawk Ave., Scotia, NY 12302.

Days/Hours: Tuesday through Sunday, 10:30 a.m.–10 p.m., closed on Monday.

Reservations accepted? No.

Restaurant size: Four tables.

Outdoor seating: No.

Menu items: The menu at Ming's Flavor Chinese Restaurant lists a seemingly endless lineup of Chinese favorites. They show a choice of twenty appetizers, nine soups, five chow mein dishes, seven lo meins, seventeen chicken entrées, twelve pork selections, fifteen beef dishes, sixteen seafood plates, twenty-five "Ming Special" plates, and twenty-seven special "combination dinners."

Ming's Flavor Chinese Restaurant, Schenectady, New York.
PHOTO BY LARRY WEILL

Price range: Appetizers are between $2 and $14 (for the "Pu Pu Platter for Two"). Chow mein and lo mein dishes are mostly $7 for a pint and $11 for a quart. Chicken and pork dinners are $7.75 for a pint and $11.95 per quart. Seafood dinners are $8.15 for a pint and $13.15 for a quart. The combination dinners are $9.95, and the Ming's Specials range between $13 and $15.

Most popular menu item: The two most popular dishes on the menu are the Sesame Chicken and the General Tso's Chicken.

Entertainment: No

Liquor license: No

Description: Ming's Flavor Chinese Restaurant is very much a local take-out spot where people order ahead and take their food home for consumption. The menu is quite extensive and offers almost everything you'd expect to see in a Chinese restaurant.

It is located very close to the canal, opposite Jumpin' Jack's Drive-in. It is not really meant to be a "dine-in" restaurant, but many boaters on the canal and bikers on the Canalway Trail will find it to be a convenient stop, especially for those who are fans of Chinese food.

MORE PERRECA'S

Phone/Address: (518) 377-9800 / 31 N. Jay St., Schenectady, NY 12305.

Days/Hours: Wednesday and Thursday 11 a.m.–7 p.m., Friday 11 a.m.–8 p.m., Saturday 10 a.m.–8 p.m., Sunday 10 a.m.–7 p.m., closed Monday and Tuesday.

Reservations accepted? Yes.

Restaurant size: About twenty tables plus seating at tables on the rear patio.

Outdoor seating: Yes.

Menu items: Perreca's serves breakfast, lunch, and dinner. Their breakfast selections include egg dishes, frittatas, and buttermilk pancakes. Later in the day, they offer a number of salads, sandwiches, and tomato pie paninis.

Price range: Most breakfast selections are $12–$13, brunch favorites run from $12 to $17, sandwiches are $11–$13, salads are $6–$16, and tomato pies are $13–$14.

Most popular menu item: Their signature dish is "Eggs in Purgatory," which is three poached eggs in a spicy tomato sauce served with toasted Perreca's bread.

Entertainment: No.

Liquor license: Yes.

Description: More Perreca's has been open for fifteen years and derives its name from the bakery located right next door. Perreca's Bakery was founded over one hundred years ago and is famous for its unparalleled Italian bread and tomato pie. The tomato pie is made with a bread crust and topped with red sauce and grated cheese, which is then served at room temperature. The bread at Perreca's Bakery is baked in an old-time wood-fired brick oven. It contributes to the authentic feel of the Italian meals, reminiscent of any Italian grandmother's kitchen.

Not only is Perreca's a family restaurant, but the employees have become part of the family as well. Employees at this establishment tend to stick around for a

More Perreca's, Schenectady, New York.
PHOTO BY LARRY WEILL

while, and most of the staff is long term. "This is a good thing," said the manager, "as the customers get used to everyone who works here. Everyone knows everyone, and we're all family."

Wednesday at More Perreca's is "Wine Wednesday" with half-price bottles of all wines.

RIVER ROAD HOUSE RESTAURANT

Phone/Address: (518) 214-4136 / 989 River Rd., Schenectady, NY 12306.

Days/Hours: Tuesday through Friday 11 a.m.–9 p.m., Saturday and Sunday noon–9 p.m., closed on Monday.

Reservations accepted? Yes.

Restaurant size: Ten tables inside with an additional six tables outside. There are even more picnic tables set out on the grass by the canal.

River Road House Restaurant, Schenectady, New York.
PHOTO BY LARRY WEILL

Outdoor seating: Yes.

Menu items: Choice of fourteen appetizers, including duck wings, nachos, and truffle fries. There is also a choice of four pizzas (with lots of toppings), and five salads. "Non-specialty pizzas" are $6 for a six-slice pizza, $14 for an eight-slice pizza, and $15 for a twelve-slice pizza. The menu also lists twelve sandwiches (including clam rolls and street tacos), and a choice of twelve dinner entrées. These include a Road House Steak and Shrimp & Scallop Alfredo.

Price range: Appetizers range in price from $6 to $14, large pizzas are $20–$23, and salads (main course) are $14–$16. The sandwiches range from $12 to $14, and the dinner entrées are from $11 (for pasta and meatballs) to $25 (for a "Black and Bleu Steak").

Most popular menu item: Wings, especially on Tuesday nights ("wings night!").

Entertainment: No.

Liquor license: Yes.

Description: People enjoy the atmosphere of the River Road House Restaurant because it reminds them of *Cheers*. Dogs are welcome in the restaurant, which also receives a lot of bicyclists and motorcyclists.

The menu items vary considerably, but most are considered pub fare. They do consider themselves to be more of a restaurant than a bar, and the place can fill up quickly around the dinner hour.

The overall feel of this restaurant is very laid-back, and everyone seems to know everyone else. (Many of the patrons live close by.) So get your food and wander out back to one of the picnic tables overlooking the canal. Your dog can join you too; everyone is welcome!

WOLF HOLLOW BREWING COMPANY

Phone/Address: (518) 214-4093 / 6882 Amsterdam Rd., Schenectady, NY 12302.

Days/Hours: Wednesday 4 p.m.–8 p.m., Thursday and Friday 4 p.m.–9 p.m., Saturday noon–9 p.m., Sunday noon–6 p.m., closed on Monday and Tuesday.

Reservations accepted? No.

Restaurant size: Fourteen tables and another twenty-five tables outside. (The tables are large so there is a high seating capacity.)

Outdoor seating: Yes.

Menu items: The real stars of the show at Wolf Hollow Brewing Company are the beers, which are almost entirely brewed on-site. At any one time, they have sixteen drafts on tap, which include creative names such as "Wolf Hollow Amber" (a red ale), "For Love Nor Money" (a New England IPA), and Campout Stout (an Irish dry stout). Only two beers are "outsourced," meaning they are brewed by another well-known brewery using their own recipe so they can brew the remaining selections onsite. They also offer two hard ciders as well as a trio of New York State wines and a selection of nonalcoholic beverages.

All foods (besides snacks) are available from the food trucks that are invited onto the property. Wolf Hollow organizes a continuous lineup of great food providers such as Burger 21, Two for the Road, Flaco's Tacos, and Sammy's Country Wagon.

Price range: Most beers are $4 for a half pint and $7–$8 for a pint. The wines are $8/glass.

Wolf Hollow Brewing Company, Schenectady, New York.
PHOTO BY LARRY WEILL

Most popular menu item: There is no one favorite. Patrons seem to enjoy all of Wolf Hollow's offerings in equal measure.

Entertainment: Yes (live music plays on the patio in back of the main building).

Liquor license: No (only the beer, wine, and cider).

Description: This is a wonderful place where the beer and "the scene" both deserve recognition. Their motto, "Your beer, brewed here" is very indicative of their mission: to brew world-class beers that will bring the community together in one place. (The founders include a school principal and a pastor!) Children are welcome too and will enjoy themselves on the walking trails that crisscross their four acres of land. It's a party that you don't want to miss.

MAX 410 AT THE WATERS EDGE

Phone/Address: (518) 370-5300 / 2 Freemans Bridge Rd., Glenville, NY 12302.

Days/Hours: Tuesday through Thursday 11 a.m.–9 p.m., Friday 11 a.m.–10 p.m., Saturday noon–10 p.m., Sunday noon–8 p.m., Monday 4 p.m.–9 p.m.

Reservations accepted? Yes (and needed).

Restaurant size: This is a large restaurant with about twenty-five tables inside and at least twenty tables outside.

Outdoor seating: Yes.

Menu items: The lunch menu lists twelve appetizers, including a crab-lobster fondue and "lollipop lamb chops." They also offer six salads, fourteen sandwiches, nine "Tavern Fare" dishes (which include everything from a "Superfood Bowl" to steak frites, plus lots of seafood and steak entrées. Their dinner menu

Max 410 at the Waters Edge, Glenville, New York.
PHOTO BY LARRY WEILL

lists many of the same appetizers and entrées but is even more extensive. It also offers several surf-and-turf dishes, more steak varieties, plus two oyster appetizers.

Price range: Many of the appetizers list between $18 and $23, while the "Tavern Fare" items are $16–$29. Most of the seafood dinner entrées are $29–$44 (king crab legs are more), and the steaks range from $31 to $49.

Most popular menu item: The Seafood 410, which is a butter-poached Maine lobster tail, sea scallops, jumbo shrimp, lobster cream, jasmine rice, asparagus, and lemon butter sauce.

Entertainment: Yes (lots of music and fun events on their outside patio).

Liquor license: Yes.

Description: Max 410 at the Waters Edge is more than just a restaurant. It is a combination of a fine dining bistro with a great outdoor facility and a party-like atmosphere. In the summer you can take your pick: dine in the stately indoor dining room or party out on the deck with music and other fun events. (But either way, make sure you get a reservation. You will need it at this popular spot.)

I must say that this was one restaurant that I returned to later, after earlier visiting to review the menu and count tables. Their menu, which is heavily slanted toward seafood, listed so many great-looking dishes that I just had to try some for myself. I ordered the Seafood 410 dish (with the lobster, shrimp, and scallops), and it was amazing. People come here for the great seafood, the superb drinks, and the relaxed cabana-like atmosphere. It is located right next to the canal, and dock slips are available to tie up your boat.

ZEN ASIAN FUSION LOUNGE

Phone/Address: (518) 280-0388 / 469 State St., Schenectady, NY 12305.

Days/Hours: Monday through Thursday 3 p.m.–10 p.m., Friday and Saturday 3 p.m.–11 p.m., closed on Sunday.

Reservations accepted? Yes.

Restaurant size: Twenty-three tables inside (including side room), plus bar seating. There are also six tables outside on the sidewalk.

Outdoor seating: Yes.

Zen Asian Fusion Lounge, Schenectady, New York.
PHOTO BY LARRY WEILL

Menu items: The menu lists a lengthy selection of nineteen appetizers and seventeen sushi dishes, and both sushi and sashimi are available à la carte. The hibachi menu lists eight dishes, including chicken, shrimp, scallops, salmon, and steak. They also have twenty-six different maki rolls, and several non-sushi dinner entrées including Thai basil fried rice, pad thai, and sesame chicken.

Price range: Appetizers are from $5 to $15, sushi rolls are $15–$17, à la carte pieces are $6–$9, and the dinner entrées range from $18 to $27. The hibachi menu goes for $17 (for tofu) to $32 for the seafood trifecta. They also have nineteen varieties of beer for $4 each.

Most popular menu item: Hibachi dinners.

Entertainment: No.

Liquor license: Yes.

Description: Zen Asian Fusion Lounge is an attractive place to get tasty dishes that run the gamut from Japanese to Chinese to Thai. They have a large sushi bar that is a nice change from the beef and burger restaurants along the State Street strip. Unfortunately, if you are coming off your boat or the Canalway Trail, this is not an option for lunch since they do not open until 3 p.m. on any day of the week.

This is also a good option to try if you have been shut out of other restaurants, as tables are usually available. They have a large bar with additional seating, where you can sit and watch your favorite cocktails being prepared. Meals are served quickly so you can get in and out if time is short. The menu is large enough so that everyone can find something that suits them.

BL'S TAVERN & GRILL

Phone/Address: (518) 374-2850 / 208 Front Street, Schenectady NY 12305.

Days/Hours: 10 a.m.–11 p.m. every day of the week.

Reservations accepted? No.

Restaurant size: Eleven tables plus bar seating.

Outdoor seating: No.

Menu items: BL's menu offers a lot of good "pub fare" items that are available at very modest prices. They have eight sandwiches, including their "BL's Deli Sandwich" (choice of turkey or corned beef with lettuce, tomato, onion, and cheese). They also list four grilled items including a build-your-own burger, along with sausage burgers, steak burgers, and hot dogs. The menu also includes six appetizers and three large salads.

Price range: Wings are $15/dozen, most sandwiches are $11–$12. The appetizers range from $8 to $11, and the three salads are $8–$14.

Most popular menu item: Wings are the most popular item on their menu. They are available in mild, hot, garlic Parmesan, barbecue, and bourbon.

Entertainment: Yes (not very often, but they do occasionally have live music).

Liquor license: Yes.

BL's Tavern & Grill, Schenectady, New York.
PHOTO BY LARRY WEILL

Description: BL's Tavern & Grill is definitely more of a pub than a restaurant. It is a neighborhood establishment where most of the customers are "regulars" who have been going there for years. The building was built in 1897. It is the oldest continuously operated tavern in the city of Schenectady.

The history of BL's is very long and colorful. It was operated as a "Speakeasy" from 1917 through 1933 when Prohibition ended. In later years it became a favorite gathering place for the local police officers and detectives.

Today, BL's can be recognized by the sign that hangs in the window. It reads "Sorry, We're Open." The sign alone draws people into the pub, which is also frequented by a nice mixture of people including GE employees, military (airborne) personnel, and neighborhood residents. Park your bike and come inside for your daily allowance of beer and wings.

ANNABEL'S PIZZA COMPANY

Phone/Address: (518) 553-0400 / 108 State St., Schenectady, NY 12305.

Days/Hours: Monday through Thursday 3 p.m.–10 p.m., Friday and Saturday noon–11 p.m., Sunday noon–8 p.m.

Reservations accepted? No.

Restaurant size: Limited seating (two tables), although this pizzeria is linked with the Frog Alley Brewing Company next door, which has almost unlimited seating capacity, so their pizzas can be ordered and consumed in the brewery.

Outdoor seating: Yes (using the brewery seating).

Annabel's Pizza Company, Schenectady, New York.
PHOTO BY LARRY WEILL

Menu items: The menu features eighteen different pizzas, including five "traditional" varieties and thirteen additional ("originals") that get more creative with the ingredients and preparation. These include a fried artichoke pizza, a cashew cream pizza, and a clams casino version. The menu also offers some great appetizers, several of which can be shared by two or three people. (I tried the fried artichokes with horseradish sauce, which would have fed three people.) The menu also advertises three salads, six sandwiches, and twenty different varieties of "frites." Oh, and let's not forget the wings either!

Price range: Pizzas range from $13.50 to $18.50, salads are $10–$13, sandwiches are $15, and wings are $16 for a plate of thirteen pieces. You can also build your own salad starting at $10.

Most popular menu item: The soppressata with burrata and hot honey pizza.

Entertainment: Not in the pizzeria, but in the connected brewery.

Liquor license: Yes (through the connected brewery).

Description: Annabel's Pizza Company appears to be a stand-alone restaurant from the outside, but it is connected (literally and figuratively) to the Frog Alley Brewing Company next door. Annabel's has a couple tables in the front of the restaurant, but most people either take out their pizzas or order them through the window in the brewery.

On the day of my visit, I made the mistake of ordering two appetizers: the fried artichoke hearts with horseradish sauce and the "pizza bites." They were both *wonderful*, but both dishes were so big that I had enough for at least three people. I would love to return to sample the pizzas from this place since the appetizers were simply amazing. It was also fun watching the pizza makers feeding logs into the wood-fired oven. What a great scene!

FROG ALLEY BREWING COMPANY

Phone/Address: (518) 631-4800 / 108 State St., Schenectady, NY 12305.

Days/Hours: Monday through Wednesday noon–10 p.m., Thursday noon–11 p.m., Friday and Saturday noon–midnight, Sunday noon–8 p.m.

Note: Brunch is also available on Sunday from 10 a.m. to 1 p.m. All food at Frog Alley Brewing Company is ordered and purchased from Annabel's Pizza Company (see previous page).

Reservations accepted? No.

Restaurant size: This is a very large facility, with about thirty large tables (and lots of bar seating) inside and an additional twenty tables outside on the patio.

Outdoor seating: Yes, in summer.

Menu (all food items are from Annabel's Pizza Company): Please see Annabel's Pizza Company (previous page) for a listing of available food items and their prices.

Beer Menu: Frog Alley's list of "Flagship Brews" describes eleven of their standard, everyday beers. These include Pilsners, lagers, porters, ales, and even a "watermelon crawl sour." There is literally something there for everyone. On the back of their menu are ten "seasonal brews," which rotate on a monthly basis throughout the year. These include a host of new brews, including their West Coast IPA, Mai Bock, Lakeside Summer Kolsch, and Pub Ale. The seasonal list also includes a "Dry Hard Cider—Indian Ladder"—although none of these may be on the menu by the time this book goes to print.

Frog Alley Brewing Company, Schenectady, New York.
PHOTO BY LARRY WEILL

Beer Prices: All brews are $8/pint, $5/half pint, and $3/4 ounces.

Most popular menu item: Take your pick! All the flagship and seasonal brews are popular, so just try one or try several.

Entertainment: Yes (music outside in the summer months).

Liquor license: Yes.

Description: This place is a beer-lover's mecca, with so many great varieties and flavors. All food is ordered through the window to Annabel's Pizzeria, which is attached to the brewery. See the previous page for descriptions of Annabel's pizza and other great entrées.

THE NEST

Phone/Address: (518) 672-3018 / 512 State St., Schenectady, NY 12305.

Days/Hours: Tuesday through Friday 11:30 a.m.–9:30 p.m., Saturday 10:30 a.m.–2 p.m. and then from 5 p.m. to 9:30 p.m., Sunday 10:30 a.m.–3 p.m., closed on Monday.

Reservations accepted? No.

Restaurant size: This is a very large restaurant, with about twenty tables downstairs, twenty tables upstairs, and another twenty tables outside on the front patio.

Outdoor seating: Yes, in summer.

Menu items: This restaurant has three different menus, with a great many "small plates" and larger fares for brunch (on Sundays), lunch, and dinner. The brunch menu lists five small plates, three biscuit dishes, four varieties of eggs Benedict

The Nest, Schenectady, New York.
PHOTO BY LARRY WEILL

(including a "Crab Cakes Gone Wild" version, and thirteen small plates (including a "Short Rib Hash" and NOLA Shrimp & Grits). Their lunch menu has ten small plates (including a "Bird Is the Word" dish), and lunch plates like jambalaya and lobster mac and cheese. Dinner lists an additional twelve small plates, three salads, and nine entrées. Several of the dishes appear on more than one of their menus.

Price range: Small plates vary in price depending on which meal of the day, but most of them list for between $4 and $19. Many of the main course entrées are between $14 and $28.

Most popular menu item: Fried chicken and short ribs are two of the most popular selections at the Nest.

Entertainment: Yes (music outside in the summer months).

Liquor license: Yes.

Description: This restaurant describes its food as "Southern-inspired cuisine," which is readily apparent as you read through the three menus. The variety of dishes and the modest menu prices enable diners to sample a variety of unique foods that do not appear on most restaurant menus.

Diners at the Nest also enjoy having a variety of seating options, including the open, spacious patio on State Street. While relaxing with dinner, don't forget to try one of their unique cocktails like their "Southern Belle" (made with vodka, house-squeezed strawberry puree, mint simple syrup, and homemade fresh-squeezed lemonade. (How can you beat that?)

SCHENECTADY COUNTY VIETNAM VETERANS MEMORIAL PARK
Located on SUNY Schenectady campus

Phone/Address: On the campus of SUNY Schenectady, between the back parking lot on campus and State Street.

Days/Hours: Twenty-four hours a day, seven days a week.

Admission: Free.

Note: This memorial, erected and dedicated in 2021, can easily be seen from State Street as you walk or bike into town from the west. It is on the opposite side of State Street from the Erie Canal.

Schenectady County Vietnam Veterans Memorial Park, Schenectady, New York.
Photo by Larry Weill

Background: Schenectady County Vietnam Veterans Memorial Park serves as a tribute to the thousands of Schenectady County veterans who served in Vietnam. It was first envisioned by Mr. Bob Becker, a United States Marine Corps first sergeant who served in the Marines for twenty-two years. He also served in numerous positions with various veterans' organizations, including the Disabled American Veterans, the New York State Council of Veterans' Organizations, the Marine Corps League, and the American Legion. Becker first proposed the idea of a Vietnam War memorial in Schenectady County to honor the 2,700 men and women from the county who served in Vietnam over the course of that tragic war.

Although the idea for a Vietnam War memorial gained immediate support in the region, progress was very slow due to the pandemic. But the effort continued and gained both political and economic support until the project came to fruition in October 2021. The memorial was completed with the aid of an $81,000 grant from the Schenectady County Legislature.

Description: The memorial is now complete and stands as a solemn reminder of those service members who paid the ultimate sacrifice. Schenectady County has approximately 8,500 veterans, of whom 2,700 are Vietnam veterans. Of those county residents who served, thirty-two were killed in action, several of whom were memorialized during the dedication ceremony.

The memorial is approached via a concrete walkway, moving north from the parking lot toward State Street. The walkway is illuminated with light posts on either side as it approaches a wide, circular concrete viewing area. A series of six marble benches surround the viewing area, providing visitors with a place to sit and reflect on the somber nature of the memorial.

At the far end of the circular viewing area is a large, black marble stone, engraved with the words: "Dedicated to the men and women of Schenectady County who proudly served our country during the Vietnam War." The stone is also engraved with a large map of Vietnam, including the names and locations of numerous important towns and bases across the country. The seals of the different U.S. armed forces branches appear across the bottom of the stone. A flagpole flying the U.S. flag and the black-and-white MIA (missing in action) flag stands directly behind the marble monument stone.

NOVEL BIBLIO BREW

Phone/Address: (518) 943-9057 / 515 State St., Schenectady, NY 12305.

Days/Hours: Thursday and Friday 8 a.m.–8 p.m., Saturday 10 a.m.–8 p.m., Sunday 10 a.m.–3 p.m., closed Monday through Wednesday.

Reservations accepted? The side room can be reserved for large parties and meetings.

Restaurant size: About ten tables (including the side room).

Outdoor seating: Yes.

Menu items: Breakfast can be ordered all day long, and five of the featured dishes are named after famous book titles. "Breakfast of Champions" is a bacon and egg scramble with sharp cheddar on warm sourdough bread. "The Sun Also Rises" is avocado, scrambled egg, cheddar cheese, microgreens, and sriracha on an everything bagel. The rest of the breakfast menu is filled with different toasts and flatbreads of every variety. Meanwhile, Novel Biblio Brew also offers an appealing lunch menu with a selection of four sandwiches, four salads, soups, and some appealing snacks. The snack column includes their "Streetcar Named

Novel Biblio Brew, Schenectady, New York.
PHOTO BY LARRY WEILL

Desire," made with corn on the cob, chipotle aioli, feta, cilantro, lime, and Tajín seasoning.

Price range: Breakfasts are available from $3.50 to $15, flatbread breakfasts are $11–$15, lunch sandwiches run from $7 to $12, and salads are $10–$12.

Most popular menu item: The Don Chipotle sandwich and their flatbreads.

Entertainment: Yes, they have live music for scheduled events, along with trivia nights and tabletop game nights.

Liquor license: Yes.

Description: Novel Biblio Brew is a fun and unique place that combines elements of many activities into a single business. It is part coffeehouse and restaurant, offering great hot and cold drinks along with a wonderful menu to satisfy any breakfast or lunch cravings. (Although any of the salads and sandwiches will also make a nice dinner.) But the fun doesn't stop there. The interior walls are lined with shelves of books, some for reading and some for purchase.

Novel Biblio Brew has also become a gathering place in the community, and many folks stop by after a night at the nearby Proctor's Theater. Before becoming Novel Biblio Brew, this used to be a bakery, and all their cookies, pastries, and muffins are baked in-house.

MOON & RIVER CAFE

Phone/Address: (518) 382-1938 / 115 S. Ferry St., Schenectady, NY 12305.

Days/Hours: 9 a.m.–9 p.m. every day.

Note: This restaurant is cash only. It is mostly vegetarian and vegan with some meat dishes.

Reservations accepted? No.

Restaurant size: Seven tables.

Moon & River Cafe, Schenectady, New York.
PHOTO BY LARRY WEILL

Outdoor seating: No.

Menu items: For a small cafe, this place has an extremely large menu. They serve all-day breakfast with thirty-nine different selections, from egg sandwiches and omelets to grits, oatmeal, and fruit with yogurt and granola combinations. They also offer a lot of hot and cold drinks to go with the food. Their lunch menu lists twenty different cold sandwiches, twenty-one hot sandwiches, and sixteen salads. It also has pizzas, paninis, and gyros. There are also numerous "house specialties" including the falafel plate, the Asian stir-fry, ratatouille, and many tofu dishes.

Price range: Many of the breakfast items average around $8, most sandwiches are listed around $6–$7, pizzas, paninis, and gyros are also around $9. Most of the "house specialty" dishes are $8–$10.

Most popular menu item: The tempeh Reuben.

Entertainment: Yes (they usually have live music seven nights a week).

Liquor license: Yes (through the connected brewery).

Description: Richard, one of the owners, describes this place as "a little arty café." He is fond of saying that "a restaurant is about food, but a café is about people." His philosophy on running the café is that "we give people what they want: each other."

The focus of this place is vegetarian and vegan dishes, but you can find almost anything you want on the menu. It is also very inexpensive, and represents one of the most price-conscious meals in town.

Richard says he enjoys seeing all the cyclists coming off the Canalway Trail in the summer, stopping in for a healthy lunch. Sometimes the entire front of the café is lined with bikes leaning up against the building. Then again, after spending a few minutes inside the Moon & River Cafe, it's obvious they enjoy everyone who walks in the door. They are that happy to see you.

20 NORTH BROADWAY TAVERN

Phone/Address: (518) 357-8992 / 20 N. Broadway, Schenectady, NY 12305.

Days/Hours: Monday 4 p.m.–midnight, Tuesday through Friday 11:30 a.m.–midnight, Saturday noon–midnight, closed on Sunday.

Reservations accepted? No.

Restaurant size: Eight tables inside (plus bar seating) and eight tables on the back patio.

Outdoor seating: Yes.

Menu items: Seven starter dishes, four burgers, chicken wings (mild, medium, hot, barbecue, chipotle bourbon barbecue, "triple threat," garlic Parmesan, and squash), plus four sandwiches.

Price range: Appetizers are $8–$11, burgers are $13–$17, wings are $16/dozen, sandwiches range between $7.50 and $15.50

Most popular menu item: More people come for the wings than anything else, but another very popular item is the Greg Allman burger, which is a half-pound burger topped with Cheddar cheese, barbecue sauce, bacon, onion rings, lettuce, tomato, and a dill pickle.

20 North Broadway Tavern, Schenectady, New York.
PHOTO BY LARRY WEILL

Entertainment: No.

Liquor license: Yes.

Description: This attractive pub has been in business for the past seventeen years, mostly with the same owner. By coincidence, the previous owner was at the pub during the time of my visit, and we got to talk about all the things that make 20 North Broadway a neighborhood hub.

It's no secret that 20 North Broadway Tavern makes world-class chicken wings. (Ask any customer in the place; they all say the same thing.) If you want proof, all you have to do is look at the long line of "chicken wing competition" prize certificates that are taped to the wall behind the bar. They've been doing this for a long time!

Another great thing about my visit to this pub was that I found myself immediately engaged with several patrons ("regulars") who immediately accepted me into their group of friends. As the bartender said, "Come prepared to enjoy yourself." It's just going to happen.

SAWMILL TAVERN

Note: Otherwise known as Don Birch's Sawmill Tavern.

Phone/Address: (518) 382-8590 / 501 South Ave, Schenectady, NY 12305.

Days/Hours: 11 a.m.–midnight, seven days a week.

Reservations accepted? No.

Restaurant size: No tables inside, but lots of bar stools and other inside seating.

Outdoor seating: One table, plus a small, covered side deck.

Menu items: This pub has no menu, although it does offer some small frozen pizzas that customers can order.

Price range: No food menu.

Most popular menu item: Pizza.

Entertainment: No.

Sawmill Tavern, Schenectady, New York.
PHOTO BY LARRY WEILL

Liquor license: Yes.

Description: The Sawmill Tavern is a comfortable bar, and only a bar. There is no food menu, but lots of cold brew and mixed drinks to satisfy the local crowd. The employees and customers both describe this place as a "five-star dive bar," which is the way the Sawmill is described online as well.

The decor inside is reminiscent of an old-time biker bar. As a matter of fact, a motorcycle hangs on the wall inside as a decoration, adding authenticity to the description.

The proximity of the Sawmill Tavern to the Canalway Trail makes it easily accessible to bikers on the trail. (The sidewalk on N. Jay Street is literally on the trail.) It is a quick-in quick-out, although there does not appear to be a place to lock a bike on the outside of the building. Regardless, the customers are friendly, and the beer is cold, so consider giving it a try.

CENTRE STREET PUBLIC HOUSE AND BIERGARTEN

Phone/Address: (518) 393-2337 / 308 Union St., Schenectady, NY 12305.

Days/Hours: Monday 4 p.m.–11:30 p.m., Tuesday through Thursday 3 p.m.–11:30 p.m., Friday 3 p.m.–midnight, Saturday 11 a.m.–midnight, Sunday 11 a.m.–10 p.m.

Reservations accepted? Yes.

Restaurant size: Twenty tables on the outside patio plus lots of tables available in the main barroom plus multiple interior private rooms.

Outdoor seating: Yes.

Menu items: Eleven starters including the Oktoberfest pretzel with cheese or mustard, truffle fries, or pierogies. They also offer a choice of six pizzas, sandwiches (including a breakfast sandwich), four wraps, three salads, and a nice selection of brunch dishes (weekends only).

Price range: Appetizers range between $9 and $17, pizzas (six-slice) are $13–$20 while eight-slice pizzas are $17–$24. Sandwiches are $15–$17 (breakfast sandwich is $12), the wraps are $13–$14, the three salads are all $11–$15, and the brunch selections are $9–$16.

Most popular menu item: Pizza and the Oktoberfest pretzels.

Centre Street Public House and Biergarten, Schenectady, New York.
Photo by Larry Weill

Entertainment: Yes (live bands on the outside patio on Saturday and Sunday and indoors during the winter months).

Liquor license: Yes.

Description: There is so much cool stuff to describe about this pub that it is impossible to do on one page. The building itself (which opened as a pub in 2013) was a brewery storage facility in the 1800s and later served as a printing factory prior to becoming a pub. Fascinating remnants of the building's past still exist today, including vast underground storage rooms discovered beneath the adjacent road. Other rooms inside the building include a speakeasy with a separate entrance. The pub uses one of these spaces as a whiskey room, where customers can sample high-end whiskey in a comfortable setting. They also have the largest outdoor patio in the city of Schenectady.

The pub houses a wood-fired pizza in the main barroom where customers can watch their pizzas be prepared over an open flame. Meanwhile, the main barroom also holds enough big-screen televisions to ensure that everyone can watch their favorite team play.

DRUTHERS BREWING COMPANY

Phone/Address: (518) 357-8028 / 221 Harborside Drive, Schenectady, NY 12305.

Days/Hours: Sunday through Thursday, noon–9 p.m., Friday & Saturday noon–10 p.m.

Reservations accepted? Yes.

Restaurant size: Thirty-four tables inside with twenty more tables on the outside patio.

Outdoor seating: Yes.

Menu items: Seven small plates including wings, nachos, and street corn dip. There are also four taco dishes, four flatbreads, six "on a bun" plates (including chicken and burgers), and three "top shelf" entrées that include salmon and steak frites. The brewing menu offers eleven different drafts on tap and eleven more that are available in cans.

Druthers Brewing Company, Schenectady, New York.
PHOTO BY LARRY WEILL

Price range: Small plates range between $14 and $18, the taco dishes are $15–$16, flatbreads are $13–$15, the "on a bun" plates are $15–$17, and the top-shelf dishes are $26–$30. Prices for the beers on tap are generally $8 or $9 for a sixteen-ounce draft. The four-packs to go (cans) are $12–$17.

Most popular menu item: Beer cheese, and their mac and cheese. Among the beverages the favorites are the beer flights and the Golden Rule Blonde.

Entertainment: Yes (live bands on the outside patio on Saturday and Sunday).

Liquor license: Yes.

Description: Druthers Brewing Company is a popular eating and drinking establishment inside the Mohawk Harbor development. They serve a large selection of their own brews with a menu of "elevated comfort food" (as described by their manager). They have a great floor plan that is divided almost equally between their inside barroom and their festive outside patio. The patio looks out over the Erie Canal, adding great scenery to everything else.

On the back side of the barroom sit the brewing tanks that produce the handcrafted beers. As their restaurant manager said, "Druthers" literally means "choices," and that is exactly what they offer to their patrons, great brews and great food.

The Schenectady location of Druthers has become extremely popular, and recent renovations have improved both the indoor and outdoor seating areas. It's right next to the canal (with boat slips), and it's also bike friendly. You'll enjoy experiencing this place for yourself.

MOHAWK HARBOR

Note: Mohawk Harbor is very different from any other "attraction" in this guide. It is an area rather than a single entity or business, containing everything from a marina and restaurants to stores, entertainment, residential units, and much more.

Phone/Address: (518) 356-4445 / 200 Harborside Dr., Schenectady, NY 12305.

Days/Hours: There are no set hours for this complex. Each restaurant or business sets its own hours. Check the website for your specific destination.

Admission: Free.

Historical Background: The site of Mohawk Harbor is centered around a mile-long stretch of the Mohawk River in Schenectady. In 1848, the Schenectady

Locomotive Works (which merged into the American Locomotive Company in 1901) began production of locomotive train engines on this site. It was a massive complex of gigantic buildings that employed thousands of workers to manufacture these engines and the area took on the appearance of a city unto its own.

The American Locomotive Company (ALCO) remained a viable, thriving business (and one of Schenectady's largest employers) well into the twentieth century. The decline in the use of trains as the major means of transporting goods forced the closure of the ALCO complex, which shuttered its operations in Schenectady in 1969. Other companies (including

Entrance to Mohawk Harbor, Schenectady, New York.
PHOTO BY LARRY WEILL

General Electric) used these same buildings for other industries until the site was abandoned in the mid-1990s.

Mohawk Harbor today: This location is now the site of an exciting project that combines a riverfront marina with a vast array of restaurants, retail businesses, entertainment options, and residential apartment space. Started in 2015, it is still under development but already offers many fun and convenient options to travelers on both the Erie Canal and the Canalway Trail.

Restaurants in and around Mohawk Harbor include the Druthers Brewing Company, the Shaker and Vine, and (slightly farther west) Dukes Chophouse. Several dining establishments are located close by with more to be built as the Mohawk Harbor nears completion.

There are also multiple entertainment options for visitors to the Mohawk Harbor area, including the Rivers Casino & Resort of Schenectady, in case you're feeling lucky during your stopover in town. You can also hone your golf game indoors at The Bunker, where you can enjoy good food and lively music between your golf swings. There is so much to do you may want to stay over!

HISTORIC STOCKADE DISTRICT OF SCHENECTADY

Address: Multiple streets in the northwest corner of Schenectady.

Days/Hours: There are no "hours of operation" since this is an entire neighborhood and section of the larger city.

Admission: Free.

History: The Stockage District of Schenectady is an area on the northwest side of the city that contains the earliest settlement of pre–Revolutionary War buildings in existence. Many of these buildings are well over two hundred years old, with the oldest dating back to the 1730s.

The term "stockade" refers to the large, heavy wooden wall that was constructed as a defensive barrier against the French and northern Indian warriors in the 1600s. The precise locations of these walls are not entirely known, although historical excavations have uncovered some buried stubs of the original foundation logs. Some sources report that this stockade originally enclosed four blocks of dwellings, although other descriptions state that the first stockade contained two rows of six houses each. In any case, this early version of the stockade was burned during the "Schenectady Massacre" of 1690.

The stockade was rebuilt by new settlers in 1704, and was larger and longer than the original version, eventually extending to the Mohawk River on the north. A complete history of the stockade and its eventual demise would require a book of its own. However, for the sake of brevity, we can summarize by stating that the wall stood its ground through the French and Indian Wars and the Revolutionary War of the 1700s, after which time it was no longer needed and was eventually removed.

The Stockade District today: While biking (or hiking or boating) through Schenectady, this is an amazing place to get off the trail or canal and just walk. Historic marker signs are everywhere, and it is immediately obvious that you are strolling through a very old neighborhood. It has been described by the National Park Service as having the highest concentration of historic period homes in the country." At least forty of those houses date back over two hundred years, and many are marked with plaques and signage explaining the dates and early ownership of the buildings.

This neighborhood can be strolled in less than an hour, including time to stop and look inside a few shops and visit the statue of Lawrence the Indian (located at 100 N. Ferry Street). It is so old and unique that it really is worth the stop.

Houses along N. Church Street in the historic Stockade District of Schenectady, New York.

SCHENECTADY COUNTY HISTORICAL SOCIETY

Phone/Address: (518) 374-0263 / 32 Washington Ave., Schenectady, NY 12305.

Days/Hours: Monday through Friday, 10 a.m.–5 p.m., Saturday 10 a.m.–2 p.m., closed on Sunday.

Admission: Adults are $6, children under age eighteen and students are free.

Background: The building that hosts the Schenectady County Historical Society was built in 1895, although it did not serve as a family residence for long. It was converted into a museum in the 1950s and remains a museum today.

The museum houses an extensive collection of artifacts from the earliest days of the city of Schenectady and the surrounding area. On display are pieces of furniture, works of art, period clothing, and dishes/utensils used in households across the region. The standing exhibits on colonial history show the diverse history of those who call this area "home."

Schenectady County Historical Society building on Washington Avenue, Schenectady, New York.

It is a community organization that also conducts walking tours, kayak tours, and numerous other activities that visitors can join as desired. These are advertised on the organization's website, and most charge an additional fee. They can fill up quickly, so check their website early.

Also housed inside the museum building is the Grems-Doolittle Library, which is a three-thousand-plus-volume collection focusing on the people, places, and history of Schenectady County. Documents contained in this library include local history, oral histories, genealogical records, newspapers and periodicals, diaries, wills, photographs, and much more. Requests to conduct research in this library must be made forty-eight hours in advance of the visit.

Other sites operated by the Schenectady County Historical Society: The Schenectady County Historical Society is a large organization that operates several historic sites inside the county. Each of these sites is further described in other pages within this book. These include the Brouwer House, which is one of the earliest homes built in the Stockade District of Schenectady. This building is open to the public, although it has not been restored as a historic landmark. Instead, it is rented out to local artists and vendors who create their crafts and sell them to visitors inside.

The Society also operates the Mabee Family Historic Site, which is located inside Schenectady County but outside the city. It dates back to 1705, and represents the oldest farm in the Mohawk Valley. (Refer to the page in this book that further describes this site.)

The Schenectady County Historical Society coordinates activities in each of these locations. Check their website for dates and additional details.

TAKE TWO CAFE

Note: This is a completely vegan restaurant. Even their "meats" (including bacon) are 100 percent plant-based.

Phone/Address: (518) 280-9670 / 433 State St., Schenectady, NY 12305.

Days/Hours: Monday through Friday, 8 a.m.–4 p.m., Saturday and Sunday 8 a.m.–3 p.m.

Reservations accepted? No.

Restaurant size: Five tables inside and three outside.

Outdoor seating: Yes, in summer.

Menu items: In addition to all their fine coffees and teas, they have an extensive breakfast lineup of twelve selections, including an Avo (avocado) Smash, specialty omelets, and the "Breakfast Crane" which is seasoned potato, bacon, and sour cream, on a crunchy tostada which is then wrapped in a flour tortilla and then grilled. Lunch includes fifteen choices including a triple-decker club sandwich, jerk chicken, and the "Jack Ass," all of which are vegan.

Price range: Breakfast items list between $4.50 and $12, while lunches are almost entirely between $13 and $15.

Most popular menu item: The Crane Street (original or Buffalo) and the Mac Wrap.

Entertainment: No.

Take Two Cafe, Schenectady, New York.
PHOTO BY LARRY WEILL

Liquor license: No

Description: The Take Two Cafe is an amazing place that offers its customers nutritious and creative meals (breakfasts and lunches) with one theme in common: everything served in the place is entirely plant-based. Even dishes listing chicken, pastrami, hot dogs, and burgers are made from plant-based ingredients!

Looking into their countertop pastry shelves, it is hard not to order one of everything. They have a wonderful selection of cookies, cakes, pies, and pastries that conform to their vegan standards. Some of these (cookies and pastries) are baked on-premises, while others are prepared by well-known area bakers. During my visit, I tried an amaretto chocolate biscotti that was superb. They also advertise "cronuts," which are donuts baked using croissant dough. Everything in this coffee shop is like this: creative, unique, flavorful, and healthy. It's one more place that you've got to try while visiting this eventful city.

JAY STREET ARTISAN MARKET

Address: Jay Street, Schenectady, from State Street north to Liberty Street.

Days/Hours: Only on Sundays from 10 a.m. to 2 p.m.

Note: Some online websites call this the Jay Street Marketplace. There is also a farmers market that is conducted on some of these same streets. The farmers market is a weekly event on Thursdays, from 9:30 a.m. to 1:30 p.m.

Admission: Free.

Description: What's more fun than spending a few hours on a laid-back Sunday than walking around an open-air market? As long as you're taking some time off the canal or

Jay Street Artisan Market, Schenectady, New York.
PHOTO BY LARRY WEILL

Canalway Trail, why not check out the many craft exhibits, stores, and other vendors participating in this unique weekly event?

Jay Street is a pedestrian, alley-like route that is lined with artistically arranged colored bricks. The exhibitors set up their tents along the alley outside the road's stores. The market has a very bohemian feel to it, with most of the exhibitors displaying handmade jewelry, wood carvings, clothing, homemade food items (jams/jellies), antiques, books, and much more. Several other vendors distill and sell local versions of alcoholic spirits, which has become a new and burgeoning business in Upstate New York. Additionally, a number of musicians play in locations along the alley, providing a festive atmosphere.

The stores along Jay Street are equally artistic and fun. They include small restaurants and cafés, music shops, bookstores, antique shops, jewelry crafts, and cozy pubs. The merchants of this micro-community have banded together over the past ten years to form the Jay Street Business Association, which hosts this weekly event.

Access to the Jay Street Artisan Market: The Jay Street Artisan Market can be found on Jay Street, starting on State Street to the south and continuing north to Liberty Street. (To find it easily, look for the sign for Johnny's Italian Restaurant on State Street. The market starts to the right of that sign.) Additional exhibitors set up their tents along Franklin Street as it runs east along the side of the Schenectady City Hall. Most of the vendors set up around the city hall building are selling produce instead of crafts. Those exhibitors display a countless array of locally grown vegetables, fruits, and flowers.

If by some chance you are driving your car (instead of hiking/biking/boating), there are conveniently located parking lots nearby. Parking is available in the Clinton North Lot (enter on Clinton Street, or the Center City Lot (enter on Franklin Street). Street parking is also available on State Street and other local thoroughfares, but open spaces are difficult to find most days.

FIRST REFORMED CHURCH

Phone/Address: (518) 377-2201 / 8 N. Church St., Schenectady, NY 12305.

Hours: Monday through Friday 8 a.m.–4 p.m., Sunday 10 a.m.–6 p.m., closed on Saturday.

Note: The church is located inside the original Stockade District of Schenectady. Several other historic buildings stand within a short walk of the church.

History: The historic marker outside this impressive building on Church Street reads "Dutch Church, Founded before 1680." From the massive stone front wall facing the road, many would be led to believe that this church has stood in the same place since that date in the seventeenth century. Yet the church has actually been destroyed by fire and other means numerous times. The structure in place today is the sixth rendition of the building.

The First Dutch Reformed Church was built nearby in 1682. It was destroyed by a fire during an Indian raid in 1690 that was dubbed the "Schenectady Massacre." Some sixty Schenectady residents (including the church minister) lost their lives on the night of February 8, 1690.

Over the course of the next 173 years, the church was rebuilt four more times, sometimes falling prey to fire while other times simply falling into disrepair. The fifth church was consumed by flames on February 1, 1948. It was rebuilt into its sixth (and current) version in 1950. This structure was built onto the

First Reformed Church, Schenectady, New York.
PHOTO BY LARRY WEILL

foundations of the previous church, using three of the remaining exterior walls, which were reinforced prior to the reconstruction.

Interesting notes: During the years of the third version of the church (from 1734 to 1814), men and women had to sit in different sections, as dictated by Dutch church rules. Likewise, Indians and slaves were seated in the balcony. This meant that families were not permitted to worship together. Another interesting item from those years was the presence of a six-hundred-pound silver bell in the belfry tower. This bell was cast in Amsterdam, New York, in 1732 using silver coins and contributions from parishioners in Amsterdam. That bell was used until it cracked in 1848.

Visitation and services: The church is open to the public and welcomes new people (whether hikers, bikers, boaters, or anyone else) to their Sunday services. Worship takes place at 10 a.m. on Sundays.

An additional gathering, called "First Forum," is conducted after the Sunday service. This is held to provide people the chance to engage with speakers about faith, the church, and service in the community and world. All are welcome to attend.

ABRAHAM YATES HOUSE

Address: 109 Union St., Schenectady, NY 12305.

Hours: This building is not open to the public.

Note: The Abraham Yates House is regarded as potentially the oldest home in the city of Schenectady. There is some debate as to whether that honor goes to this home or to the Brouwer House at 14 N. Church Street.

History: The Abraham Yates House was built by a Schenectady tanner, Abraham Yates, around 1725. The property had remained in the same extended family throughout most of its existence, although it has since been sold to new owners outside the family.

Abraham Yates House, Schenectady, New York.
PHOTO BY LARRY WEILL

Numerous building designs and techniques identify this house as an example of colonial Dutch architecture. The gabled roof and the brick facade facing the street, along with the black cross brick ties have been preserved to the current day, despite numerous rounds of upgrades and reconstruction. Additionally, many of the inside beams and floor planking are original, although much of the footage (3,462 sq. ft interior) was added to the house in the centuries since its construction.

Several excavations have taken place on the property of the Yates House and have yielded a number of interesting artifacts. Among the items recovered were clay pipes, shards of pottery, and a 1744 Spanish coin.

Visitation: As of now, the house is privately owned and is not open to the public. However, it is still an interesting place to stroll past, especially since it is located next door to the First Reformed Church. You may want to stop by and enjoy the architecture as long as you're there. It is located only two short streets off the Canalway Trail.

ALBANY COUNTY

MILLER'S BACKYARD BBQ

Phone/Address: (518) 238-3613 / 1 Niver St., Cohoes, NY 12047.

Days/Hours: Tuesday through Saturday 11 a.m.–8 p.m., closed on Sunday and Monday.

Reservations accepted? Yes.

Restaurant size: Five tables inside, seven tables on front porch, and ten tables under covered pavilion.

Outdoor seating: Yes.

Menu items: This is a barbecue restaurant with all kinds of tasty items from the barbecue grill. They list five appetizers including smoke-fried chicken wings and fried pickles. They also offer six sandwiches including the Rhode Island Hog, Nashville Chk'n, and a brisket Reuben. Also on the menu are four mac and cheese bowls and eight dinner entrées, which can include brisket, pulled pork, ribs, chicken, turkey breast, and cheddar sausage. They also list combo platters with either two, three, or four meats.

Price range: The appetizers range from $9 to $17, sandwiches are $13–$18, mac and cheese bowls are $14–$16, and the dinners run from $12 to $30.

Most popular menu item: Pulled pork sandwiches and brisket cheesesteak sandwiches.

Entertainment: No.

Liquor license: No.

Description: Miller's is pure barbecue, through and through. They got their start years ago grilling barbecue meats in their backyard before graduating to a food truck. The food truck quickly gained popularity as people became accustomed to their unique seasonings and slow-cooked barbecue flavors.

In 2022, Miller's Backyard BBQ moved into its current location, which is a full restaurant on Niver Street (located right next to the Canalway Trail). It's a busy place around mealtimes as the local population and the Canalway bikers pile in for lunch and dinner. They offer all the standard barbecued meats, plus

Miller's Backyard BBQ, Cohoes, New York.
PHOTO BY LARRY WEILL

"combo platters" that will test your appetite by piling up to four meats onto the same plate.

One more sign that this restaurant has great, authentic barbecue fare: The walls are lined with certificates, trophies, and ribbons from various barbecue competitions dating back many years. And just when you think you've seen them all, just wait until you use the bathroom. There are even more ribbons and award certificates on the walls in there—the "auxiliary trophy room!"

SARATOGA COUNTY

MOHAWK LANDING NATURE PRESERVE

Phone/Address: (518) 371-6651 / 640 Riverview Rd., Rexford, NY 12148.

Note: This park is listed under multiple addresses in different towns. Another address found online is "Riverview Road, Clifton Park, NY." However, simply entering "Mohawk Landing Nature Preserve" into most GPS systems will lead you to this park.

Days/Hours: 5 a.m.–10 p.m., according to the signs at the start of the trail. It's best to go by the "dawn-to-dusk" rule, just to be safe.

Admission: Free.

Mohawk Landing Nature Preserve, Rexford (Clifton Park), New York.
PHOTO BY LARRY WEILL

Background: The Mohawk Landing Nature Preserve is a relatively small parcel of land that serves as host to some nice hiking trails and convenient places to rest and enjoy a picnic lunch. The entire tract is only six acres, and it's possible to view houses and other structures through the trees in many locations.

There is a wide and fairly level gravel path that leads into the preserve from the parking lot along Riverview Road. Farther down that trail is a nice picnic area that looks over the Mohawk River. A loop trail then leads hikers on a circuit that follows the outer edges of the property and eventually returns to the original trail. It is all relatively short and level and requires no special footwear. This trail is also gentle enough for children of all ages (but watch the small "cliffs").

The picnic area is shaded and contains three picnic tables. There are no garbage receptacles, so users must carry out their own trash.

Warning: One of the picnic tables was set up next to a short wooden fence, with a sign warning of a cliff. The fence does not completely protect the table from the drop-off, so supervise your children at all times.

There is a short trail leading from the picnic area about twenty feet down to the river, making it convenient for paddlers of small boats and kayaks to pull their craft ashore and use the picnic area. However, no signs were visible from the river, so users may have to hunt for the park's location or rely on GPS from the water.

Rules:

- The preserve is open from dawn to dusk. "Trespassers" will be prosecuted after dark.
- All dogs must be leashed at all times.
- Please pick up any waste after your pet.
- No hunting is allowed inside the preserve at any time.

DON & PAUL'S COFFEE SHOP

Phone/Address: (518) 233-1040/ 68 Broad St., Waterford, NY 12188.

Days/Hours: Monday through Saturday 7 a.m.–7:30 p.m., Sunday 7 a.m.–2 p.m.

Reservations accepted? Yes.

Restaurant size: Eight tables plus counter seating.

Don & Paul's Coffee Shop, Waterford, New York.
PHOTO BY LARRY WEILL

Outdoor seating: No.

Menu items: The breakfast menu includes nine egg dishes, four omelets, and seven pancake/French toast items. The menu for lunch or dinner has nine appetizers (including shrimp cocktail and jumbo wings), salads, soups, sixteen different sandwiches, subs, hot sandwiches, and burgers. There are also numerous specials (including a lobster roll, fried shrimp, and scallops) on the board behind the counter.

Price range: Egg dishes range from $3 to $10, pancakes or French toast are $3–$8, appetizers are $3.50–$9.50, sandwiches run from $4.50 to $8.50, and burgers are around $6. Prices are posted on the board behind the counter for specials, with most being $10–$15.

Most popular menu item: Their $3 eggs-and-toast special is always one of their best sellers. People also go for their hamburgers, cheeseburgers, and fish fry.

Entertainment: No.

Liquor license: No.

Description: Don & Paul's is a uniquely Waterford restaurant and gathering spot that's been a fixture in the community for forty-five years. Both the canal and the Canalway Trail pass by just up the street, and many travelers from both visit there every day.

This is another hometown diner where everyone knows everyone else. The waitresses joke with the patrons and often seem to know what they're about to order before a word is spoken.

The decor of Don & Paul's has an old-time feel to it, right down to the wooden floor planks and painted sign above the entrance. I had a chance to speak with Don during my visit, and he expressed his love for the restaurant, his customers, and his employees. This is a great place to go if you want a quick and inexpensive meal in a comfortable setting.

MCGREIVEY'S

Phone/Address: (518) 238-2020 / 91 Broad St., Waterford, NY 12188.

Days/Hours: Generally open from 11:30 a.m. to 9 p.m., but those hours can vary based on business and time of year. Closed on Sunday.

Note: The hours of operation are listed differently on various websites. Call to confirm before visiting.

Reservations accepted? Yes.

Restaurant size: Twenty-seven tables, divided between the barroom and the side dining rooms, plus twenty tables on the rear patio.

Outdoor seating: Yes.

Menu items: The lunch menu lists soups, nine appetizers (including fried calamari and chicken nachos), eight salad dishes, and sixteen other lunch selections including everything from cheeseburgers to Cajun jambalaya. The Irish side of the menu includes staples like shepherd's pie and "The Knickerbocker," which is New York State corned beef with Swiss cheese, coleslaw, and Thousand Island dressing on grilled rye. Gluten-free wraps are also on the menu. They also offer ten dinner entrées including everything from Jack Daniel's steak to crab-stuffed haddock.

McGreivey's in Waterford, New York.
PHOTO BY LARRY WEILL

Price range: Appetizers are between $8 and $19, the salad dishes are $11.50–$21, and the lunches range from $16 to $20. The ten dinner entrées run between $22 and $29.

Most popular menu item: The Knickerbocker sandwich.

Entertainment: No.

Liquor license: Yes.

Description: McGreivey's is a genuine Irish pub and restaurant located in a historic building that dates back to the 1800s. People visit this pub for great food in large portions that will ensure you do not leave hungry. It is just a short distance from the canal and the Canalway Trail, so you won't lose time getting off and on again. They also have a spacious back patio with lots of tables, so you can enjoy the fresh air while dining here.

I had lunch at this restaurant and enjoyed the Knickerbocker sandwich, which came with a mountain of French fries. Friendly service and a lively bar atmosphere complete the scene here.

KLAM'R TAVERN & MARINA

Phone/Address: (518) 930-0577 / 32 Clamsteam Rd., Clifton Park, NY 12065.

Days/Hours: Wednesday and Thursday 3 p.m.–10 p.m., noon–11 p.m. on Friday and Saturday, noon–10 p.m. on Sunday, closed on Monday.

Reservations accepted? Yes (for large parties).

Restaurant size: Twenty-two tables inside plus eight more on the outside deck.

Outdoor seating: Yes.

Menu items: The menu starts with a large selection of sixteen appetizers, including "clam shooters" (which is a raw Rhode Island littleneck clam in a shot glass topped with cocktail sauce). Buffalo breaded cauliflower, or a basket of sweetfries. They offer nine soups and salads, six different quesadillas, twenty-two sandwiches ("and more"), which include everything from mac and cheese to the "Rachel," which is turkey breast, bacon, melted Swiss cheese, and Russian dressing on grilled rye bread. The menu is rounded out with a selection of seven different burgers.

Price range: The appetizers range from $8 to $16, sandwiches are $13–$21, the quesadillas are $13–$15, the soups/salads range from $8 to $16, and the burgers are $15–$17.

Most popular menu item: Clams and fish fry.

Entertainment: Yes (every other weekend they have live bands).

Liquor license: Yes.

Description: The Klam'r Tavern & Marina is a bright, high-end place that offers a lot to its customers. Located right up the hill from both the canal and the Canalway Trail, it is an easy-on, easy-off location to rest and grab your favorite eats and drinks. (Boat slips are available for your use.)

This restaurant/pub/marina has been under the same management for seven years, although its history as a restaurant dates back to the 1930s. Paul, the

Klam'r Tavern & Marina, Clifton Park, New York.
PHOTO BY LARRY WEILL

owner, enjoys running the place as a high-end establishment with "good food and a great family-friendly environment."

Klam'r sponsors a number of special events throughout the year, but their most popular is the ClamFest, which takes place the second weekend in October. Many patrons of the restaurant arrive via boat, Jet Ski, or kayak. The restaurant is not marked on the canal, so enter through the Diamond Reef Marina to pull into the boat slips. Welcome ashore!

FESTIVALS AND SEASONAL EVENTS ACROSS THE ERIE CANAL

This section has been added to provide a brief schedule of festival-type activities that are conducted for limited periods of time (days or weeks) along the Erie Canal. This listing has been organized in chronological order throughout the year without regard to location. For additional details on any one event, search online using the event name.

This listing has been compiled from multiple online sources, including New York State and private websites. The dates for many events change on an annual basis, so check the dates and locations of events before traveling to attend.

Some of the festivals and other events listed on public websites advertise programs that take place in towns and cities that are on the Erie Canal, but the festival itself does not take place on the canal. These events have not been included in this list.

Additionally, some of these events may have been suspended or even been terminated due to factors related to the pandemic and public health concerns. Once again, validate the dates of any event before making plans.

Location	Festival Name	Dates
Entire Canal	Canalway Challenge	February (entire month)
Schoharie	Towpath Tuesday Hike	February (3rd week)
Schoharie	Intro to Snowshoeing	February (3rd week)
Schoharie	5-Miler Sunday Hike at the Schoharie Crossing State Historic Site	February (4th week)
Schenectady	Mohawk River Living History Weekend	May (1st week)
Brockport	Low Bridge High Water Festival	May (2nd–3rd week)
Utica	Erie Canal Half Marathon, 5K and Relay	May (3rd week)
Fairport	Fairport Canal Days	June (1st week)
Queensbury	Canoe/Kayak Race & Family Recreational Paddle	June (1st week)
Schoharie	Canal Day	June (1st week)
Fort Hunter	Paddle Along the Mohawk	June (1st week)
Albion	Strawberry Festival	June (1st–2nd week)
Lockport	Rock the Lock	June (2nd week)
Palmyra	Heritage Weekend at Historic Palmyra	June (2nd–3rd week)
Chittenango	Boat Float Bash	June (2nd–3rd week)
Macedon	Erie Canal Family Fun Day	June (2nd–3rd week)
Schoharie to Schenectady	Paddle the Canals: Mohawk River Expedition	June (3rd week)
Newark	Wine, Craft Beverage, and Artisan Festival/Music on the Erie	June (3rd week)
Fairport	Full Moon Social Paddles	June (3rd week)
Fairport	Adaptive Paddling Extravaganza	June (4th week)
Buffalo to Albany	Journey Along the Erie	June (4th week)
Newark	Music on the Erie	June through August (every Friday)
Lockport	Lockport Arts & Crafts Festival	June (4th week)
Lyons	Peppermint Days	July (2nd week)
Schoharie	Schoharie Crossing Canal Days	July (2nd week)
Rotterdam Junction	CanalFest at Mabee Farm	July (2nd week)
Macedon	Sound Waves on the Erie Canal	July (2nd week)
Entire Canal	Cycle the Erie Canal (Buffalo to Albany)	July (2nd–3rd week)
Tonawanda	Canal Fest of the Tonawandas	July (2nd–3rd week)
Ilion	Annual Ilion Days	July (2nd–3rd week)
Utica	Erie Canal Half Marathon	July (3rd week)
Niagara Falls to Saratoga Springs	Great Bug FANY Ride	July (4th week)
Amherst	Row, Row, Row Your Boat	July (4th week)
Rome	CanalFest	August (1st week)
Albion	Albion's Annual Rock-The-Park Festival	August (1st week)
Little Falls	Annual Little Falls Canal Celebration	August (1st–2nd week)

(Continued)

Location	Festival Name	Dates
Little Falls	Annual Little Falls Canal Celebration	August (2nd week)
Sylvan Beach	CanalFest	August (2nd week)
Sylvan Beach	Towpath Day, The Legacy of the Erie Canal	August (2nd week)
Schuylerville	Annual Cardboard Boat Race	August (2nd week)
Camillus	Tow Path Day	August (2nd week)
Clyde	Clyde Fire Department Community Festival	August (2nd week)
Buffalo	Traveling the Erie Canal: 200 Years of Journeys	August (3rd week)
Fonda	Fonda Fair	August (4th week) though September (1st week)
Entire Canal	Canal Splash	September (2nd–3rd week)
Fairport	Scarecrow Festival	September (2nd–3rd week)
Waterford	Annual Kayaking 4 Meso	September (2nd week)
Albion	Old Timers Fair	September (2nd week)
St. Johnsville	St. Johnsville Fall Celebration of the Erie Canal	September (2nd week)
Waterford	Waterford Tugboat Roundup	September (2nd–3rd week)
Palmyra	Canaltown Days	September (3rd week)
DeWitt to Rome	Tour the Towpath	September (3rd week)
Rome	Locktoberfest 2019	October (1st week)
Little Falls	Little Falls Cheese Festival	October (1st week)v
Amherst	Erie Canal Music and Stories	October (2nd week)
Rexford	Mohawk Towpath Byway Duathlon	October (3rd week)
Chittenango	Annual Erie Canal Run	October (4th week)

PUBLIC HARBORS AND MARINAS

This book mentions the occasional marina or docking facility in order to provide notice of camping areas, restrooms, and showers that are open to the public. These few pages are by no means a comprehensive listing of all such resources available for hikers, bikers, and boaters on the Erie Canal.

The New York State Canal Corporation provides an extensive listing of such facilities on its website: https://www.canals.ny.gov.

This is a superb website that provides an updated compendium of all things related to traveling on the Erie Canal. It also lists similar information for the following:

- Oswego Canal
- Champlain Canal
- Cayuga-Seneca Canal (and Seneca and Cayuga Lakes)
- Hudson River

These listing include municipal facilities, parks, marinas, clubs, and services. Additionally, each location is listed according to its mile marker on the canal and lists the services offered at each location, including:

- Electrical
- Water
- Pump out
- Restrooms
- Showers
- Laundry
- Wi-Fi
- Fuel (whether gasoline or diesel)
- Repair services are also listed, including electrical, hull, mechanical, mast stepping, and towing

A phone number for each of these facilities is listed, along with the VHF radio channels on which they may be contacted.

BOAT RENTAL FACILITIES

If you are hiking or biking the Erie Canal and feel the sudden urge to get out on the water, there are several ways to do this. The two primary means are to either take a cruise where you are simply the passenger, or rent a boat of some kind. There are thirty-nine companies listed on the Canal Corporation's website that would be happy to rent you one of the following platforms:

- Canoe
- Kayak
- Paddleboat
- Rowboat
- Water bike
- Stand-up paddleboard
- Fishing boat
- Houseboat
- Pontoon boat
- Jet Skis
- English-style narrowboat
- Twenty-four-foot trawler

Obviously, the choices are many, as are the companies providing these options. You can view all the vendors by visiting https://www.canals.ny.gov/wwwapps/boatong/boatsforhire.aspx.

CRUISES

If you are looking to have someone else do the work while you simply sit back and enjoy the view, the same website (www.canals.ny.gov/wwwapps/boatong/boatsforhire.aspx) lists thirty-two companies that will take you out for a guided cruise. (Note: Not all of the cruises listed are on the Erie Canal. Some are as far removed as the Finger Lakes.)

These cruises vary greatly in duration and focus. Some are even available with a full meal served while a guide narrates the complete voyage. Look online to find the cruise that suits your needs.

CAMPING ALONG THE CANALWAY TRAIL

The following information on camping has been provided courtesy of the New York State Canals Corporation.

The New York State Canals Corporation website lists four types of campgrounds accessible to travelers on the Erie Canal or the Canalway Trail. These are the Cycler-Hiker-Boater Campsites distributed across the state (free of charge), various Municipal Parks and Marinas (which range in cost from free to $20/night), State Campgrounds (which always charge a nightly fee), and Private Campgrounds (which also levy a nightly fee). Each of these camping options offers different facilities and services, so make certain to access their websites to ensure that your needs are met by the site you select.

The New York State Canal Corporation offers seventeen Cycler-Hiker-Boater Campsites along the Canalway Trail and waterways. These campsites are designed to make touring along the Canal System easier for trail users, boaters, and paddlers during the navigation season (May–October). The Canal Corporation offers camping/campsites designated as "primitive," with limited on-site amenities. Porta johns are provided at the designated campsites, but visitors should be prepared with their own potable water, first aid kits, and camping and cooking supplies. The sites include an area for four tents. Stays are limited to forty-eight hours and are available on a first come, first served basis. Please provide advanced notice by contacting the sites at the phone numbers on the following page prior to arrival.

The Cycler-Hiker-Boater Campsites also vary in the types of access they provide to the canal and Canalway Trail. These may include boat access, paddler access, cyclist access, and trail access. The most current updates are available online at https://empiretrail.ny.gov/trip-planning.

Upon arrival, see the Lock Operator (if present), then take a one-minute online survey.

If the Lock Operator is unavailable, scan the posted QR Code to access the survey.

General Rules:

- Camping is first come, first served; lock operators should be contacted in advance so you can receive information on the campsite's status as open. Weather or safety conditions can close campsites unexpectedly.
- Campsites are limited to four tents and ten people.
- Campers must be at least eighteen years old unless accompanied and supervised by an adult.
- Stays are limited to forty-eight hours.
- No campfires or bonfires are allowed.
- Campsite sites are carry-in, carry-out for garbage unless a waste receptacle is present.
- Quiet hours must be observed between 10 p.m. and 7 a.m.
- No motorized vehicles are allowed in the campsites
- For camping space for groups larger than ten people/four tents, you must reach out to the Canal Real Property Management Department to obtain a permit: (518) 449-6000
- Primitive Campsites: These are campsites that provide no amenities with the exception of a porta john. Campsites require carry-in and carry-out and campers to bring their own water or water purification

The list of available campsites can change on an annual basis. Rather than risk providing information that may be outdated, the following phone numbers represent the offices for each region across the canal. Call these offices directly for information regarding camping inside each district:

- Section 1 Fort Edward (518) 747-4613
- Section 2 Waterford (518) 233-8575
- Section 3 Fonda (518) 853-3823
- Section 4 Utica (315) 329-1878
- Section 5 Lysander (315) 695-2210
- Section 6 Lyons (315) 871-4300
- Section 7 Pittsford (585) 586-6877

For the most current information on camping locations and facilities, visit https://empiretrail.ny.gov/trip-planning.

ADDITIONAL PUBLICLY OPERATED CAMPGROUNDS

The following information on camping has been provided courtesy of the New York State Canals Corporation.

These camping locations require advance reservations, and they do charge a fee. Contact the appropriate sites and reserve your campsite in advance to ensure a site.

Name	Location	Phone	Services
Waterford Canal Visitor Center	At the waterfront at the eastern gateway to the canal and Canalway Trail	(518) 233-9123	Potable water, toilets, and showers
Verona Beach State Park	On the eastern shore of Oneida Lake	(800) 456-CAMP or (315) 762-4463	Full restroom facilities, water fill-up station, dumping station
Cayuga Lake State Park	Seneca Falls	(800) 456-CAMP or (315) 568-5163	Full restroom facilities, water fill-up station, dumping station
Green Lakes State Park	Fayetteville, New York	(315) 637-6111	Full restroom facilities, water fill-up station, dumping station

ACKNOWLEDGMENTS

This book could not have been written without the cooperation of dozens of individuals who are involved in the many aspects of the management, operations, and development along the Erie Canal. From the historical background to the facility management, and finally, to the businesses that serve the canal's end users, they have all provided their unique thoughts, outlooks, and experiences from their many years on "the Ditch" to make this work possible.

John McKee, an operations supervisor and chief lock operator (Locks 34 and 35) in the Lockport section of the canal provided key information on the historical background of the "Flight of Five" locks and the development of the canal over the many years of expansion.

Richard Sullivan, mayor of Sylvan Beach, New York, contributed his thoughts on the historical development of the Erie Canal in the eastern end of Oneida Lake and the community of Sylvan Beach. Pat Goodenow provided insights into the background of the Sylvan Beach Amusement Park and its development and expansion from the 1870s to the present day.

Members of the Fort Brewerton/Greater Oneida Lake Chamber of Commerce discussed the development of the parks and lighthouses on and around Oneida Lake, and facilities available for use by the hikers and bikers on the Canalway Trail.

Numerous employees of the New York State Canal Corporation, including Hank Brummer (deputy, Western Region canal engineer), Nick Melson and Joell Murney-Karsten (Public Affairs, Western Region), Shelby Moore, and William Sweitzer provided detailed insights into various aspects of the Erie Canal and the New York State Canalway Trail. Connie Cullen, director of Integrated Communications for the New York Power Authority suggested numerous improvements to the section detailing camping locations and resources along the Erie Canal and Canalway Trail.

Thanks go to Edward Heinrichs, the Living History & Volunteer Coordinator of the Herkimer Home State Historic Site near Little Falls, New York. Ed spent considerable time detailing the history of the mansion at the Herkimer Home site and the plans for future programs and development.

Many thanks to Paul Banks, historic site manager at the Schoharie Crossing State Historic Site near Amsterdam, New York. Paul provided descriptions of the past and present sites of interest around the Schoharie Crossing as well as the Putman Canal Store. He also supplied photographs of the reconstructed Putman store and the area around the original Lock 28 on the enlarged Erie Canal.

Derrick Pratt, who serves as the museum educator of the Erie Canal Museum in Syracuse, led me through their exhibit halls and explained the museum's collections as well as the various programs they coordinate in Syracuse and around the state.

Ian Seppala, executive director of the Herschell Carrousel Factory Museum in North Tonawanda, served as my personal tour director through the many rooms and workshops of their facility.

Mary Alexander, curator of Education and Public Engagement at the Arkell Museum in Canajoharie, explained the origins of the museum and the factors that shaped its growth over the years. Eileen Chambers, who serves as the historian for the village of Fort Plain, New York, supplied her time and materials to explain the background of the Fort Plain Free Public Library.

Norm Bollen, chairman of the Fort Plain Museum, provided detailed information about the origins of the museum and also the extensive archaeological works on the grounds surrounding the facility.

Pat Goodenow of the Sylvan Beach Amusement Park supplied photographs and detailed historical background of that popular local attraction. Les Bearclaw Stewart, president of the Fort Klock Historic Restoration, graciously opened the fort's doors to me and led me through a private tour of the facility and its grounds.

Michael Diana, education director, Schenectady County Historical Society, lent his time and expertise to serve as my guide through the Schenectady County Historical Society Museum and also discussed the background and stewardship of the Mabee Farm Historic Site and the Brouwer House Creative.

The proprietors of Sweet Sprig in Schenectady led me on a tour of the Brouwer House Creative (the oldest house in the historic Stockade District) and detailed the history and architectural background of the residence.

Tammee Poinan Grimes, the captain of the *Colonial Belle* in Fairport, not only led me on a tour of their canalboat but also provided the recommendation and thoughts on including the *Seneca Chief* in this book.

Patrick Russell Walsh, executive director of the Corn Hill Waterfront and Navigation Foundation, discussed the history of the nonprofit organization's origins and operations on the Erie Canal and Genesee River in Rochester.

Burt Lewis, proprietor of Montezuma Anchorage, added insights into the history and development of the area surrounding the canal as it transits through Cayuga County and the Montezuma Heritage Park.

While I have undoubtedly failed to mention every person who has contributed to this book, I'd like to conclude with a blanket statement expressing my gratitude to everyone who has aided me in this endeavor. To the restauranteurs, pub owners, museum curators, and historians, not only was your knowledge and experience critical to the accuracy of this volume, but your friendliness and exceptional cooperation made this project a wonderful experience. I cannot thank you enough for your collaboration and support.

www.ingramcontent.com/pod-product-compliance
Lightning Source LLC
Chambersburg PA
CBHW062103160225
21802CB00002BA/2

* 9 7 8 1 4 9 3 0 8 9 0 7 9 *